Coriolanus

ARDEN EARLY MODERN DRAMA GUIDES

Series Editors:
Andrew Hiscock, University of Wales, Bangor, UK and
Lisa Hopkins, Sheffield Hallam University, UK

Arden Early Modern Drama Guides offer practical and accessible introductions to the critical and performative contexts of key Elizabethan and Jacobean plays. Each guide introduces the text's critical and performance history, but also provides students with an invaluable insight into the landscape of current scholarly research, through a keynote essay on the state of the art and newly commissioned essays of fresh research from different critical perspectives.

A Midsummer Night's Dream, edited by Regina Buccola
Doctor Faustus, edited by Sara Munson Deats
King Lear, edited by Andrew Hiscock and Lisa Hopkins
Henry IV, Part 1, edited by Stephen Longstaffe
'Tis Pity She's a Whore, edited by Lisa Hopkins
Women Beware Women, edited by Andrew Hiscock
Volpone, edited by Matthew Steggle
The Duchess of Malfi, edited by Christina Luckyj
The Alchemist, edited by Erin Julian and Helen Ostovich
The Jew of Malta, edited by Robert A. Logan
Macbeth, edited by John Drakakis and Dale Townshend
Richard III, edited by Annaliese Connolly
Twelfth Night, edited by Alison Findlay and Liz Oakley-Brown
The Tempest, edited by Alden T. Vaughan and Virginia Mason Vaughan
Romeo and Juliet, edited by Julia Reinhard Lupton
Julius Caesar, edited by Andrew James Hartley
The Revenger's Tragedy, edited by Brian Walsh
The White Devil, edited by Paul Frazer and Adam Hansen
Edward II, edited by Kirk Melnikoff
Much Ado About Nothing, edited by Deborah Cartmell and Peter J. Smith
King Henry V, edited by Karen Britland and Line Cottegnies
Tamburlaine, edited by David McInnis
Troilus and Cressida, edited by Efterpi Mitsi

Further titles are in preparation.

Coriolanus

A Critical Reader

*Edited by
Liam E. Semler*

THE ARDEN SHAKESPEARE
LONDON • NEW YORK • OXFORD • NEW DELHI • SYDNEY

THE ARDEN SHAKESPEARE
Bloomsbury Publishing Plc
50 Bedford Square, London, WC1B 3DP, UK
1385 Broadway, New York, NY 10018, USA
29 Earlsfort Terrace, Dublin 2, Ireland

BLOOMSBURY, THE ARDEN SHAKESPEARE and the
Arden Shakespeare logo are trademarks of Bloomsbury Publishing Plc

First published in Great Britain 2021
This paperback edition published in 2022

Copyright © Liam E. Semler and contributors, 2021

Liam E. Semler and contributors have asserted their right under
the Copyright, Designs and Patents Act, 1988, to be
identified as the authors of this work.

For legal purposes the Acknowledgements on p. xiii constitute
an extension of this copyright page.

Cover image taken from the 1615 title-page of *The Spanish Tragedy*,
by Thomas Kyd

All rights reserved. No part of this publication may be reproduced
or transmitted in any form or by any means, electronic or mechanical,
including photocopying, recording, or any information storage or retrieval
system, without prior permission in writing from the publishers.

Bloomsbury Publishing Plc does not have any control over, or responsibility
for, any third-party websites referred to or in this book. All internet
addresses given in this book were correct at the time of going to
press. The author and publisher regret any inconvenience caused if
addresses have changed or sites have ceased to exist, but can accept no
responsibility for any such changes.

A catalogue record for this book is available from the British Library.

A catalog record for this book is available from the Library of Congress.

ISBN:	HB:	978-1-3501-1119-6
	PB:	978-1-3502-1365-4
	ePDF:	978-1-3501-1121-9
	eBook:	978-1-3501-1120-2

Series: Arden Early Modern Drama Guides

Typeset by Integra Software Services Pvt. Ltd.

To find out more about our authors and books visit www.bloomsbury.com
and sign up for our newsletters.

CONTENTS

List of Figures and Tables vii
Series Introduction ix
Notes on Contributors x
Acknowledgements xiii
Timeline xiv

Introduction *Liam E. Semler* 1

1 The Critical Backstory *Huw Griffiths* 15

2 Performance History *Robert Ormsby* 45

3 State of the Art *Graham Holderness* 71

4 New Directions: Putting Tongues in Wounds: The Search for an Honest Body in *Coriolanus* *Anna Kamaralli* 95

5 New Directions: 'As if a man were author of himself': Fantasies of Omnipotence and Autonomy *Evelyn Gajowski* 117

6 New Directions: Hegel's Rome and Shakespeare's *Coriolanus*: Grounds for Tragedy *Jennifer Ann Bates* 139

7   New Directions: *Coriolanus* and the
    Datasphere *Hugh Craig* 165

8   'Teach my mind': Approaches and Resources
    for the *Coriolanus* Classroom
    Claire Hansen 191

Notes 217
Bibliography 259
Index 284

LIST OF FIGURES AND TABLES

Figures

7.1 Word-variable weightings for a Principal Component Analysis of 100 very common words in 531 character parts each of 2,000 words or more 168

7.2 Character scores for a Principal Component Analysis of 100 very common words in 531 characters each speaking 2,000 words or more 169

7.3 Proportions of *has* to *hath* in four sets of plays 177

7.4 Proportions of *does* to *doth* in four sets of plays 177

7.5 Proportions of *you* forms to *thou* forms in four sets of plays 178

7.6 Proportions of verb forms ending in *-s* to verb forms ending in *-th* for a set of 180 verbs in four sets of plays 179

7.7 Percentage of verse lines which are shared between characters in twenty-seven Shakespeare plays 180

7.8 Percentage of speeches in *Coriolanus* consisting of one word, two words, three words etc., up to thirty words 182

Tables

7.1 Identification of labels in Figure 7.2 170

7.2 The ten highest and lowest scoring words in comparisons of regularity and rarity between *Coriolanus* and four sets of plays 173

7.3 The Information Entropy scores of three 500-word segments of *Coriolanus* 184

SERIES INTRODUCTION

The drama of Shakespeare and his contemporaries has remained at the very heart of English curricula internationally and the pedagogic needs surrounding this body of literature have grown increasingly complex as more sophisticated resources become available to scholars, tutors and students. This series aims to offer a clear picture of the critical and performative contexts of a range of chosen texts. In addition, each volume furnishes readers with invaluable insights into the landscape of current scholarly research as well as including new pieces of research by leading critics.

This series is designed to respond to the clearly identified needs of scholars, tutors and students for volumes which will bridge the gap between accounts of previous critical developments and performance history and an acquaintance with new research initiatives related to the chosen plays. Thus, our ambition is to offer innovative and challenging guides that will provide practical, accessible and thought-provoking analyses of early modern drama. Each volume is organized according to a progressive reading strategy involving introductory discussion, critical review and cutting-edge scholarly debate. It has been an enormous pleasure to work with so many dedicated scholars of early modern drama and we are sure that this series will encourage you to read 400-year-old play texts with fresh eyes.

Andrew Hiscock and Lisa Hopkins

NOTES ON CONTRIBUTORS

Jennifer Ann Bates is Professor of Philosophy at Duquesne University, Pittsburgh, and General Editor of *Idealistic Studies: An Interdisciplinary Journal of Philosophy*. Jennifer is the author of *Hegel and Shakespeare on Moral Imagination* (2010) and *Hegel's Theory of Imagination* (2004), and co-editor (with Richard Wilson) of *Shakespeare and Continental Philosophy* (2014). She has chapters in *The Routledge Companion to Shakespeare and Philosophy* (2018) and *The Philosophy of Theatre, Drama and Acting* (2017), and articles in *Wallace Stevens Journal*, *The Journal for Environmental Ethics*, *Criticism: A Quarterly for Literature and the Arts*, *Memoria di Shakespeare*, *Philosophy Compass*, *Angelaki: Journal of the Theoretical Humanities* and *Philosophy Today*.

Hugh Craig is Emeritus Professor of English at the University of Newcastle, Australia. He has worked on attribution problems for many years, most recently on the authorship of the classic Chinese novel *The Dream of the Red Chamber*. Some of the more controversial authorship proposals in *Shakespeare, Computers, and the Mystery of Authorship* (2007), co-edited with Professor Arthur F. Kinney, are championed in *The New Oxford Shakespeare* (2016–present). His current projects include a digital mapping platform, the Time-Layered Cultural Map of Australia, and a stylometric study of the text of the Shakespeare First Folio, in collaboration with Professor Gabriel Egan.

Evelyn Gajowski is Professor of English Emerita at the University of Nevada, Las Vegas. Her fifth book is *The Arden*

Research Handbook of Contemporary Shakespeare Criticism (The Arden Shakespeare, 2020). She has previously published *The Merry Wives of Windsor: New Critical Essays*, with Phyllis Rackin (2015); *Presentism, Gender, and Sexuality in Shakespeare* (2009); *Re-Visions of Shakespeare: Essays in Honor of Robert Ornstein* (2004); and *The Art of Loving: Female Subjectivity and Male Discursive Traditions in Shakespeare's Tragedies* (1992). She serves as Series Editor of Arden's Shakespeare and Theory series and is currently writing *Shakespeare and Presentist Theory* for the Series.

Huw Griffiths is Senior Lecturer in Early Modern Literature at the University of Sydney. He is the author of *Shakespeare's Body Parts: Figuring Sovereignty in the History Plays* (2020).

Claire Hansen is Lecturer in English at the Australian National University, Canberra. Her first book, *Shakespeare and Complexity Theory*, was published in 2017. Claire is a member of the Shakespeare Reloaded project, a collaboration exploring innovative approaches to teaching and learning Shakespeare. She is currently working on a place-based education project.

Graham Holderness is the author or editor of some sixty books of literary criticism, theory, scholarship and theology; 'creative criticism'; and creative writing in fiction, poetry and drama. His key critical works include *The Faith of William Shakespeare* (2016), *Shakespeare: The Histories* (2000), *The Politics of Theatre and Drama* (1992) and *The Shakespeare Myth* (1988). Graham's works of creative criticism, which are half criticism and half fiction, include *Tales from Shakespeare: Creative Collisions* (2014), *Re-writing Jesus: Christ in 20th Century Fiction and Film* (Bloomsbury, 2014) and *Nine Lives of William Shakespeare* (The Arden Shakespeare, 2011).

Anna Kamaralli gained her Master's degree from The University of New South Wales, Sydney, and her PhD from Trinity College Dublin. She is the editor of *Much Ado About Nothing* for the Arden Performance Editions (2018). She is the author of *Shakespeare and the Shrew* (2012), and has chapters in the *Palgrave Handbook of the History of Women On Stage* (2019) and the *Feminist Companion to Shakespeare* (2016).

Robert Ormsby is Associate Professor of English at Memorial University of Newfoundland, Canada, where he teaches early modern drama. His research includes Shakespearean performance and Shakespearean tourism. In 2014 he published a performance history of *Coriolanus*. In 2017 he co-edited with Jill L. Levenson *The Shakespearean World*. His articles have appeared in various journals and essay collections.

Liam E. Semler is Professor of Early Modern Literature at the University of Sydney. His recent publications include *The Early Modern Grotesque: English Sources and Documents 1500–1700* (2019) and *Teaching Shakespeare and Marlowe: Learning versus the System* (The Arden Shakespeare, 2013).

ACKNOWLEDGEMENTS

To the health workers around the world who served the sick and dying during the COVID-19 global pandemic (2019–20). Thank you.

Fifth century BC. Early Roman Republic. Grain shortages. Pestilence. Civil unrest.

           Coriolanus myth begins.

1605–10. Jacobean England. Grain shortages. Plague. Midlands Rising.

          Shakespeare writes *Coriolanus*.

2019–20. Australia. Megafires. Coronavirus. Lockdown.

        Semler edits Coriolanus: *A Critical Reader.*

Coriolanus is surely a play for our times. I am deeply grateful to Huw Griffiths, Rob Ormsby, Graham Holderness, Anna Kamaralli, Lynn Gajowski, Jennifer Bates, Hugh Craig and Claire Hansen who wrote such lively and original chapters for this collection in such difficult times. My sincere thanks to Lara Bateman and Mark Dudgeon at Bloomsbury and to the series editors Lisa Hopkins and Andrew Hiscock for all their grace and professionalism.

              Liam E. Semler
              Sydney, Australia

TIMELINE

509 BC	Expulsion of the last Roman King, Lucius Tarquinius Superbus, and the foundation of the Roman Republic.
493 BC	Roman capture of Corioli from the Volsci for which Gnaeus Marcius Coriolanus wins his cognomen.
492 BC	Coriolanus's banishment for tyrannical conduct in relation to the distribution of corn to starving plebeians.
59 BC	Livy (Titus Livius), the Roman historian, born.
17	Livy dies.
c. 46	Plutarch (Lucius Mestrius Plutarchus), the Greek biographer, born.
120	Plutarch dies.
1564	William Shakespeare born.
1595	Plutarch, *The Lives of the Noble Grecians and Romanes*, trans. by Sir Thomas North – Shakespeare's primary source. The first edition was 1579.
1606–9	Recurrent visitations of plague and closure of theatres in London.
1606	Bad harvests in England.
1607	Midlands Rising against land enclosures and resulting depopulation and loss of livelihoods.
1607–8	The Great Frost.
1608	Severe dearth in England and high grain prices.

TIMELINE

c. 1608	Probable composition of Shakespeare's *Coriolanus* (estimates vary from 1605–10). Possible first performance in 1608 or 1609, but no record of a performance during Shakespeare's lifetime survives.
1616	Shakespeare dies.
1623	First mention of *Coriolanus*, in the Stationers' Register (8 November). First publication of *Coriolanus* in *Mr. William Shakespeares Comedies, Histories, & Tragedies* ('the First Folio').
1632	*Coriolanus* published in Shakespeare's Second Folio.
1655	John Cotgrave publishes *The English Treasury of Wit and Language*, containing extracts from *Coriolanus*.
1657	Joshua Poole publishes *The English Parnassus*, containing extracts from *Coriolanus*.
1663	*Coriolanus* published in Shakespeare's Third Folio.
1681	Nahum Tate, *The Ingratitude of a Commonwealth; or the Fall of Caius Martius Coriolanus*, performed at Drury Lane. Published 1682.
1685	*Coriolanus* published in Shakespeare's Fourth Folio.
1719	John Dennis, *The Invader of His Country, or The Fatal Resentment*, performed at Drury Lane. Published 1720.
1749	James Thomson, *Coriolanus*, performed at Covent Garden. Composed 1747.
1752–4	Thomas Sheridan, *Coriolanus: or, the Roman Matron*, a blend of Thomson's and Shakespeare's versions, performed at Smock Alley Theatre Dublin. Performed at Covent Garden 1754–5. Published 1755.

1754	David Garrick's production of *Coriolanus* at the Theatre Royal, Drury Lane, London.
1789–1817	John Philip Kemble's production of *Coriolanus* at Drury Lane and Covent Garden, with him as Coriolanus and Sarah Siddons occasionally as Volumnia. This long run had a number of interruptions.
1819	William Charles Macready plays Coriolanus at Covent Garden, and returns to the role numerous times thereafter.
1901	Henry Irving performs Coriolanus, with Ellen Terry as Volumnia, at the Lyceum, with a significantly cut text and impressive Etruscan-inspired sets.
1933–4	Émile Fabre (dir.), *La Tragédie de Coriolan*, performed at La Comédie-Française in Paris.
1951	Bertolt Brecht begins composing his *Coriolan* for the Berliner Ensemble. It is unfinished at his death in 1956. Published in German in 1959.
1959	Peter Hall (dir.), *Coriolanus*, Stratford-upon-Avon, with Laurence Olivier in the title role and Dame Edith Evans as Volumnia.
1963	BBC television miniseries, *The Spread of the Eagle*, including *Coriolanus*.
1964	Berliner Ensemble stages a version of Brecht's *Coriolanus* in Berlin.
1965	Berliner Ensemble performs its *Coriolanus*, directed by Manfred Wekwerth and Joachim Tenschert, at the Old Vic in London.
1966	Günter Grass, *The Plebeians Rehearse the Uprising* performed in Berlin. Performance for the RSC at Aldwych Theatre in London in 1970.

TIMELINE

1971	Manfred Wekwerth and Joachim Tenschert's revised, English-language version of the Berliner Ensemble's *Coriolanus* performed for the National Theatre in London, with Anthony Hopkins in the title role and Constance Cummings as Volumnia.
1972	John Osborne, *A Place calling itself Rome*. Unstaged script. Published 1973.
	Trevor Nunn (dir.), *Coriolanus* for the RSC with Ian Hogg as Coriolanus.
1977	Terry Hands (dir.), *Coriolanus* for the RSC with Alan Howard as Coriolanus.
1983	Elijah Moshinsky (dir.), *Coriolanus* for BBC Television Shakespeare, with Alan Howard as Coriolanus, Irene Worth as Volumnia and Mike Gwilym as Aufidius.
1984–5	Peter Hall (dir.), *Coriolanus* for the National Theatre, with Ian McKellen as Coriolanus.
1988–9	Steven Berkoff (dir.), *Coriolanus* for the New York Shakespeare Festival at the Anspacher Theater, New York, with Christopher Walken as Coriolanus and Irene Worth as Volumnia.
1992–4	Robert Lepage (dir.), *Cycle Shakespeare*, including *Coriolan*.
2007	Yukio Ninagawa (dir.), *Coriolanus* at the Barbican, London, with Toshiaki Karasawa as Coriolanus and Kayoko Shiriashi as Volumnia.
2007–17	Ivo van Hove (dir.), *Roman Tragedies*, including *Coriolanus*, and played in Dutch for Toneelgrope.
2011	Ralph Fiennes (dir.), film *Coriolanus*, with Fiennes as Coriolanus, Vanessa Redgrave as Volumnia and Gerard Butler as Aufidius.

2012	Motoi Miura (dir.), Chiten Company's *Coriolanus* at the Globe to Globe Festival.
2013	Josie Rourke (dir.), Donmar Warehouse production with Tom Hiddleston in the title role.
2017	Angus Jackson (dir.), *Coriolanus* for the RSC, with Sope Dirisu as Coriolanus, Hadyn Gwynne as Volumnia and James Corrigan as Aufidius.
2018	Robert Lepage (dir.), *Coriolanus* at Ontario's Stratford Festival, with a French-language transfer to Montréal's Théâtre du Nouveau Monde in 2019.

Introduction

Liam E. Semler

Shakespeare's *Coriolanus* is a compelling and intriguing play.[1] From its turbulent opening scene of desperate citizen revolt – 'all resolved rather to die than to famish' (1.1.3–4) – and Martius's venomous slapdown – 'What's the matter, you dissentious rogues' (1.1.159) – the audience is strapped in for an intense character study of a protagonist who thrives on conflict or, to put it more emphatically, violent contest. The play stages scene after scene of emotional intensity reaching from the battle cries of heroic military leaders through to the heavy silences of domestic encounters and everything in between. Class resentments, strained friendships, patriotic drive, pragmatic scheming and family ties are all on show. The play holds its audience not just by the ferocious masculinity of its protagonist, but also by the panoply of feelings Shakespeare invites us to witness and share.

Our guide through this bumpy, yet quintessentially dramatic terrain of agon and emotion, is Caius Martius, later named 'Coriolanus': he leads the play as he leads his soldiers and is everywhere talked of. *Coriolanus* is a long play, but it is driven speedily to its inexorable conclusion by the intensity of its dialogue and the decisiveness of its protagonist.[2] The bluntness of this character and the clarity of his progress through highly charged scenes carry the audience swiftly on and tend to hide another substantial achievement. This is Shakespeare's representation of the early Roman Republic as a live, political entity entailing the state, family and individual. It is the assured theatrical combination of strident character, lucid plotting and vivid setting, each highly specific, yet each contributing in just the right proportions to create a compelling story and subtle interrogation of the political, which makes the play, *as a play,* so impressive. It is on this basis that I can understand T. S. Eliot's famous provocation:

> *Coriolanus* may be not as interesting as *Hamlet*, but it is, with *Antony and Cleopatra*, Shakespeare's most assured artistic success. And probably more people have thought *Hamlet* a work of art because they found it interesting, than have found it interesting because it is a work of art. It is the 'Mona Lisa' of literature.[3]

Setting aside *Antony and Cleopatra* for simplicity's sake, we should be able to agree (at least) that *Coriolanus* and *Hamlet* are compelling in different ways and that the tag, 'most assured artistic success', can be defended in respect to *Coriolanus*, especially if we take it to mean '*dramatic* success'. Further confirmation might be found in Harley Granville-Barker's view that '[t]he play contains little or no superfluous matter' and its 'verse in the main is vigorous, and it drives hard and exclusively at its dramatic purpose'.[4]

The on-stage death count is peculiar for a Shakespearean tragedy and unique among his Roman tragedies which tend to regard the dramatis personae as a hit list. In *Coriolanus*, while thousands of distant extras are casually slaughtered offstage (be they Volscian or Roman soldiers, or the inhabitants of Corioles or provincial Roman towns), only one named character dies and that is Coriolanus. This fact serves to underline the play's primary interest in one man's story which is neatly bookended by a Roman citizen's opening demand, 'Let us kill him' (1.1.9), and the Volscian conspirators' closing cry,

'Kill, kill, kill, kill, kill him!' (5.6.131). In Roman politics and Volscian councils of war, in his family, among his friends and in the public eye, Coriolanus cannot be ignored and must, in fact, be constantly managed in person or in absentia. *Must* be managed. He is an existential threat, colliding with friend and foe 'like a planet' (2.2.112): no other Shakespearean play – not *King Lear*, not *Julius Caesar* – is so much about the one being managed by the many.

Kenneth Burke's classic essay on the play addresses this issue of Coriolanus's singularity (and how it relates to the genre of tragedy) when he argues that Coriolanus exemplifies 'the paradox of substance', a theory that the starring role 'is in large measure defined, or determined, by the other characters who variously assist or oppose him'.[5] Burke then analyses all the main characters in metadramatically functional terms, indicating how their construction and behaviour may be understood to be thus '"derived from" the character of Coriolanus',[6] which is to say designed for the primary purpose of co-constructing the titular character as someone suitable to carry the burden of tragedy and be its 'scapegoat'.[7] Another angle on the same issue is provided by Brian Vickers who illustrates how the play presents a number of distinct 'perspectives' – from the patricians, the plebeians, Volumnia and Aufidius – on Coriolanus as 'conflicting groups in the play are trying to dominate each other by using Coriolanus as a tool'.[8] He concludes that 'we cannot take anything that any of them say about him as constituting the truth, for each group has its own image, used for a specific purpose'.[9] While we might quibble that there are indeed truths uttered about Coriolanus, it is clear that they are inflected by perspectives that are intensely political in this play. Whatever the approach – and Burke's and Vickers's theses enrich rather than undo each other – it is true that critics often return to the fact that this is a play uniquely focused on one man's story. With no subplot to aerate the experience – Menenius's fable (1.1.84–158), the ladies' sewing scene (1.3) and the banter of Aufidius's servants (4.5.150–237) give little relief – the audience is subject to a surging, masculinist agenda of Roman war and politicking. All this is stepped through sequential climaxes aligned with the five acts: the spectacular victory at Corioles; the tribunes' devious plotting; the trap sprung and banishment achieved; the partnership of Coriolanus and Aufidius which threatens Rome; and the extraordinary family confrontation that precipitates the death of Coriolanus.

Coriolanus rightly compares himself to 'a lonely dragon' (4.1.30); Menenius confirms he is 'grown from man to dragon. He has wings' (5.4.12–13); and Aufidius knows all too well that he '[f]lights dragon-like' (4.7.23). Such mythologized intensity is naturally fascinating to observers (even if many are also repulsed and terrified) and Shakespeare builds into this figure an intriguing array of personal traits – Coriolanus's devotion to his mother, his erotically charged obsession with combating Aufidius, his patrician contempt for the common people, his resistance to showing his wounds, his rigid view of himself and his dry humour – that inveigle the audience into constructing psycho-social explanations of his behaviour.

When these details of character are considered within the highly political story arc, we see that Shakespeare's *Coriolanus* is a powerful lens through which to view the so-called 'Conflict of the Orders' that bedevilled, yet also valuably animated, the Roman Republic. This long-running class tension saw the plebeian order agitating in various ways to improve its structural position vis-à-vis the patrician order in the Republic. The creation of the tribunate was a key, early reform that Shakespeare makes essential to his plot: thus the tribunes, not Aufidius, are the real counterweight to Coriolanus and what they think he stands for. We will never know if he would have proved a tyrant had he become consul, but we do know that he loves Rome, has a genuine (albeit imperfect) nobleness of character, and was not ambitiously craving consulship. All in all, he is a hero apt for the early Republic, a larger-than-life figure straddling legend and history, and struggling against enemies inside and outside the city.

Shakespeare got his story from Plutarch, a writer he knew well. His primary, but far from sole, source for his Roman tragedies is Sir Thomas North's English translation (1579; but especially the second edition of 1595) of Jacques Amyot's French translation (1559) of Plutarch's *Lives*. This ancient Greek, prose masterpiece comprises biographies of notable Greeks paired with biographies of notable Romans. While Shakespeare primarily relies on Plutarch's 'Life of Coriolanus', he also draws on other authors. The ancient historian Livy and the Elizabethan author William Averell seem of particular use when he decides to transform Plutarch's account of Menenius's 'Fable of the Belly' into a more prominent and interactive exchange that builds Menenius's character and triggers some key themes of the play.[10] Plutarch's construction of Coriolanus's biography (paired with the life of the Athenian statesman and general Alcibiades) provides a compelling narrative template that comes to Shakespeare in the modern and at times gripping Tudor prose of his slightly older contemporary North. Reading North's text is one of the most illuminating things a student of Shakespeare's play can do.

Cynthia Marshall explains how Plutarch's 'Lives' are capacious, inclusive and complex representations to which Shakespeare applies a deft theatrical hand producing streamlined plots, less ambiguous characters, oppositional structures, sensational conflicts, key moments of decision-making for characters and a 'more violent and masculinist' image of Rome.[11] As surely as Shakespeare adopts and dramatizes some key aspects of Plutarch's storytelling, so also does he incorporate, at times verbatim, apt turns of phrase or passages of speech from North's prose. Peter Holland is right to say that Shakespeare read North's 'Life of Coriolanus' 'with quite exceptional attentiveness' such that '[a]t times he is, in effect, turning North's language into drama'.[12] This makes Shakespeare's deviations from Plutarch all the more significant. In the play, to pick up on some of Kenneth Muir's insights: Aufidius is introduced much earlier as a long-term rival of Coriolanus; the common soldiers become more cowardly, the tribunes more conniving and Coriolanus more intolerable; the vignette of the young Martius tearing the butterfly is invented; Coriolanus goes into exile alone rather than accompanied; the embassies sent to Coriolanus to plead for Rome's preservation are restructured more succinctly; Menenius gets an expanded role as a trusted confidant; and Volumnia is newly burdened with 'the fatal relationship between mother and son' that underpins the play.[13] Shakespeare relies on Plutarch, yet transforms the sprawling prose narrative into tight and compelling theatre that vividly reimagines the relationships between Coriolanus and Menenius, Aufidius and Volumnia.

The most consequential of these reimagined relationships is that between Coriolanus and his mother. It is a defining feature of Shakespeare's play and has spawned an enormous amount of interpretation.[14] While the erotically charged, battle-built partnership of Coriolanus and Aufidius is magnetic, the relationship between Volumnia and her son is deeper: it shapes his subjectivity and destiny; drives the play's images of disease, feeding and dependency; and contributes significantly to the idea of Rome in the play. Volumnia is a strong, intelligent, female role: her son was Rome's saviour (via his military prowess) at the start of the play and she is Rome's saviour (via her wise rhetoric) at the end.

Shakespeare also maximizes the contemporary relevance to Jacobean audiences by commencing with the plebeians rioting due to dire grain shortages and prohibitive food prices that they blame on the patrician class. David George puts the connection succinctly: 'Violent insurrection had taken place in the Midlands in June 1607, and severe dearth in all England in 1608. Most of 1.1 of *Coriolanus* is devoted to England's two troublesome years.'[15] Richard Wilson explores how the play reflects class tensions associated with the rise of market forces in Warwickshire of which Shakespeare was all too aware.[16] The play's composition is most often dated to 1608, although Wilson suggests *c.* 1604–7, and others suggest *c.* 1605–10. Its first performance may have been between plague closures at the public, open-air Globe Theatre or the private, indoor

Blackfriars Theatre. Whatever the case, the bad harvest (1606), the Midlands Rising against land enclosures (1607), the Great Frost (1607–8), severe dearth and inordinate grain prices (1608), and recurrent visitations of plague (1606–9) would have primed public audiences to respond viscerally to the citizens' plight and all audiences would understand the class tensions between them and patricians such as Menenius and Coriolanus.[17]

Gordon Braden observes that 'no other English dramatist demonstrates anything like Shakespeare's interest in Plutarch' and he provides a survey of scholarship that addresses 'Shakespeare's Plutarchan plays' – *Julius Caesar*, *Antony and Cleopatra* and *Coriolanus* – as 'a special phenomenon worth studying on its own'.[18] Three views include: J. L. Simmons's idea that the main characters 'have transcendent aspirations but find themselves in a world in which no genuine transcendence is possible' and so live out 'deluded ambitions that cannot do anything but fail';[19] Geoffrey Miles's idea that the plays address the venerable Renaissance theme of 'constancy' which manifests excessively in Coriolanus as 'wilful obstinacy';[20] and Paul A. Cantor's idea that the three plays collectively dramatize 'the rise and fall of the Roman Republic' and thus represent 'the tragedy of Rome itself'.[21] Braden notes that Cantor presents Shakespeare as something of 'a political theorist'[22] who documents in *Coriolanus* a Republic 'with major internal contradictions that are inseparable from its virtues and make its demise inevitable; the story in question, after all, is of how the city cannot accommodate the purest product of its own system and is almost destroyed as a consequence'.[23] The human tragedy associated with this is, in Cantor's words, 'that the Republic seems to offer men nobility only at the price of wisdom and self-knowledge'.[24]

Coriolanus has sometimes been regarded as a character of military prowess and rhetorical poverty.[25] A close look at the text suggests this claim is off target. Coriolanus may be no Antony ('Friends, Romans, countrymen, lend me your ears'),[26] and may appear linguistically awkward in some key scenes, but he's not without rhetorical versatility. Witness his zinging invectives against the plebeians (1.1.159–60, 162–83; 3.3.119–34); his well-turned repartee with Cominius (1.6.29–32, 34–9); his cursing and enthusing of the troops before Corioles (1.4.31–46; 1.6.66–85); his consoling of his wife and mother at his banishment (4.1.1–11, 14–33); his suppliant's case put to Aufidius in Antium (4.5.67–103); and his pained concession to his mother's plea for the sparing of Rome (5.3.182–93). He has his soliloquies too, brief and uneven though they be, where he: complains resentfully and in rhyming couplets about the custom of seeking plebeian 'voices' (2.3.110–22); reflects on the world's 'slippery turns' as he prepares to join forces with his enemy (4.4.12–26); and struggles with his emotions, in semi-soliloquy, as his family approaches to seek Rome's preservation (5.3.20–37). Some critics point out Coriolanus's distinctive reluctance to use conjunctions, transitions and connectives with the result that his speech has a non-Ciceronian tendency toward asyndeton (lack of conjunctions) and anacoluthon (interruption to expected sentence sequence and grammar) and thus a certain terseness and abruptness.[27] His dynamic and idiosyncratic speech sits within the play's broader rhetorical texture that includes colloquial exchanges between citizens and servingmen, intense politicking in Acts 2 and 3, and polished set pieces by Menenius, Cominius, Aufidius and Volumnia.

Two, perhaps counterintuitive, components of Coriolanus's personal style add further richness to his characterization: humour and silence. Wilbur Sanders is right to pick up on and positively value both as components of the play overall and of Coriolanus's manner. There is indeed a 'sardonic, laconic Coriolanian sense of humour' that 'keeps cropping up in this play', and 'Coriolanus's silences – his moments of steadfastly *not* soliloquizing – may be filled with something just as important as Hamlet's loose-souled lucubrations'.[28] These qualities are well appreciated in performance, but no less present and enjoyable for attentive readers too. All this should be enough to show that Coriolanus possesses the linguistic skills appropriate to his patrician class despite the disproportionate time he has spent in war rather than debate.[29]

In any case, the greater point is not that he suffers, or actually does not suffer, from impoverished rhetorical capacity, but that he harbours a deep-seated aversion to what he sees as rhetoric's inauthenticity. In John Plotz's powerful reading, Coriolanus finds himself in a world where 'words are not used to *express* but to *get* things': Rome exhibits 'an exceptionally unscrupulous sort of politics-as-usual, where interest rules and deceit has the drop on sincerity any day' and Coriolanus cannot abide it and calls it out (to his detriment).[30] It would be too simplistic, of course, to laud Coriolanus as a beacon of purity in a sullied world, but his desire for a type of universal plain dealing is as attractive as it is unrealistic. When immersed in the duties of war this presents no particular difficulty, but once among the politicians it all feels tainted: 'I will go wash' (1.9.66) he says, deadpan, in response to publicly receiving his glorious cognomen.

Coriolanus has a solipsistic, class-based notion of Rome and society that allows him little latitude in social relations and burdens him with such scorn for the civic rights and rites of his wider community as will ultimately undo him. Rome imagined him and, through his mother's tutelage and the school of war, realized him. That he flourishes so extraordinarily does not mean he lies beyond Rome's assumptions or its power to call him to heel.

Shakespeare places Coriolanus in a republic that, for all its class and wealth inequities, remains genuinely invested in democratic values and thus capable of structural developments that benefit the masses such as the emergence of the tribunes. That Brutus and Sicinius are adept political schemers, whose office had to be won by popular protest rather than mere rational argument, does not discount the fact that Coriolanus finds himself within a state that is larger than him and determined to persist as a whole-of-society structure able simultaneously to value its inherited processes and allow incremental change for the maintenance of social order.

Compromising, temporizing, negotiating, talking-the-talk and making concessions – these tedious, slow, difficult and, yes, often deceptive, strategic and cruel processes are the very lifeblood of the Republic (witness Menenius!) and cannot be imagined away. The 'one' must come to terms with the 'many' and there is, unless one would banish all society and live and die alone, no other way. This home truth is delivered in its most powerful form by Coriolanus's mother as she coaches him to 'war' for Rome (1.3.1–17), 'dissemble' for gain (3.2.63) and give up all for mother and motherland (5.3.94–182). This coming to terms will necessarily be most painful – and even personally and generically tragic – for those comets of heroic masculinity that Rome produces, needs, celebrates and, when the time comes, shovels aside like rubble before the onward march of collective statehood. As Cynthia Marshall puts it, 'Martius's conflict is *with the political* – with the requirements of life in a social group' rather than with any particular person, group or event.[31]

A play as political as *Coriolanus* necessarily resonates across parties, territories and centuries because everyone has a view on the relationship between society, family and individual. This capacity of the play to be read diversely is a recurring theme throughout the chapters of this collection, which I will briefly describe here. In 'The Critical Backstory', Huw Griffiths shows how the difficulty of achieving a settled view of the play and its protagonist – because of their inherent paradoxes and ambiguities – has generated a diverse body of scholarship from the seventeenth century to the present. While many early responses faulted the play for its failure to adhere to neoclassical standards of taste, from the early nineteenth century onwards a range of more positive and disparate critical traditions began emerging that valued its complexity of character and ambiguity of meaning.

In the second chapter, Robert Ormsby provides a 'Performance History' of *Coriolanus* which confirms the play's political versatility on stage from early adaptations by Nahum Tate and John Dennis, through to the influential nineteenth-century actor-managers John Philip Kemble and Edwin Forrest and ground-breaking work by the Comédie-Française and Berliner Ensemble. He concludes by surveying a dynamic array of British, North American, Québécois, Dutch and Japanese productions.

Graham Holderness rounds out the first half of the book with his account of the 'State of the Art' of *Coriolanus* scholarship. He outlines some foundational late-twentieth-century criticism before unpacking, with numerous examples, the three broad, interpretative trends – political, gendered and creative – that he sees as currently shaping modern approaches to the play.

The second half of the book comprises four original essays articulating 'New Directions' in *Coriolanus* research. The first of these is Anna Kamaralli's chapter which is attuned to the salience of gender and the acting profession as it interrogates selfhood in the play. Coriolanus is in every way a staged body, condemned to performing being (and to being performed) for multiple onstage and offstage audiences.

In the next chapter, Evelyn Gajowski takes a presentist approach as she overlays the tale of Coriolanus, a triumphant warrior and patrician so inflated by the early Roman Republic that he believes he can override its rites or persist alone, with the tale of Donald Trump, a wealthy businessman and president so empowered by his late-capitalist republic that he believes similarly. The parallel calls for urgent reflection on the impact of 'strongman' leaders on society and the natural world.

In the third 'New Directions' chapter, Jennifer Ann Bates uses G. W. F. Hegel's speculative and phenomenological accounts of ancient Rome as intellectual tools via which to examine Coriolanus's world and the grounds of his failure within it. Her philosophical analysis demonstrates how conditions and challenges of mediation and self-mediation are critically important to the play and of ongoing relevance to us today.

In the final 'New Directions' chapter, Hugh Craig brings cutting-edge, stylometric methodologies to bear on the linguistic fabric of the play. He demonstrates what can be uncovered when one explores *Coriolanus* as a collection of words, rather than a drama script. The analysis, since it is not grounded in traditions of literary-critical debate around the play's characters and themes, has the ability to throw up new insights, indeed facts, about the play that are not limited to serving current critical arguments, but may be considered in relation to such arguments or indeed to other bodies of knowledge entirely.

The seven chapters just described illustrate how artistically and conceptually fertile *Coriolanus* is in performance and scholarship from the earliest times to the present. Let's return to a few closing reflections on the play. One could say that Coriolanus's overvaluing of himself is expressive of the sort of disastrous misrecognition expected in a tragedy. His flaws are not entirely of his own making. Rome is mediated to him through his mother, his patrician status and the act of warring, and all three, in glorious combination, have misguided him to a false sense of reality in which he overestimates his own value and independence. He does experience some self-recognition at the end when confronted by his mother and family: it is partial and too late for him to benefit personally, but not too late for Rome. After a celebrated stage direction, '*holds her by the hand, silent*' (5.3.182 SD), that guides and yet leaves so much to the actor, Coriolanus makes the right ethical call with aching words straight out of North's Plutarch: 'O, mother, mother! / What have you done?' (5.3.182). Shakespeare and Thomas North are true collaborators in this artistic moment, as Muir well knew.[32]

And so Rome is redeemed – and yet it can be hard for audiences to feel either elated at its rescue or depressed by the cost. More true, perhaps, to say that Rome has dodged a spear it launched at itself. Coriolanus, heroic and patrician, had little vulnerability or insight via which to endear himself to the audience: he did not invite us in like Hamlet, nor did he come round to feel what wretches feel like Lear. If we lack sympathy for him and find little in Rome to admire, does it come down to a mere question of numbers? One death to prevent a war is worth it. An inequitable, yet relatively stable society, is better than none at all. Politics is what it is and we are the wiser for considering it. Why do these truths feel unsatisfying in this context?

Forty years ago James Holstun argued that critics have variously felt the play lacks 'the lyric meditation, tragic recognition, and figurative language we generally associate with Shakespearean tragedy', omits serious inclusion of the gods and the supernatural, does not present an Aristotelean protagonist, and refuses to conclude with the possibility of transcendent values or movement toward better social order.[33] These thoughts are provocative enough (because we may sense Aristotelean tragic qualities in Coriolanus and feel that the evolving Republic has a future), but Holstun went further to claim that the play aligns less with tragedy and more with political satire. Rather than presenting any grand tragic vision, he felt it 'satirizes tragedy and the tragic affiliations of the body politic by placing a tragic king-figure within a satiric plot as its gull'.[34]

More recently, David Scott Kastan tackled the same problem of the play's tragic uniqueness from a different angle. He noted that 'after the metaphysical density and poetic richness of the so-called "great" tragedies' some see the stylistic or poetic 'harshness' of *Coriolanus* and *Timon of Athens* 'as evidence of a decline in Shakespeare's artistic powers, or, less judgementally, of a change in his conception of tragedy'.[35] In reply, Kastan argued that 'in their stylistic severity these two plays uncompromisingly display the fullest extension of Shakespeare's tragic understanding' because even that final consolation, when all else is lost, of 'remarkable artistic control' and beautifully 'ennobled' form, is withheld.[36] There is no consolation provided at the end, not even 'the consolations of art'.[37] What we get is a messy, yet politically effective murder, a baldly undignified victory stomp ('*Aufidius stands on him*'; 5.6.131 SD), and continuation of routine politics. The views of Holstun and Kastan are not miles apart and when we add them to the plethora of interpretations already presented in this Introduction and scattered through the chapters of this book, it is clear that this intriguing play, over centuries, has never lost its grip on us.[38]

But does it grip students? Well, the final chapter in this collection aims to help teachers facilitate that. Claire Hansen shares her experience of having taught the play and enriches it with a survey of useful editions, productions, contexts and approaches to enable multiple routes through the text in the classroom.

I hope this Introduction has made its case that *Coriolanus* is something of a TARDIS, far bigger on the inside than it appears on the outside (even for a long play). The *Doctor Who* analogy goes further because the play travels in time: its protagonist and politics are able to speak to – indeed *for* – all of us, even though we may occupy radically differing mindsets, states and centuries. The 'New Directions' chapters in this collection require the reader's passage to new worlds. This is an important point: the chapters do not just give different literary interpretations of the play, they require us to occupy different disciplinary standpoints and rhetorics from which to consider the play. If you have been trained in or lean toward one particular discipline – such as English or Drama – you will need to be patient and perhaps even reread the chapters that speak in other disciplinary tongues because Craig's chapter relies on the mathematical language of data analysis, Gajowski's piece is driven by a presentist cultural imperative, Bates's mode is decidedly philosophical, Kamaralli's understanding is performative, and Hansen's chapter is oriented to the pedagogical. A play like *Coriolanus* deserves such an orchestra of disciplines.

1

The Critical Backstory

Huw Griffiths

Interpreting *Coriolanus*

Coriolanus, the play, and Coriolanus, the character, are two things that seem to demand interpretation. They want us to work hard at making sense of them. At the same time, however, they both frustrate efforts to bring them clearly into focus. They are, you might say, 'open to interpretation'.

Take the play's final scene. Within barely a couple of minutes of stage-time, Coriolanus moves from defiantly inviting his enemies to 'Cut me to pieces' to being ignominiously trampled on as he is killed, and then to being lifted off stage as a military hero. Aufidius, his nemesis, makes a confused attempt to summarize his story:

> Though in this city he
> Hath widowed and unchilded many a one,
> Which to this hour bewail the injury,
> Yet he shall have a noble memory.
>
> (5.6.152–5)

The conspicuous paradoxes contained in Aufidius's final speech, as he is preparing to help carry Coriolanus's body offstage, not only frustrate our capacity immediately to grasp the meaning of the performance, they also anticipate the interpretative work that audiences and critics have undertaken ever since. How is it possible to reconcile the man who 'hath widowed and unchilded many a one' with the man of 'noble memory'? How is a character who clearly revels in violence and who displays an all-consuming contempt for the Roman people, particularly the plebeians against whom he pits the values of his own patrician class, to be squared with the celebration of him as a man of honour and virtue? If people are still 'bewailing the injury', how can his death become an occasion for tragic reconciliation? Even as the play seems to come to a conclusion, further interpretation is invited.[1]

In this chapter, I examine some aspects of how *Coriolanus* has been discussed from the period when the first Shakespeare criticism appeared – the late seventeenth and early eighteenth centuries – and will consider how those critical debates have developed through the centuries. I will pay particular attention, throughout, to the way that critics have variously responded to the fragmentary, open-ended or ambiguous nature of the play and its central character. From John Dennis in 1712 (who considered the play to be 'without moral' because of its inconsistencies) through to current readings of the play, writers have contended with the difficulties of interpreting one of the most enigmatic of Shakespeare's plays, and the seeming resistance of both the play and its central protagonist to clear explanation.

But I want, first, to dwell on a particular moment that constitutes a turning point in Shakespeare criticism more broadly, and in *Coriolanus* criticism in particular. The late eighteenth and early nineteenth century is a moment in which the critical debate around this play crystallizes, when writers respond to the work of earlier critics but when they also start to formulate the questions that still dominate our understanding of the play. This period in Europe and Britain witnessed a number of revolutions: political, social and cultural. The French Revolution of 1789 that overturned the monarchy, replacing it with a republic, was both the culmination of long-standing political unrest and the starting point of significant political change across the continent. Old orthodoxies were questioned and traditional political forms overturned. In the arts, these political changes were reflected in the Romantic movement. In writers' approaches to Shakespeare, this included a new approach, away from an emphasis placed by writers of the previous age on the moral implications of his plots, and toward a focus on the psychology of individual characters. Also bolstered by the very early beginnings of the academic study of English literature, and the development of the public lecture as a major cultural form, this period saw a pronounced interest in Shakespeare as a topic of discussion. And, given the topicality of many of the events that are central to the plot of *Coriolanus* – popular riots against the patrician class; patrician disdain for popular dissent; the politics of domestic upheaval and of international conflict – it is no surprise to find that the play featured prominently in those discussions.

In an introduction to an 1808 edition of the play, Elizabeth Inchbald captures the potential for topical interpretation occasioned by the play at this time. Inchbald was a successful novelist, a very successful playwright and a less successful actor. The edition – from her twenty-five-volume collection *The British Theatre* – records the text adapted by Richard Brinsley Sheridan and used by a famous production that had John Philip Kemble in the lead role. The Kemble production had been running since 1789 and would last on the stage until 1817. However, Inchbald is writing just after an eight-year hiatus in the run (from 1797 to 1806) which she explains as follows:

> This noble drama, in which Mr. Kemble reaches the utmost summit of the actor's art, has been withdrawn from the theatre of late years, for some reasons of state. When the lower order of people are in good plight, they will bear contempt with cheerfulness, and even with mirth; but poverty puts them out of humour at the slightest disrespect.

Certain sentences in this play are therefore of dangerous tendency at certain times, though at other periods they are welcomed with loud applause.[2]

Inchbald's account of the play's 'dangerous tendency at certain times' confirms the 'openness' of *Coriolanus* to interpretation. At times of political unrest, the 'lower order of people' might see in it some justification for violent complaint; at less fraught periods, they might consider the harsh treatment of the plebeians by the patricians in the play with greater equanimity. How the play is interpreted depends upon context and the kinds of question that you bring to it. This account of a particular production also confirms the undecidability of the play's politics. If Emma Smith is right that the play often tries, but somehow fails, to 'get to know' its central protagonist, then the same might be said of its political significance.[3] That it is a play about politics and, particularly, about the relationship of the people to the ruling classes is without question. But how the play thinks about that relationship, or what it wants us to think about this, is unclear. The paradoxes in Coriolanus's character go hand in hand with the undecidability of the play's politics.

William Hazlitt, another early-nineteenth-century writer working among the after-effects of the French Revolution, took the paradoxes in Coriolanus's character to be a virtue of the play. In his influential book from 1817, *Characters of Shakespear's Plays*, he writes that, 'Coriolanus himself is a complete character' and then goes on to derive what he sees as the 'complete' nature of Coriolanus from an itemized list of interrelated contradictions in his motivations and actions:

> Coriolanus himself is a complete character: his love of reputation, his contempt of popular opinion, his pride and modesty, are consequences of each other. His pride consists in the inflexible sternness of his will; his love of glory is a determined desire to bear down all opposition, and to extort the admiration both of friends and foes. His

contempt for popular favour, his unwillingness to hear his own praises, spring from the same source. He cannot contradict the praises that are bestowed upon him; therefore he is impatient at hearing them. He would enforce the good opinion of others by his actions, but does not want their acknowledgements in words.[4]

Hazlitt sees Coriolanus as innately contradictory but also sees in these seeming contradictions the makings of a unique character. So, even though he appears both prideful and modest, this irregularity is derived from what Hazlitt calls Coriolanus's 'inflexible sternness'. This is also true for Inchbald, who sees Coriolanus as a 'spoiled child' whose 'vices and virtues ... are blended':

> The vices and virtues of Coriolanus are blended, by the poet's hand, with the nicest observance of filial similitude, as well as of filial piety. He possesses in his military character all the fire, courage, and ambition of his mother – and, as a politician, all the woman's vanity and petty pride. Yet no one can be offended with this spoiled child for his humours, as he retains a most grateful sense of that maternal tenderness which inspired his thirst of fame; though it possibly had impeded the philosophical strength of mind which would have rendered his valour of importance.[5]

Inchbald might be skewering the character of Coriolanus with this very faint praise, but she celebrates Shakespeare's capacity to produce a complex, multifaceted character. The way that she sees Coriolanus's character as something that is dependent on an assessment of the character of his mother, Volumnia, is something that I will look at again in the part of this chapter devoted to a twentieth-century psychoanalytic reading of the play.

Hazlitt's book, *Characters of Shakespear's Plays*, comes at a turning point in the history of Shakespeare criticism. Like Inchbald, he moves the critical discussion away from the very precise concerns with plot – and particularly with the moral implications of plot – that so much occupied writers in the eighteenth century. Duncan Wu writes of Hazlitt's work on Shakespeare as being part of a shift toward a recognizably modern understanding of the plays:

> Here was a new approach responsive to the Romantic fascination with psychology. And therein lies the key to Hazlitt's modernity. He saw that Shakespeare's gift lay in his understanding of the mind, and interpreted the plays in that light.[6]

In terms of *Coriolanus* criticism, Hazlitt's modernity certainly does predict later tendencies to resolve the play's perceived problems or contradictions within an understanding of the central character's complex psychology. In this, his work not only foreshadows the 'character criticism' of early-twentieth-century critics like A. C. Bradley but also the influential psychoanalytic approaches taken by later-twentieth-century critics like Janet Adelman, both of which will be covered in more detail below.

There are other ways in which Hazlitt's approach to the play foreshadows later developments. He is also concerned to isolate the play's problematic politics. Together with the elusive nature of Coriolanus's character, the precise politics of the play have been a constant concern in *Coriolanus* criticism. Hazlitt opens his essay on *Coriolanus* with the idea that the play is a 'store-house of political common-places':

> The arguments for and against aristocracy or democracy, on the privileges of the few and the claims of the many, on liberty and slavery, power, and the abuse of it, peace and war, are here very ably handled with the spirit of a poet and the acuteness of a philosopher.[7]

However, he determines that ultimately the play comes down against the 'many' and in favour of the 'privileges of the few'.

Hazlitt's essay pre-dates by two years Percy Bysshe Shelley's poem, 'The Mask of Anarchy', with its famous invocation to the people that they should continue to rise up against their aristocratic oppressors following the Peterloo Massacre which had seen government troops open fire on workers: 'Ye are many – they are few!'[8] But the same juxtaposition of the 'many' and the 'few' is an indication of the extent to which Hazlitt's essay on *Coriolanus* is similarly involved with his contemporary political moment, as much as it is with the play itself. He even claims, albeit a little facetiously, that reading the play could be a useful substitute for reading either Edmund Burke's *Reflections on the Revolution in France* or Thomas Paine's *Rights of Man*, the two key English political texts responding to the political upheaval and opportunities of the French Revolution, from conservative and radical perspectives, respectively. Ultimately, though, Hazlitt claims that Shakespeare comes down on the side of the aristocrats rather than the people. 'Shakespear', he writes, 'himself seems to lean to the arbitrary side of the question'.[9] But this claim, too, is founded as much on Hazlitt's engagement with contemporary political arguments as on a treatment of Shakespeare's play. As Hazlitt claims to see it, one of the reasons for Shakespeare, in *Coriolanus*, coming down on the side of the conservative traditions of hereditary rule rather than on the side of the people's democratic rights is because, '[t]he principle of poetry is a very anti-levelling principle'.[10] 'Poetry', he writes, 'is right-royal' in that its bias in favour of representing extreme positions prevents it from adopting more equitable visions of the world. His sardonic treatment of poetry as necessarily 'royal' or 'arbitrary' is, for his contemporary readers, a not-so-subtle attack on the poet, Samuel Taylor Coleridge, who had abandoned the radical cause in the years following the revolution, becoming a target for younger Romantic writers like Hazlitt. The essay also has the John Kemble production of the play in mind and is, in fact, an extended version of a review that had already appeared in the journal *The Examiner*. That production was, as Jonathan

Sachs describes it, an 'emphatically aristocratic staging of the play'.[11] Hazlitt would have seen this production in the last year of its run, when it had returned to the stage after its hiatus. But, as we have seen in Inchbald's account of the play and the production, the politics of the production were not so straightforwardly 'on the arbitrary side' as Hazlitt claims. Her account points toward the ways in which the play might have, rather, in the political contexts of the early nineteenth century, given impetus to political action on behalf of the 'many' against the 'few'. That this judgement of the play is based on the same production that Hazlitt identifies as, for him, leaning distinctly toward what he considers to be the play's own natural tendency toward supporting the 'few' over the 'many' is a good indication of the complexities involved in identifying the politics of *Coriolanus*.

The undecidability of the play's politics at this moment – what Sachs calls the 'culture wars that accompanied the reception of the French Revolution in Britain' – can be partly explained by the immediate concerns of the early nineteenth century.[12] But that *Coriolanus*, whether in Hazlitt's somewhat tetchy essay, or in the famous Kemble production, or in Inchbald's mediation of that production, proved to be a particularly fertile site for political engagement also has something to do with the play itself. If *Coriolanus* has a particular political 'moment' in the years following the French Revolution, this is because questions of its political interpretation might already be built into it.

The contradictions of Coriolanus's character leave him 'open to interpretation'; this is also the case with politics of the play. The example of the early-nineteenth-century, post-French Revolution response to the play indicates the indeterminacy of the play's politics, even as it shows the play's capacity for topical application. And, as with the presentation of Coriolanus's character, the complexities of political interpretation are, themselves, considered within the play. One particular moment where this happens is early on in *Coriolanus*, in the 'Fable of the Belly' (1.1.84–150) that Menenius, a Roman patrician, relates to the people who are rioting against the State because they do not have enough to eat. In what is a conservative version of the time-worn metaphor of the 'body politic', Menenius explains to the assembled rioters the need for all parts of the polity to stick to their station in life. The Roman senators are the 'belly' of the body politic – 'the store-house and the shop / Of the whole body' (1.1.128–9) – from which all benefits are distributed to the rest of the body. But, as with all productive political metaphors, Menenius is unable fully to control how his patrician pleas for a restoration of law and order might be interpreted. When, for example, he disparagingly refers to one of the rioters as 'the great toe of this assembly' (1.1.150), his partisan hostility to the rioters is revealed, and they seem ready to answer back. For Stanley Cavell, a critic with a particular interest in the question of 'interpretation' and in sceptical approaches to knowledge, this episode is illustrative of the way in which the play's politics might always have multiple interpretations:

> I take the telling of the parable of the belly as a sort of play-within-the-play, a demonstration of what Shakespeare takes his play – named for Coriolanus – to be, for *Coriolanus* too is a tale about food, with competing interpretations requiring application, told by one man to a cluster, call this an audience, causing them to halt momentarily, to turn aside from their more practical or pressing concerns in order to listen.[13]

Cavell is right that food and eating are ideas that permeate the play, particularly its dense metaphorical language.[14] But the main argument that he advances here is that the play has an ambiguous politics built into it. The sceptical responses of the 'many' to Menenius's fable, as they pause to hear this allegorical explanation of their situation, are all of our responses to the play as a whole, as we watch, read or write about it. Even as the play clearly advances specific political concerns and ideas, it turns us over onto our own capacities to interpret what those ideas might mean. It probably seems trite to say that a play by Shakespeare invites multiple, potentially contested, interpretations. This is self-evidently true, given the enormous amount of critical activity that has been undertaken over centuries. But what I have been suggesting, here, is that this is more than usually true of *Coriolanus*. As Cavell writes of the 'Fable of the Belly': 'The tale has competing interpretations.'[15] Before moving on to some twentieth- and twenty-first-century approaches to the play, I want to turn to some competing interpretations from the very beginnings of Shakespeare criticism in the late seventeenth and early eighteenth centuries.

Coriolanus and Shakespeare's first critics

If what we mean by literary criticism is the discussion and evaluation of a text that is at some remove from the critic's own immediate experience, then the first criticism of Shakespeare's work was written in the period known as the Restoration. The public theatres that Shakespeare would have been familiar with were closed in 1642. London theatres reopened in 1660. During the intervening time, there were no public theatres operative in London. When they reopened, Restoration theatre companies adapted the plays of Shakespeare and of some other Elizabethan and Jacobean contemporaries as part of their new repertoire. And they altered them in ways that fit their new theatrical, social, cultural and political circumstances. The contexts for staging and for understanding the work of Shakespeare were now sufficiently distant from their original situation that they required both adaptation for the stage and also an explanation for those otherwise interested in them as objects in their own right. And, so, this period also witnessed the first pieces of writing that sought to understand and to explain the drama of Shakespeare and his contemporaries.

The sense of what might make a good play had so altered that the critical reaction generated a range of responses. John Dennis, in a public letter published in 1721, encapsulates the situation. Dennis was himself a dramatist as well as a critic and wrote his own adaptation of Shakespeare's *Coriolanus* which was performed in 1719. He argues that his contemporaries who claim to like Shakespeare would, in fact, reject his plays if they were written now:

> A very great Part of those who pretend to be in Love with *Shakespeare*, if he were now living, and his most celebrated Plays were to be acted *De novo* without a Cabal, without Character or Prepossession wou'd Hiss and Damn the very Things of which they are now the fashionable Admirers; which seems plain to me from this very Reason, because the modern Plays which they most approve of are the very Reverse of *Shakespeare's*, with respect either to his Excellencies or his Faults.[16]

Dennis's point is that the judgement of his contemporaries is superficially fashionable, rather than the product of rational evaluation. In particular, he singles out something that was a commonplace in this period: Shakespeare was good at natural dialogue – at fitting suitable words to particular characters – but not very good at constructing narratives. Admittedly, Dennis is also taking aim at two of his literary rivals – Alexander Pope and Joseph Addison – but the source of this bitter and long-standing literary slanging match was a difference over the way that plots should offer a sense of moral justice. Dennis's view is the orthodox view for the time: that in plays it is better that the guilty get punished and the innocent rewarded. Addison offered an alternative view, to which Dennis took exception, both in general and, as I will illustrate in a moment, with regard to *Coriolanus*. Addison finds it absurd that plays should obey these kinds of narrow moral precept:

The *English* Writers of Tragedy are possessed with a Notion, that when they represent a virtuous or innocent Person in Distress, they ought not to leave him till they have delivered him out of his Troubles, or made him triumph over his Enemies. This Error they have been led into by a ridiculous Doctrine in modern Criticism, that they are obliged to an equal Distribution of Rewards and Punishments, and an impartial Execution of poetical Justice. Who were the first that established this Rule I know not; but I am sure it has no Foundation in Nature, in Reason, or in the Practice of the Ancients.[17]

He goes on to criticize Nahum Tate's 1681 rewriting of *King Lear*, in which Tate provides Lear and Cordelia with a happy ending. Cordelia survives and Lear returns to the throne. Addison writes of this adaptation: 'as it is reformed according to the chymerical Notion of Poetical Justice, in my humble Opinion it has lost half its Beauty'.

Now, in the twenty-first century, we might be inclined to agree with Addison, but it was Dennis who had the weight of critical tradition on his side. Even when critics praised Shakespeare, they did so in the knowledge that his work was lacking the kind of moral control that they might otherwise have required. When, in one of her 'Sociable Letters' from 1662 (just two years after the reopening of the theatres), the writer Margaret Cavendish praises Shakespeare's 'Wit, to Express to the Life all Sorts of Persons, of what Quality, Profession, Degree, Breeding, or Birth soever', she is already doing so in the knowledge that others would attack him for presenting this same variety on stage and that his sometimes clownish characters were not fitting for the polite stage.[18] The poet and dramatist John Dryden is chief among Shakespeare's defenders in the period, but even he has to admit that the work lacks something. He writes that 'the raising of Shakespeare's Passions are more from the Excellency of the Words and Thoughts, than the Justness of the Occasion'.[19] Dryden, like Cavendish, sees the value in Shakespearean dialogue but admits that his plots are not 'just' or 'reasonable'. He is responding to the vehement attack on the earlier drama by Thomas Rymer who compares the plays of Shakespeare and of his Jacobean contemporary, John Fletcher, unfavourably with classical precedent, believing them to fall severely short of his idea of a good play:

> ... beside the *purging* of the *passions* something must stick by observing that constant order, that harmony and beauty of Providence, that necessary relation and chain whereby the causes and the effects, the vertues and rewards, the vices and their punishments are proportion'd and link'd together.[20]

These critics are all, in various ways, applying neoclassical attitudes to their understanding of drama and, for some, Shakespeare falls so below the standards set by Aristotle and, also, by contemporary French drama, that his work should be rejected. His failure to conform his plots to ideas of poetic justice, his willingness to represent indecorous behaviour, and the way that his plays refuse to observe unified understandings of time and place: all of these things mark him down. Even those who defend him have to admit that his strengths do not allow for presenting sound moral precepts.

In attitudes toward *Coriolanus*, a focus for this critical debate was the character of Menenius, described in Charles Gildon's 1710 account of the play as 'an old humorous Senator'.[21] Writing in 1765, Samuel Johnson provides an overview of the critical conflict and mentions Menenius as a potential sticking point:

> *Dennis* is offended that *Menenius*, a senator of *Rome* should play the buffoon; and *Voltaire* perhaps thinks decency violated when the *Danish* usurper is represented as a drunkard. But *Shakespeare* always makes nature predominate over accident; and if he preserves the essential character is not very careful of distinctions superinduced and adventitious. His story requires Romans or kings, but

he thinks only on men. He knew that *Rome*, like every other city, had men of all dispositions; and, wanting a buffoon, he went into the senate-house for that which the senate-house would certainly have afforded him.[22]

Perhaps buffoons *shouldn't* be in the senate but, as Johnson claims, they might have been and, in any case, Shakespeare is more interested in the idea of a buffoonish character than he is in a sense of decorum. That Johnson sees the play as exceeding the moral structures that might ordinarily attach themselves to a neoclassical model for tragedy is also indicated in his famous, if surprising, assessment, in his edition of the play that *Coriolanus* is 'one of the most amusing of our author's performances'.[23] 'Amusing', in this context might mean something more like 'a pleasant distraction', but it still allows for a comic confutation of genres that neoclassical criticism would usually disallow. What Johnson is looking back to is Dennis's account of *Coriolanus* in his 1712 *Essay On the Genius and Writings of Shakespear*. Much of this book is taken up with a discussion of *Coriolanus*, a play that was of particular interest to Dennis, given his rewriting of it. Dennis uses *Coriolanus* as an example of where Shakespeare's work offends against ideas of decorum, claiming that these faults are not because Shakespeare lacks any talent as a writer, but because he has not had the education in the 'Poetical Art' from which later writers have benefited:

> For want of the latter our Author has sometimes made gross Mistakes in the Characters which he has drawn from History, against the Equality and Conveniency of Manners of his Dramatical Persons. Witness *Menenius* in [*Coriolanus*], whom he has made an errant Buffoon, which is a great Absurdity. For he might as well have imagin'd a grave majestic *Jack-Pudding* [a stock-name for a clown], as a Buffoon in a *Roman* Senator. *Aufidius* the General of the *Volscians* is shewn a base and profligate Villain. He has offended against the Equality of the Manners even in

his Hero himself. For *Coriolanus* who in the first part of the Tragedy is shewn so open, so frank, so violent, and so magnanimous, is represented in the latter part by *Aufidius* which is contradicted by no one, a flattering, fawning, cringing, insinuating Traytor.[24]

That a Roman senator should act like a buffoon, Dennis considers to be a 'great Absurdity'. While most critics concede Shakespeare's capacity to draw characters from nature, some critics see it as a risk. For them, he sometimes privileges rich characterful dialogue over probability. That this kind of judgement is also linked to potential problems with the moral content of the plays is evident when Dennis, in the quotation above, moves on to discuss Coriolanus himself. Here, the discontinuities in his character – what Romantic and even modern critics might see as his rounded, 'blended' character – Dennis uses as evidence for the play's lack of moral purpose.

When Dennis adapted *Coriolanus* for the stage, he substantially changed the plot. Given what he says in his critical essay on Shakespeare, this comes as no surprise. Dennis sets out his rules for what he calls, 'Poetical Fiction' as opposed to a mere 'Historical Relation'. In the former, the action should be seen to be guided by 'Providence', by some guiding moral force that exceeds mere historical accident:

> The Good must never fail to prosper, and the Bad must be always punish'd: Otherwise the Incidents, and particularly the Catastrophe which is the grand Incident, are liable to be imputed rather to Chance, than to Almighty Conduct and to Sovereign Justice. The want of this impartial Distribution of Justice makes the *Coriolanus* of *Shakespear* to be without Moral.[25]

What is it about the play that Dennis so objects to? He concedes that Coriolanus does get 'punish'd' for siding against Rome, his own country:

> 'Tis true indeed *Coriolanus* is kill'd by those Foreign Enemies with whom he had openly sided against his Country, which seems to be an Event worthy of Providence, and would look as if it were contriv'd by infinite Wisdom, and executed by supreme Justice, to make *Coriolanus* a dreadful Example to all, who lead on Foreign Enemies to the Invasion of their native Country.[26]

But the problem lies with the other characters. Aufidius, 'the principal Murderer of *Coriolanus*, who in cold Blood gets him assassinated by Ruffians', 'not only survives, and survives unpunish'd, but seems to be rewarded for so detestable an Action'.[27] Likewise, Dennis believes that the Roman tribunes, Sicinius and Brutus, appear 'to cry aloud for Poetick Vengeance' but are left unscathed by the play's action. Dennis goes into great detail on the apparent methods and motivations that the tribunes use to oppose Coriolanus and to secure his banishment. If they had opposed him openly Dennis would have approved but, given the underhand methods that they used, then they should not have been left unpunished by the plot.

When Dennis revises the plot of the play for his own version, which he calls *The Invader of His Country, or The Fatal Resentment*, he revises it in a way that responds to the problems he sees with the moral workings of Shakespeare's original. His title reveals the intended message: Coriolanus, in particular, is to be 'punish'd' for invading his own country, but not before he has dispatched a number of treacherous tribunes and, also, leaves Aufidius dead on the ground. Dennis's plot is determined as much by his political intent – an attack on Jacobitism – as by his own moral and aesthetic criteria. He rewrites the play in order to direct sympathy away from Coriolanus, who he turns into a representation of Jacobite rebellion enlisting foreign forces to overthrow the government of his own country. The politics of Dennis's play are in marked contrast to an earlier Nahum Tate version, *The Ingratitude of a Commonwealth* (1682), which, as its title suggests, sympathizes more with Coriolanus than with the people. Although Coriolanus still dies at the end, he does so in a way that sees him embracing his family as a form of royal dynasty. Tate's version looks back on the period of the Civil Wars and he uses the play to attack the government of the Cromwellian Interregnum, and to celebrate the return to the throne of the Stuart monarchy.

In order to produce a version of *Coriolanus* with a more consistent message, both playwrights have to iron out the inconsistencies that they see in Coriolanus's character. When Dennis writes that Coriolanus appears as one kind of person at the start of the play and as another at the end, he is making an aesthetic judgement about what constitutes a good play: a character that performs a clear and logical role within a plot that articulates a particular moral vision of the world. He cannot accept a character who is 'open' and 'magnanimous' at one time and then 'fawning' and 'cringing' at another. Rather than, as later critics do, resolve these apparent contradictions within the complex psychology of the central character, Dennis sees incongruities as being a problem with the plot that can only get resolved through a radical rewriting. He sees Shakespeare's Coriolanus and *Coriolanus* as so fragmentary that they require interpretation but, rather than taking this as a virtue – as both Inchbald and Hazlitt do – he corrects Shakespeare's 'mistakes'.

Having already looked at the ways in which writers in the early nineteenth century understood the potentially fragmentary nature of Coriolanus, in the next section I move on to look at a variety of ways that, through the twentieth century and into the present, critics have used the fragmented nature of the play's protagonist as an occasion for productive critical engagement.

Coriolanus in the early twentieth century: Bradleyan ignorance

When, in 1922, the writer and critic, Lytton Strachey wrote that '*Coriolanus* is certainly a remarkable, and perhaps an intolerable play', he was, as we have seen, writing after centuries of critics' efforts to make sense of it. Strachey's disgruntlement with the play condenses into a singular judgement that 'The hero is no human being at all':

> ... he is the statue of a demi-god cast in bronze, which roars its perfect periods, to use a phrase of Sir Walter Raleigh's through a melodious megaphone.[28]

Strachey would have seen his distaste for the play echoed in the writings of his contemporary, the foremost and most influential Shakespeare critic of the early twentieth century, A. C. Bradley. *Coriolanus*, Bradley writes, 'is scarcely popular', declaring that 'no reader ever called it his favourite play'.[29] Bradley's influence on Shakespeare criticism in the first half of the twentieth century is hard to overestimate and, while his star waned in the academy from the 1970s onwards, his influence lingers on in high school education and, sometimes, in the theatre. What makes his approach to Shakespeare so enduring and attractive is, partly, that his work unites the two different sets of assumption espoused by neoclassical and Romantic critics: the primacy of appropriate plot in eighteenth-century critics and the reorientation to a consideration of specific characters' attributes and motivations that occurred in the early nineteenth century. His formulation for successful drama comes in his famous and often reprinted book, *Shakespearean Tragedy*: 'The centre of the tragedy, therefore, may be said with equal truth to lie in action issuing from character and character issuing from action.'[30] What Bradley means is that the tragic action of a play – what Dennis calls its 'catastrophe' – is (or should be) dependent on the character of its central character. It is because of the kind of person that they are that the tragedy happens; and the kind of person that they are is to be understood as the product of the events in which they are found.

Part of Bradley's circumspection about *Coriolanus* – and about Coriolanus – lies in the connections that he sees between the action of the play and how that issues from the character of the protagonist. 'There must', he writes, 'be some ... reason why this drama stands apart from the four great tragedies and *Antony and Cleopatra*':

> And one main reason seems to be this. Shakespeare could construe the story he found only by conceiving the hero's character in a certain way; and he had to set the whole drama in tune with that conception.[31]

The story that Shakespeare 'finds' is one in which an apparently noble man turns against his own country and attacks it. The 'catastrophe' – the tragedy – is precipitated by this basic sequence of events and, for Bradley, there must be something about Coriolanus himself that makes this inevitable. As with most critics discussed so far, Bradley does not shy away from the apparent contradictions in Coriolanus's character:

> Though he is the proudest man in Shakespeare, he seems to be unaware of his pride, and is hurt when his mother mentions it. It does not prevent him from being genuinely modest, for he never dreams that he has attained the ideal he worships; yet the sense of his own greatness is twisted round every strand of this worship. In almost all of his words and deeds we are conscious of the tangle.[32]

What Inchbald calls 'blended' and Hazlitt calls the 'complete' character of Coriolanus, Bradley calls a 'tangle'. For Bradley, it is from these characteristics that the tragic action of the play must be derived and, so, he identifies in Coriolanus a lack of self-awareness. Coriolanus stumbles into tragedy because he is not aware of these contradictory impulses in the 'tangle' of his character. 'Unfortunately', Bradley writes, 'he is altogether too simple and too ignorant of himself.'[33] He argues that this can be seen in one of the play's defining moments, when Coriolanus is seemingly too proud to acknowledge the acclaim of the Roman people:

> There is a greatness in all this that makes us exult. But who can assign the proportions of the elements that compose this impatience of praise: the feeling (which we are surprised to hear him express) that he, like hundreds more, has simply done what he could; the sense that it is nothing to what might be done; the want of human sympathy ... ; the pride which makes him feel that he needs no recognition, that after all he himself could do ten times as much, and that to praise his achievement implies a limit to his power? If any one could solve this problem, Coriolanus certainly could not. To adapt a phrase in the play, he has no more introspection in him than a tiger.[34]

His failure to assess his own capacities in relation to the events that surround him leads him blindly into a conflict with the very things that he claims to want to protect: Rome, and his family. The audience of *Coriolanus* is 'expected to see in the hero a man totally ignorant of himself, and stumbling to the destruction either of his life or of his soul'.[35] Bradley's answer to the conundrum of Coriolanus's contradictions and the invitation to interpretation provided by the play's difficulties is that what we are witnessing is a central hero who is deeply unaware of his own character and motivations. The play's unknowability derives from Coriolanus's failure to know why he does what he does.

Interestingly, at the edges of his account of *Coriolanus*, this vacuum in the main character allows Bradley to suggest an alternative source of responsibility for his actions: his mother. 'Though the play is by no means a drama of destiny', Bradley writes, 'we might almost say that Volumnia is responsible for the hero's life.'[36] In what follows, I look at the ways in which our sense of Coriolanus's fragmentary personhood has, at times, been ascribed to the prominent place given to his mother in the play and, also, an influential psychoanalytic reading that draws on this idea.

Coriolanus, Volumnia and psychoanalysis

As we saw in Elizabeth Inchbald's 1808 'Remarks' on *Coriolanus*, she understands Coriolanus's character as a blend of ambition and vanity. Where he gets these characteristics from is his mother:

> The vices and virtues of Coriolanus are blended, by the poet's hand, with the nicest observance of filial similitude, as well as of filial piety. He possesses, in his military character, all the fire, courage, and ambition of his mother – and, as a politician, all the woman's vanity, and petty pride.[37]

Coriolanus is not himself; he is his mother's son. The importance that Inchbald gives to Volumnia in our understanding of the play's complexities is something that is picked up by many critics, sometimes by writers who value the characterization of Volumnia as, for various reasons, more obviously successful than that of Coriolanus. The subtitle for Kemble's version of the play was, tellingly, 'The Roman Matron', indicating that Volumnia might be a character who makes a strong claim on our attention such that she might almost be considered a second protagonist. In his notes to the 1710 complete edition of Shakespeare's works, Charles Gildon, in a common assessment of her character from the eighteenth century, describes her as having a 'noble spirit' that is, 'well express'd in her speech'.[38] More recently, in twentieth-century psychoanalytic work on the play, Volumnia has been seen as a projection of masculinist fears of dependence on women and on the mother in particular. She is a woman, as Janet Adelman describes her, 'who lives through her son' but who has also created him 'as the enactment of the role that she has imagined for him'.[39] One of the key insights of this psychoanalytic work is that characters are not necessarily in full possession of their own motivations but can also be considered projections of others' fantasies, and that who they are is dependent on matters that exceed their control. Whether in the discontinuities identified by Dennis as a fault of Shakespeare's learning, or in the paradoxes of Hazlitt's version of Coriolanus, or in Bradley's understanding of him as deeply unaware of his own motivations, we can see that this play is readily available to readings that construe people, or characters, as determined by aspects of themselves that are beyond their own understanding or control. If Coriolanus's character seems always to be understood as indeterminate, or as fragmentary, then psychoanalytic approaches to the play provide a way into thinking about how a person is never self-identical, never quite their own person.

In *Suffocating Mothers*, Janet Adelman outlines the ways in which masculine personhood, as represented in some of Shakespeare's plays, is dependent on a rejection of a mother figure that, nevertheless, returns to trouble and disturb the realization of that masculine identity. Prominent in her discussion are Hamlet's relationship with Gertrude and the haunting of Macbeth by the monstrously maternal weird sisters and by Lady Macbeth. With *Coriolanus*, she argues that the protagonist's quest for solitary military glory is predicated on a fear of maternal influence that can never be escaped because, at least in this play, that quest is also the explicit desire of the mother in question. Coriolanus, she writes, 'attempts to recreate himself through his bloody heroics, in fantasy severing the connection with his mother even as he enacts the ruthless masculinity that is her bidding'.[40] As Coriolanus dreams of autonomy – away from his mother, from Rome, from the demands of the people – he is only ever demonstrating his inability to escape those origins. This version of Coriolanus reads, in some ways, like an amalgamation of Strachey's empty metallic shell of a man and Bradley's tragically unaware hero. As already mentioned in Cavell's focus on this aspect of the play, Adelman identifies food and hunger as an important motif in the play. But, rather than use this as a means to consider the politics of scarcity that determine the play's political engagements, she sees in it a realization of the play's concern with the maternal:

But although Volumnia [unlike *Macbeth*'s witches or Lady Macbeth] does not make stews out of body parts or threaten to dash Coriolanus's brains out while he is nursing, her less melodramatic disruptions of the feeding situation give her a power over her son that is the psychic equivalent of theirs: 'framed' (5.3.63) by her equation of starvation and masculinity, he becomes the man her fancy builds (2.1.192–4). By failing to feed him enough, she makes hunger the sign of his vulnerability, creating him as a virtual automaton who cannot tolerate his own ordinary human neediness and who thus is compelled to act out needs he can neither understand nor satisfy. Under her tutelage, any acknowledgment of need – starting with the acknowledgment that he, like the crowd he so despises, needs food – threatens to undermine his masculine autonomy, in effect returning him to the maternal breast from which he could never get enough.[41]

Coriolanus's attack on Rome and his destructive desire to set it on fire – to burn the whole thing down – is a final attempt to regain control. The difficult political question of the play – how can such an apparently honourable Roman turn on his own city? – is understood not through the paradoxes of his individual character, nor through the politics of the 'few' versus the 'many' but, rather, as the fantastic projection of a crisis in masculinity. Since the 1980s, the critical accounts of the play that have paid the most determined attention to the play's complicated identification with masculinity are queer readings, and it is to these that I turn in the next section.

Coriolanus: Queer readings and future Coriolanuses

When Coriolanus is exiled from Rome, he approaches his archenemy, Aufidius, to form an alliance. Aufidius greets him with open arms and with some of the most palpably homoerotic lines in Shakespeare's writing:

> But that I see thee here,
> Thou noble thing, more dances my rapt heart
> Than when I first my wedded mistress saw
> Bestride my threshold. ...
>
> ... Thou has beat me out
> Twelve several times since and I have nightly since
> Dreamt of encounters 'twixt thyself and me –
> We have been down together in my sleep,
> Unbuckling helms, fisting each other's throat –
> And waked half dead with nothing.
>
> (4.5.117–20, 123–8)

This writing is excitingly physical and, when in these sentences, Aufidius's dream lands on the loaded word, 'nothing', the erotic impact of them is hard to ignore. Some early adaptations (Tate's *Ingratitude* and Sheridan's *Roman Matron*, but not Dennis's *Invader*) omit or substantially alter this speech, averting their gaze from some of its impact. Queer critics have, rather, used it as a springboard for analysing the play in ways that, again, work to undo the tattered remains of Coriolanus's 'character'.

Bruce Smith associates the play and particularly its characterization of Coriolanus through his relationships with men, as a version of one of the six 'myths' that he sees early modern culture inherit from classical literature as a language for the representation of same-sex male desire. Unsurprisingly, *Coriolanus* is a play that he associates with the myth of 'Comrades and Combatants'. Smith sees this particular myth as all-encompassing for the homosocial world of early modern England:

> Since all men in Elizabethan and Jacobean society participated in patriarchy, the Myth of Combatants and Comrades incorporated them all, high and low, literate and illiterate alike.[42]

Ultimately, Smith sees Shakespeare's masculinist plays about military comrades and combatants as pursuing 'safe, well charted courses through the treacherous waters of sexual desire', but this is not before he mounts a compelling case for the ongoing investment that this play has in homoerotic representation. In particular, he points out the purposeful alterations that Shakespeare makes to Plutarch's *Parallel Lives*, the main source for the play:

> Plutarch's life of Coriolanus, though suggestively set in parallel with the life of Socrates' protégé Alcibiades, is altogether innocent of the homoerotic images in which Shakespeare has bodied forth the Roman hero's military career. In Plutarch's account, Aufidius's speech to Coriolanus is one simple sentence:
>
>> Stande up, O Martius, and bee of good chere, for in proffering thy selfe unto us, thou dost us great honour: and by this meanes thou mayest hope also of greater things, at all the Volsces' handes.
>> (2.170)
>
> No embracement, no declaration of love, no dream, no struggle. ... Nowhere in these parallel lives ... is there any suggestion of the volatile connection Shakespeare makes between male aggression and male sexual desire.[43]

While Smith traces the ways in which homoeroticism might occupy the mainstream of early modern literary production, other critics have seen some more subversive potential in the play's language. Paul Hammond demonstrates that the play sufficiently scandalized the norms of the 1660s (just fifty years after its initial production) that, as mentioned above, early adaptations attempted variously to draw a veil over the play's explicit physicality. He describes Aufidius's speech as 'an ecstatic fusion of enmity, rivalry, comradeship, and sexual desire', before outlining the ways in which Nahum Tate, in 1682, removed all of these suggestions.[44]

In a book chapter that was a catalyst for connecting queer theory with Shakespeare studies – 'The Anus in *Coriolanus*' – Jonathan Goldberg pushes the disruptive potential of some of the dialogue in this play still further. Goldberg claims that Aufidius's speech 'motivated [his] inquiry from the start':

> It is clearly no overstatement to regard these lines as sexual, or to see a relationship between the wedded mistress (whom, Aufidius assures Coriolanus, he loved – 'Know thou first, / I lov'd the maid I married' [4.5.115–16]) and the nocturnal enemy now crossing the threshold like a bride, or between the fisted throat and the vagina.[45]

Goldberg's account draws inspiration from psychoanalytic approaches to the play in order further to expand the range of implications that might be derived from this speech, connecting it in particular to Menenius's 'Fable of the Belly' in which, he writes, 'the belly assumes the position of the anus, receiving what is normally expelled'.[46] This is because the body politic that Menenius conjures up is a weirdly 'closed economy' in which waste itself becomes consumed by the belly; it is described as 'the sink of the belly'. Paying close attention to a short note on the idea of waste in Cavell's discussion of food, eating and consumption in the play – an account which in turn derives some of its material from Adelman – Goldberg elaborates a metaphorics of the body that sees the play refusing to present a discrete, coherent idea of personhood:

> Coriolanus's career of attempted self-authorship represents a desire to become a machine, to 'live' in some realm that is not the biological. The fantasy of the play involves a dream of authoring and of self-authoring that transgresses even the transgressive desire that the play suggests in its equation of womb and bowels. For in paralleling the loves of Aufidius and of Volumnia, in equating hetero and homo desire and its betrayal, the play looks beyond these forms of sexuality,

or, perhaps imagines an 'inhuman' sexuality that would not be subject to betrayal.[47]

Goldberg's 'inhuman' Coriolanus is derived from the insights of queer theory, which asks us to rethink what it means to be a person in the world. It is telling that, in doing this, he returns us to the paradoxical narrative of the play: a play about a man that betrays both his country and his supposed enemy, both his family and his intimate rival. The difficult politics of this play are, at the close of Goldberg's chapter, being reoriented toward a question for the future: how might bodies continue to be implicated within intractable political equations?

That question has been answered in a couple of ways by critics writing more recently – in Jason Edwards's contribution on *Coriolanus* to the collection, *Shakesqueer*, and in work such as that of James Kuzner – that might require us to think about the fate of biological life within ruinous political systems.[48] Kuzner takes as his starting point recent critical interest in the way that early modern drama might engage with theories of liberal or even democratic republicanism, particularly thinking of work by Annabel Patterson. Such theories, Kuzner tells us, depend on an idea of 'bounded personhood'. Even though the play, *Coriolanus*, is set at the birth of the Roman republic, the idea that a person might be a coherent and comprehensible entity is not something to which the play readily lends its support. Instead Kuzner turns his attention to the political theories of the contemporary Italian writer, Giorgio Agamben, whose influential idea of 'bare life' has underpinned recent thought about what is at stake in any political system. For Agamben, all political systems, however they might relate the 'many' to the 'few', depend on the existence of forms of life that are placed beyond the law, rendering them vulnerable to killing that is neither legal nor illegal. This understanding of political formations is sometimes called, by Agamben and others, the 'state of exception', a state in which sovereign power exists through its capacity to exclude, kill and exile outside of a rule of law that these actions, nevertheless, bring into being. In our world, we might think of stateless people of various kinds. Ironically, it is in the exiled Coriolanus that Kuzner locates the glimpse of a possibility that we might be able to think outside of this situation:

> As an exploration of the emerging appeal of bounded selfhood, *Coriolanus* has proven exceptionally provocative to early modernists. While the play's eponymous hero is usually read as the character most attracted to the wish for such selfhood, he is, I argue, just the opposite: a figure who represents practices of self-undoing that could clear a path out of the state of exception, however tortuous that path might prove. He gestures toward life after and outside its production in Rome as bare life, toward ways of speaking and acting that do not depend on a construct of personal boundedness through which the public can locate and manipulate its subjects.[49]

At the start of this chapter, I looked at the paradoxes of Coriolanus's character – both prideful and full of humility, both enemy and champion of Rome – and throughout the chapter I have shown the ways in which these intractable contradictions are, for many critics, played out in the unsolvable politics of *Coriolanus*: is it for the many or for the few? Kuzner invites us to see that, in his path of self-annihilation, in the way that the play blasts apart the integrity of political personhood, we might glimpse the possibility of a politics that escapes these relationships completely. This is echoed in a speculative piece on the play that I think might help guide us toward future understandings of it. Jason Edwards, like Kuzner, takes his cue from Goldberg's radical re-evaluation of the concept of personhood and the integrated body, and seeks a more utopian vision that is gestured to, not by Coriolanus's own actions in the play, but in our capacities to reinterpret it and to rethink how we treat paradox and contradiction via the queer possibilities of giving in to our bodies as always open, never discrete:

If more of us could develop a taste for these queer possibilities, if more of us were, unlike Coriolanus, able to understand part-part and part-whole relations in desirable, democratic, intersubjective terms, rather than as disgusting or the inevitably degenerative interplay of mutually 'monstrous members' (2.3.12) in 'mutinies and revolts' (3.1.127), there might be the hope of a happier ending. We would have to risk opening ourselves up in spite of the fear, reality, and proximity of infection, impingement, bombardment, and the often toxic nourishment provided by other people.[50]

So much of the play's action, and of the critical story that I have told here, is/has been motivated by this fear. Edwards asks us to reinterpret the play – one more time – in a way that provides a comically 'happy ending' in the place of the constraining paradoxes of tragedy.

2

Performance History

Robert Ormsby

Introduction

Coriolanus may not be the most frequently staged Shakespeare play, but the history of its stagings has been well chronicled by scholarship. Besides numerous shorter accounts, two monographs provide in-depth analyses of productions from the seventeenth to the early twenty-first century: John Ripley's and my own.[1] Those accounts, and this chapter, illustrate that *Coriolanus* has enjoyed memorable and important productions for centuries. While many leading actors have recognized the title role as a star vehicle, some of *Coriolanus*'s most-remembered productions are notable for their politics. The nature of and differences between productions of *Coriolanus* have depended on circumstances that include broad historical context, theatre companies' institutional priorities, individual artistic talent and theatregoers' expectations. While these circumstances are so diffuse that the play does not have a singular, overarching identity in the theatre, artists have repeatedly exploited the protagonist's antagonistic relationships to generate explicitly political stagings that explore the family as the basic social unit, class divisions and war as an extension of policy.[2] Adapters, directors and actor-managers have employed the theatrical means at their disposal to adjust this relationship between the hero's personal antagonisms and their political consequences to devise productions that are, by turns, conservative, provocative and purportedly free of politics altogether.

Coriolanus on the early modern stage

So little is known about *Coriolanus*'s original staging that its early theatrical history is a matter of conjecture.[3] Scholars have speculated about whether or not it was performed at all during Shakespeare's lifetime, if so which venue(s) it appeared in and to what extent such performances were affected by plague-related theatre closures.[4] We can only make informed guesses about what effects the play might have had on the relatively empty early modern stage. Shakespeare combines an urgent narrative drive, spectacular processions, intermittent violence, two climactic scenes (5.3, 5.6) and the harsh language of personal and political conflict that defies moral certainty. This dramatic strategy has led to an extensive literature about *Coriolanus*'s topicality, though it is impossible to know how such topicality might have registered in Jacobean performances.[5] However, as R. B. Parker argues, it is clear that Shakespeare scripts numerous potentially theatrically exciting moments in his depiction of Rome's politics through Coriolanus's relationships of mutual reliance and conflict with his family, the people and their tribunes, and Aufidius.[6]

Shakespeare introduces these relationships early on, moving quickly to Rome's battles with the Volsces, the first of many public scenes in which Martius (soon to be Coriolanus) demonstrates that his singularity must be performed in relation to a collective. The battles provide opportunities for the hero and the actor playing him to flaunt his soldierly skills; overcoming Aufidius and impossible odds wins Martius his cognomen. Yet his military exceptionalism is played out in relation to the Volscian and Roman soldiers; his comrades cheer him and, in a memorable stage image, lift him up as an instrument of war when he cries 'O, me alone! Make you a sword of me?' (1.6.76). These battles are followed by spectacular second-act processions in which Romans celebrate Coriolanus and, like audiences in the theatre, watch him perform in these political ceremonies.[7] Establishing the hero's importance for Rome in these scenes allows Shakespeare to ironize them in Act 5: in the ladies' procession where spectators witness Volumnia replacing her son as Rome's saviour when she returns home victorious; and in the following scene when Aufidius baits Coriolanus before an audience of Volscians who call for Coriolanus's death.[8] The latter metatheatrical scene potentially has great theatrical vitality and clarity; besides the thrilling rhetoric of Coriolanus's last speeches, Aufidius's standing on the dead hero is a blatant image of early modern English stage warriors' violent competitiveness and a brutally obvious sign of the Volsce's delight in his victory.

Coriolanus's relationship with the plebeians sheds more light on the theatricality of politics in the play. After his 1.1 confrontation with the people, his next encounter with them occurs when he must ask them for their voices and reveal his scars in 2.3, a scene Oliver Arnold compares to early modern English elections.[9] The symbolic violation of the people imagining that they will put their tongues into Coriolanus's wounds and speak for them implies the plebeians seizing control of the scar ritual's interpretation; as Cynthia Marshall argues, Shakespeare devises the scene to reveal how subjectivity and politics emerge through transactions with social and theatrical audiences.[10] The tribunes' manipulation of the people's response to Coriolanus's performance in the scar ceremony converts metaphorical tongues-in-wounds violence to the theatrically exciting physical danger of Act 3 in which the plebeians chant to banish Coriolanus and support their tribunes in the fight that erupts with Coriolanus.[11]

The play's intimate scenes, too, would have provided early modern actors opportunities for engrossing (meta-)theatrical tension. In 4.5 at Antium, Shakespeare exchanges physical combat for Coriolanus's stagey unmuffling before Aufidius who replies with a set speech of erotic language that effeminizes his former enemy.[12] Any Jacobean theatregoers who regarded this scene as comprising self-conscious demonstrations of the players' artistry likely perceived Volumnia's treatment of Coriolanus in the same way. Her third-act clear-eyed advice to her son about dissembling before the people to regain his consulship reveals Volumnia's understanding that the social and political are fundamentally performative.[13] This chastisement prefigures the harangue she delivers in 5.3 to persuade Coriolanus to halt the Volsce invasion. Elsewhere, she instils in Coriolanus 'the masculinist, militarist ideology of Rome'; here, she seems a *matrona docta*, the exemplary early modern English female literary figure who transmits her learning, including a knowledge of rhetoric, to her son, proving it with a fatal lesson in how to deliver persuasive speech which defeats her equally verbose child.[14] Volumnia's victory in the scene would have been densely meaningful in its original staging to the extent that early modern spectators were conscious she was played by a boy, a young player who outperformed the company's long-established leading actor, Richard Burbage (assuming he played Coriolanus). Whether or not the King's Men performed *Coriolanus* during the seventeenth century, the play's military heroism, personal conflict and political debate would give the tragedy a remarkable career in performance during the next four centuries.

Coriolanus, the Jacobite cause and the Kemble tradition

Twenty years after England's theatres reopened following a nearly two-decade hiatus during the Civil War and Interregnum, Nahum Tate reworked *Coriolanus*'s personal relationships for contemporary political purposes.[15] Tate's *The Ingratitude of a*

Commonwealth, performed in early 1682 at London's Theatre Royal, Drury Lane, is the first known staging of *Coriolanus*. In 1681, Charles II was fighting with members of Parliament who sought to exclude his Catholic brother James from succession to the throne. The theatres supported Charles, and Tate's play was 'one of a number of dramatic contributions' to the King's cause.[16] Avoiding direct allusions to James, Tate improves Coriolanus and renders his enemies more unsympathetic to demonstrate the injustice of excluding a worthy leader. Tate emphasizes Coriolanus's conflicts with his Roman enemies, reduces those with the Volsces and makes Volumnia's arguments with him more about love of Rome than filial piety.[17] No records of the production details or its reception survive, though Restoration theatre was quite different from Shakespeare's: women played female roles; a short apron jutted beyond the proscenium, behind which much of the action occurred; and painted flats connoting location ran in stage-floor slots and could be drawn to discover tableaux. Tate placed his plebeians close to the audience to give theatregoers a sense of their danger and scripted discoveries of grouped actors to elevate Coriolanus at their centre.[18] In the final scene, Tate reunites Coriolanus's family to achieve what were surely gripping theatrical effects. Tate's Aufidius gloatingly plans to rape Virgilia and the newly scripted figure Nigridus tortures Young Martius, driving Volumnia mad. Yet, poetic justice prevails: Aufidius dies shortly after deciding against rape and Volumnia kills Nigridus; to amplify this pathos, Tate scripts Coriolanus's valedictory speech with his dead son and wife by his side.[19]

John Dennis and James Thomson subsequently altered Shakespeare's play in opposition to the cause of James and his Stuart successors whose failed attempts to recapture the crown through armed conflict after James's 1688 deposition provides the background for these plays.[20] Dennis's *The Invader of his Country* (staged at Drury Lane in 1719 with Barton Booth in the lead) and Thomson's *Coriolanus* (staged at London's Covent Garden in 1749 with James Quin in the lead) cuts

Shakespeare's script to maintain the neoclassical unities of action and place: the former is shortened to ten scenes; the latter excluded Shakespeare's first three acts.[21] There are other similarities: both employ spectacular discoveries to glorify Coriolanus in accordance with neoclassicism's need for a noble hero; and both emphasized the drama's pathos through the embassy scene, as in each play, Coriolanus's mother offers him a dagger to kill her.[22] Furthermore, the plays includes characters who straightforwardly deliver their authors' didactic messages. Dennis alters Cominius's lines to lecture Coriolanus on democracy; Thomson adds the Volscian Galesus who urges Coriolanus not to treat Rome too harshly. Cominius and Galesus appear in the endings of their respective plays to remind playgoers of the conclusions' poetic justice: Coriolanus was noble, but was destroyed for planning to invade his homeland.[23]

John Ripley contends that, from the mid-eighteenth century to the early twentieth century, influential actor-managers, particularly John Philip Kemble, developed theatrical traditions that diminished the play's 'potential political subversiveness'.[24] During this era, England hardly 'lacked urgent political and military struggles that could' be read into the play.[25] The French Revolution, the Napoleonic wars and the expansion of the British Empire that entailed so much armed conflict all seem apt contexts to be read into productions of *Coriolanus*. Yet, Ripley argues that the play became a means not for polemic, but to display star actors' individual talent before appreciative audiences at the expense of Shakespeare's dramatization of 'class conflict'.[26] Kemble, the preeminent actor of his era, made the play his own, starring in it repeatedly between 1789 and 1817 (when he played Coriolanus for his Covent Garden retirement performance) and was matched until 1811 by his sister, the renowned Sarah Siddons, as Volumnia.[27] Kemble arguably established the text and visual traditions for the play that lasted until the First World War. His treatment of the text downplays democratic ideals and he devised impressive displays that suited his acting style characterized by 'a deliberate and majestic step, a statuesque grace of action, and formal, stately declamation'.[28] Painted backdrops depicted Imperial Rome, while massive processions glorified Kemble's Coriolanus as a military leader; he maintained the lead's dignity in these scenes by conveying his steadfastness. The best-known visual effect was a discovery of Kemble's exiled hero standing next to a statue of Mars at Antium, and spectators at his retirement performance witnessing such blatant comparisons between Coriolanus and the god of war, praised the actor in superlatives and expressed their sense that a theatrical era was over.[29]

In Ripley's view, what succeeded Kemble was largely a continuation of the performance conventions he established, particularly aspects of Kemble's scenography and his diminishment of partisan politics in favour of actor-managers' heroic performances.[30] However, accounting for decades of English productions by labelling them part of the 'Kemble tradition' does not do them service, especially when the productions were mounted in diverse circumstances and starred such a range of actors, including: Edmund Kean (1820), whose acting was so different from Kemble's; Charles Macready (1838); Samuel Phelps (1848–61); Henry Irving, opposite Ellen Terry's Volumnia (1901); and Frank Benson, who toured *Coriolanus* for years (1893–1919). Nor can the label account for productions in America where it was performed since the 1760s by the likes of Thomas Abthorpe Cooper (1794–1831); William Conway (1824–7); Thomas Hamblin (1825–31); and Tomasso Salvini (1885), who spoke Coriolanus's lines in Italian.[31] While space limitations prevent lengthy discussion of those productions here, Edwin Forrest's contribution to the 'Kemble tradition' warrants consideration. Forrest's actorly prestige in the United States is associated with his vocal power, athletic heroism and his embodiment of an idealized American democratic ethos.[32] He is best remembered for his nationalist, class-inflected competition with Briton Charles Macready; their rival interpretations of Macbeth led to Manhattan's notorious Astor Place riots (1849).[33] In stagings between the

1830s and 1860s, Forrest balanced his own populist instincts with Coriolanus's disdain for the people, though Forrest devised lavish processions that rivalled Kemble's in elevating the hero above his fellow citizens.[34] Forrest's most spectacular scene was his funeral procession that concluded with choral song as Coriolanus's body was lit on a pyre which lowered into the stage's trap. Moments later, a papier-mâché phoenix emerged from the fire to suggest the redemption that would follow the hero's martyrdom.[35]

Elements of the actor-manager tradition continued to shape major *Coriolanus* productions in the twentieth century, though new political influences and related scenographic innovations would affect the play's fortunes on stage, especially after the Second World War. Scenographic changes that appeared starting in the 1960s were anticipated in productions by the 'Elizabethan Methodists' Nugent Monk, William Bridges-Adams and Robert Atkins, though these directors' attempts to recreate early modern staging conditions had different assumptions about theatre than did the productions of their postwar counterparts.[36] A more obvious development in subsequent *Coriolanus* productions was the combination of a widespread desire for magnetic lead actors and assertions of the tragedy's relevance for a world that had witnessed decades of catastrophic political events.[37]

Politics, star actors and *Coriolanus*'s 'relevance' on twentieth-century stages

Coriolanus at Paris's Comédie-Française (1933–4) was, arguably, the first major twentieth-century production of the play to become politically partisan, though it was not intended as such. Swiss scholar René-Louis Piachaud's translation renders the tribunes more hypocritical[38] than they are in Shakespeare and his alterations 'stress Coriolanus's heroism and downplay his treason'.[39] Isabelle Schwartz-Gastine relates that the production did not employ elaborate sets typical of Comédie-Française shows, but relied on painted backdrops of Rome to convey an 'atmosphere of dignity and nobility'.[40] There was also a large central flight of stairs, 'allowing for extremely solemn movements that underlined the hierarchical supremacy of the hero'.[41] In Coriolanus's second-act victory procession, more than 200 actors and supernumeraries crowded both sides of the steps to greet the returning hero, their right arms raised in a gesture resembling the Nazi salute.[42] Schwartz-Gastine observes that such staging followed the Comédie-Française tradition of designing its production to show off star performers, an effect accentuated by the single-named star Alexandre's delivery of Coriolanus's harsh dialogue. She argues that this focus on a talented star with an 'emphatic and vigorous style' of speech 'resulted in a one-sided interpretation that was bound to kindle the emotions of an already very sensitive audience'.[43]

France's unstable political situation made comparisons between the well-received production and events in the country virtually inevitable.[44] The Comédie-Française's director, Émile Fabre, was himself concerned that the play could stir political outrage, and with good reason: Parisian audiences had interpreted other recent politically innocuous productions as highly topical; there were two changes of government in October and November, shortly before the play opened on 9 December; and matters worsened when the Stavisky scandal broke early in *Coriolanus*'s run.[45] Alexandre Stavisky had committed serious financial fraud and died, supposedly by suicide, early in 1934. However, there were suspicions that government officials and the police had protected Stavisky until it became too dangerous and someone in power had him killed.[46] Angry response inside the theatre to Coriolanus's attack on both the tribunes and an incompetent ruling class was matched by the national press, which encouraged such interpretations; one paper even compared Coriolanus and Hitler, suggesting that fascism could eliminate government corruption.[47] Such reaction sharpened as the political situation worsened. The disturbances that erupted in the theatre when another government fell on 27 January 1934 grew louder on 4 February, when it was announced that Fabre had been replaced by Georges Thomé, director of the Sûreté générale; that night, *Coriolanus*'s performance was repeatedly interrupted by shouts of 'Vive Fabre' and the audience demanded numerous curtain calls.[48] On 6 February, huge crowds rioted in Paris protesting the left-wing government, resulting in sixteen deaths and more than 1,200 people injured.[49] On 9 February, newspapers announced that *Coriolanus* performances were suspended indefinitely, though another change of government returned Fabre and the production to the Comédie-Française. Although *Coriolanus* played from 11 March into the autumn without further disturbances, its early run demonstrates how the 'production became not simply the analysis of the politics of the stage but a vehicle for the playgoers' political engagement'.[50]

Mainstream mid-century British productions were largely free of such political engagement. Foremost among these stagings was Laurence Olivier's 1959 performance in the lead at Stratford-upon-Avon's Shakespeare Memorial Theatre (SMT), twenty-one years after he first played Coriolanus.[51] The SMT would soon become the Royal Shakespeare Company (RSC) under the direction of Peter Hall, who would attempt to establish an ensemble company that could create 'radical' Shakespeare. But *Coriolanus*, directed by Hall, exemplified what Ripley sees as mid-century audiences' desire for 'film stars in romantic stage roles' and the 1959 SMT season was full of stars, including Dame Edith Evans, Charles Laughton and Paul Robeson.[52] Olivier, however, stood above them all: with a remarkable stage and film career, especially in Shakespearean roles, he had solidified his reputation as the twentieth century's greatest English actor. The SMT in 1959 may have produced 'escapist Shakespeare', but the company was shaped by politics insofar as a deeply inequitable class division was built into the star system it perpetuated.[53] Hall's production was clearly designed to elevate its star. The set connoted the classical world and featured stairs connecting playing spaces on three levels. This arrangement was not useful for massive processions, but, like the Comédie-Française set, it encouraged the visual representation of social hierarchies. Olivier first appeared on the top platform from where he scolded the people. It was also on this spot that his Coriolanus met his end: after the Volsce conspirators stabbed him, the 52-year-old actor plunged headfirst from the platform dangling above the stage floor; as the Volsces held his ankles, Anthony Nicholls's Aufidius made the fatal stab.[54] The fall, consistent with Olivier's physical bravado in the production, complemented his powerful and varied vocal delivery.[55] Evans's Volumnia was a match for Olivier in switching between verbal pyrotechnics, formal intonation and subtly moving speech. Together, they led the show to its first climax, when Coriolanus held Volumnia's hand silently for a long time before dramatically speaking 'O mother, mother! / What have you done?' (5.3.182–3).[56] Critics reinforced the star system by focusing on Evans and Olivier, praising their performances, especially the latter's charisma. Yet some disliked Olivier's supposed self-conscious theatricality, and sensed he was relying on a set of stale mannerisms.[57]

If criticism of Olivier hinted at a desire for theatrical revolution, Bertolt Brecht and the Berliner Ensemble were preparing one that would have lasting effects on *Coriolanus*'s history in the theatre.[58] When Brecht started adapting *Coriolanus* in 1952, he was Europe's foremost living dramatist-director-theatrical theorist. Having fled Germany in 1933 because his socialist intellectual credentials made him an enemy of the Nazis, he returned from exile in 1948 to Soviet-controlled East Berlin where he and his wife Helene Weigel soon established the Ensemble.[59] When Brecht died in 1956, his unfinished *Coriolanus* included about 60 per cent of Shakespeare's dialogue and 17 per cent new material.[60] While Brecht viewed Shakespeare as 'the measure of peerless dramatic excellence', he nevertheless altered the play to make Coriolanus and the patricians less appealing, the plebeians more sympathetic and united, and the tribunes less politically self-serving.[61] The adaptation also highlights social forces at the expense of some of Shakespeare's emphasis on the personal. For instance, Brecht sets the final scene in Rome to show the Senate, specifically Brutus, dismissing news of the hero's death as insignificant to the routine but important business of legislating.[62] Darko Suvin argues that Brecht's adaptation is a veiled criticism of Joseph Stalin's dictatorship, with the tribunes as stand-ins for committed Marxist artists like Brecht and his peers, whose 'pristine revolutionary impulse' inspires their support for the people.[63] Brecht and Weigel knew how hard it was to remain ideologically pure in Stalinist East Germany: they struggled successfully against the machinations of Walter Ulbricht's East-German Socialist Unity Party (SED) to make the Ensemble Europe's most prestigious theatre company when it first toured to London in 1956.[64]

The Ensemble's 1965 London *Coriolanus* tour, meanwhile, reveals Shakespeare becoming embroiled in the Cold War.[65] Following Brecht's death, East Germany undertook economic collectivization, halted movement to and from West Germany and, in 1963 the German Shakespeare Society split into East and West groups. SED bureaucrats treated Shakespeare, who had long been a surrogate national poet in Germany, as a proto-socialist 'cultural monument ... not to be critically examined'.[66] Suvin argues such developments meant Ensemble artists had to be careful when criticizing authoritarian rule through *Coriolanus*.[67] The risks were real: an Ensemble member who defected in London was later found dead in East Germany.[68] The situation helps explain why Ensemble members made politically anodyne comments about the production to the British public, though they might also have feared putting off Western audience members with explicit statements about Marxist Shakespeare.[69] The 1965 script that directors Manfred Wekwerth and Joachim Tenschert reworked maintains aspects of Brecht's text, such as Volumnia (Weigel) explaining to Coriolanus that Rome's people intend to resist the Volsce invasion.[70] However, they reversed Brechtian alterations by making the people less politically savvy and the tribunes less politically influential, though the sound recording reveals that the people and Brutus (Günter Naumann) and Sicinius (Martin Flörchinger) were steadfastly rational when delivering their lines.[71] Significantly, the directors restored the personally motivated struggle between Ekkehard Schall's Coriolanus and Hilmar Thate's Aufidius, especially in the battle scenes, which were thrillingly loud and action-filled.[72] However, Wekwerth and Tenschert employed anti-realistic Brechtian 'estrangement' techniques to emphasize the means by which theatrical artifice is produced: although costumes were identifiably Roman, the monochromatic set's stockade that revolved to show Rome and Corioles on opposite sides, was illuminated brightly, and scene changes occurred behind a half-curtain, making the artistic means of production continuously visible.[73] Other tactics, including the use of military symbols and intercutting battle scenes with domestic ones to emphasize the socially produced and contingent nature of human experience, are also typically Brechtian.[74] English critics were, however, more interested in Schall's and Weigel's star performances, dismissing the production's politics as simplistic and criticizing the battles as reminiscent of Nazi militarism.[75]

This *Coriolanus* reappeared on London stages in different guises half a decade later. The National Theatre's 1971 production featured scenography virtually identical to the Ensemble's, but returning directors Wekwerth and Tenschert adapted the 1965 script using Shakespearean dialogue.[76] In this staging, the people were less appealing than before, the tribunes lost political significance, the production did not have Constance Cummings's Volumnia telling Anthony Hopkins's Coriolanus that the people would withstand his invasion of Rome and performances concluded with Coriolanus's assassination.[77] Additionally, performers gave more weight to personal psychological conflicts than to political analysis compared to the Ensemble's version: Hopkins was enthralled by the battles and overwrought when asking for the people's votes; Cummings's final exchange with Hopkins was all about their characters' familial dynamic; and the conclusion depicted a personal triumph for Dennis Quilley's Aufidius.[78] One year earlier, the RSC staged Günter Grass's *The Plebeians Rehearse The Uprising* at London's Aldwych Theatre.[79] Grass's drama, which depicts the 1953 East-German workers' protests over increased government production quotas, imagines the protest spilling over into the Ensemble's *Coriolanus* rehearsals where Brecht's avatar, The Boss, incorporates their revolution into revolutionary Shakespeare. In a play about adaptation, rehearsal and relationships between Shakespearean performance and politics, The Boss finally acknowledges that he cannot foment rebellion against the Soviet-backed state, leaving for his country house.[80] With a set that realistically depicted rehearsal space containing an approximation of the Ensemble's stockade and plausible lookalikes for Brecht and Weigel in Emrys James and Peggy Ashcroft respectively, theatregoers could ponder their own relationships to recent Shakespearean political theatre.[81] Yet, director David Jones did not stress such comparisons, although the RSC supposedly purveyed radical Shakespeare in the 1960s, while following Brecht in trying to develop a stable ensemble of actors for the company.[82] Journalists reacted to these revisions of the Brecht-Ensemble *Coriolanus* as before, expressing more interest in characters' personal psychology than in political analysis, except to deem both works foreign to Shakespeare and English theatrical sensibilities.[83]

The tendency to diminish the specific politics of these productions, a phenomenon related to a British tradition of employing Brecht's aesthetics while discarding his Marxism, continued in major English performances over the next fifteen years.[84] Trevor Nunn's 1972 RSC production featured a white performance space resembling the Ensemble's, though the company fitted Stratford's mainstage with a mechanical system that shapeshifted into myriad configurations.[85] Nunn arranged his large cast into tableaux and choreographed battles and processions that delivered arresting stage images; in a variation on Forrest's funeral pyre, the Volsces grilled Ian Hogg's Coriolanus over flames shooting from the stage.⁸⁶ However, the production was more about making Shakespeare 'relevant' to contemporary theatregoers by emphasizing his supposedly timeless representation of human nature. This belief in relevance was manifested in acting styles meant to stimulate audience empathy by conveying personal rather than political-social conflicts, and relied on a rhetoric of Shakespeare's intentions for character, said to be encoded in the text. In practice, this approach amounted to theatre companies' and critics' preference for powerful star actors. For *Coriolanus*'s 1973 London transfer, Nunn replaced Hogg with Nicol Williamson who gave just such a performance, which reviewers greeted enthusiastically.⁸⁷ When Terry Hands staged *Coriolanus* for the RSC in 1977 he relied on Alan Howard to deliver a similar performance.⁸⁸ Hands devised masterful scenography that thoughtfully paralleled action and stunning lighting of his monochromatic stage for this production that also toured Europe, but it was Howard who won most praise, including the London Theatre Critics's Best Actor Award (1978).⁸⁹

The situation repeated itself when Peter Hall revisited *Coriolanus* for a 1984–5 National Theatre staging.⁹⁰ Britain's political situation was tense: Margaret Thatcher's government had been battling striking coal miners since March 1984 and Hall publicly criticized the government for what he regarded as its politically motivated underfunding of the Arts Council.⁹¹ This *Coriolanus* set was a large central sandpit with upstage doors which, reminiscent of the Ensemble's gates, were painted gold on one side for Roman scenes, black on the other for Volscian ones. Hall filled the space with anachronistic spectacle, most obviously by placing onstage part of the paying audience who participated in scenes of conflict between Ian McKellen's Coriolanus and the people.⁹² The rest of the production highlighted McKellen's centrality, both in battle and in his personal relationships with Greg Hicks's Aufidius and Irene Worth's Volumnia.⁹³ Critics responded as they had for decades, praising the actors' psychologically compelling performances (McKellen won 1984's Evening Standard

Best-Actor Award) and scorning Hall's onstage audience for disrupting Shakespeare's fictional world.[94]

The New York Shakespeare Festival's (NYSF) 1988-9 *Coriolanus* challenged British theatrical practices discussed so far.[95] *Coriolanus* was part of the Festival's Shakespeare Marathon, a plan to stage all of Shakespeare's plays between 1988 and 1993 with the intention of democratizing and popularizing Shakespeare for American audiences. However, NYSF Artistic Director Joseph Papp hired Steven Berkoff, known for his highly physical avant-garde theatre, to direct. Berkoff commented he was doing 'the audience a favour' in cutting the text and he decried both naturalistic acting and the star system's theatrical classism.[96] His subsequent recollections of 'text-bound' actors who lacked sufficient physical training reflects his approach, which diminished verbal textual meaning to the advantage of actors' physical signification.[97] Besides cutting more than 1,000 lines of speech, Berkoff costumed actors in modern dress and the set in the small Anspacher Theatre was almost bare throughout.[98] He organized part of the cast into an ensemble that executed synchronized anti-realistic mimed action which defied individual characterization with collective behaviour that saw them transformed from one group to another, and their dance-like movement was linked to Larry Spivak's live percussion-and-synthesizer music.[99] Still, the performance of Christopher Walken, an eccentrically charismatic star, was central to the action, and much of the ensemble's reactive behaviour kept attention focused on him. Dressed in black, with a full-length leather coat, Walken, too, performed anti-realistically, for instance by miming battles against actual and imagined enemies, while parodying both Coriolanus's neuroses and his own New Yorker identity and accent.[100] Many critics appreciated his magnetic performance, though others disliked his parodic ad-libbing of clichéd American mannerisms for ostensibly interfering with Shakespeare's textual meaning.[101] Reviewers were hostile to Berkoff, responding as though they had to protect Shakespeare from the 'perversity' of his high-concept theatre, and some praised Irene Worth as a contrast to the whole production for her supposed ability to convey Shakespeare's intentions appropriately.[102] There is irony in American journalists safeguarding England's foremost playwright against a British director by lauding the acting of the American-born Worth, who strengthened her reputation for performing classical drama as Volumnia in both Hall's 1984–5 production and the BBC's 1983 television version. Such complexities would repeat themselves in subsequent 'intercultural' *Coriolanus* stagings.

Millennial *Coriolanus*: Spectacle, interculturalism and multiculturalism

In the late twentieth and early twenty-first centuries, *Coriolanus* acquired new political significance in international touring productions devised by high-profile directors who were, like Berkoff, more interested in scenography than fidelity to Shakespeare's text. The longest-running such work was Toneelgrope's modern-dress Dutch-language *Roman Tragedies*, a six-hour performance combining *Coriolanus*, *Julius Caesar* and *Antony and Cleopatra*; directed by Ivo van Hove, it played Amsterdam and toured to England, Europe, the United States and Australia between 2007 and 2017. Van Hove and his dramaturgs mostly removed the common people and battles from the plays to depict politics as a media spectacle conducted by ruling classes.[103] The set's anonymous space suggested a corporate-lounge-cum-broadcast-studio, placing the action almost anywhere in the then-current moment.[104] Van Hove constantly juxtaposed live action with projections on a large screen above the stage and smaller ones onstage. Projections included Afghanistan war footage, announcements of characters' impending deaths, historical information, images of the audience and live-streamed video of actors performing and preparing between scenes (thus erasing the line separating onstage and offstage worlds).[105] Screened close-ups of Fredja van Huêt's Coriolanus and Frieda Pitoors's Volumnia contributed to the characters' intense emotion,[106] while the video of the dead Coriolanus (his death, like the others, was bloodless) contrasted with Aufidius's (Chico Kenzari) moving final speech delivered downstage, 'unmediated', to the audience.[107] The director juxtaposed these scenes with moments of sudden violence, such as the press-conference brawl between Coriolanus and the tribunes that caused real physical injuries.[108] The production encouraged audience participation, evidently to reveal democracy's participatory limits. While theatregoers could sit in furniture and buy food and drink onstage, watch the actors up close and tweet or email comments that became part of the projection feed, company members restricted spectators' movement.[109] Furthermore, audience members could not affect the plays' outcomes, their views of live actors and screens were frequently blocked, and they battled for viewing space, thereby mirroring the characters' struggles for political advantage.[110] The production attracted much political commentary, including Thomas Cartelli's scepticism about whether or not van Hove's quasi-Brechtian exposure of the 'corporate, mediatized' world actually perpetuated a politics of 'exclusionary representation' by ignoring ordinary characters.[111] Yet, other than one article celebrating van Hove's challenge to British text-bound Shakespeare, reviewers did not forcefully nationalize their response, as critics had done to the Ensemble's Coriolanus.[112] That is, rather than treating Roman Tragedies as an intercultural work located between a fundamentally English Shakespeare and some Netherlandish essence, critics regarded the world Toneelgrope evoked as part of a widely shared experience of Western modernity.

Other productions were more explicitly bound up in the politics of national culture. For instance, Québécois director Robert Lepage's 1992–4 staging of the play, one-third of the 'Cycle Shakespeare' that included *The Tempest* and *Macbeth*, anticipated many elements of *Roman Tragedies*.[113] However, Lepage mounted *Coriolanus* as a way to claim for Québec part of a prestigious repertoire, using Shakespeare's plays to display Québec culture by touring it overseas.[114] The early to mid-1990s were a politically tumultuous time for Canadian federalism, when Québec nearly voted to separate from the country. The scripts Lepage used for the Cycle, Michel Garneau's French-language 'tradaptations', can be read in light of the era's cultural-linguistic politics, as the tradaptations would purportedly naturalize Shakespeare for Québécois French.[115] If Garneau repurposed Shakespeare's textual prestige, Lepage challenged the text's primacy by cutting one-third of the *Coriolanus* adaptation and foregrounding the spectacle visible in the oblong aperture he created by framing the stage in black fabric.[116] Spectators watched actors in modern dress perform in settings – a radio station, a locker room, a restaurant – that could be from anywhere in the contemporary world.[117] With fewer than a dozen actors, there were no processions, no plebeians visible and the cramped performance space encouraged horizontal blocking and intensely personal relationships, including a homoerotic one between Jules Philip's Coriolanus and Gérald Gagnon's Aufidius.[118] Lepage employed some video projection, but the production's singular effect was to put on display the creation of character.[119] By repeatedly moving actor's faces in and out of the frame as they stood on tables and lowered themselves again, the director showed bodies losing and acquiring individuality, a technique particularly effective in rendering the power struggle between Coriolanus and Anne-Marie Cadieux's emotional Volumnia.[120] English reviewers of *Coriolanus*'s Nottingham performance expressed a sense of cultural superiority in criticizing Lepage's supposed diminishment of Shakespeare's characterization.[121] Québec critics, however, treated Lepage's international exposure of local culture on tour as a source of pride that, ironically, revealed anxiety over perceived cultural inferiority and debated the 'faithfulness' of Garneau's script to Shakespeare and whether or not it represented an outdated nationalism.[122] This diverse reaction makes evident the production's cultural-political stakes, revealing the complexity of the ways that global intercultural Shakespeare can activate ideas about cosmopolitanism and local identity.

Two Japanese *Coriolanus*es offer somewhat different perspectives on how intercultural Shakespeare can signal national identity theatrically. When Yukio Ninagawa's 2007 *Coriolanus* travelled to the Barbican, London audiences witnessed an impressive spectacle. A huge staircase, which literalized hierarchical relationships, dominated the set, while mirrors multiplied the dozens of actors who depicted a samurai-era Japan. They fought 'thrilling', precisely choreographed battles to a soundtrack that emphasized emotions throughout.[123] The mirrors, which also reflected the audience back at itself, and a prominent soundscape featured in Ninagawa's earlier Shakespeare productions, as did the samurai setting.[124] However, the director insisted he used Japanese elements to make Shakespeare understandable to Japanese, not Western audiences.[125] According to Tomonari Kuwayama, Japanese critics of Ninagawa's Shakespearean work, including *Coriolanus*, differed from English ones: the former were not harshly critical, provided plenty of information and appreciated isolated aspects of the performance; the latter demonstrated a 'custodial' approach to Shakespeare, were concerned with actors' intonations and the relationship between text and performance, and desired a consistent treatment of the text that manifested a coherent and plausible play-world.[126] While some English critics thought that Toshiaki Karasawa's Coriolanus and Kayoko Shiriashi's Volumnia (and the production overall) lacked emotional depth and complexity, they appreciated the spectacle, the heroic displays in battle, actors' vocalizations and the magic of Ninagawa's mirrors. Moreover, English reviewers wanted a coherent world that explained the play and insisted that what they saw as Ninagawa's samurai code of honour and the feudal Japanese setting made sense of the play's relationships between warriors, family members and different political classes. They thus deemed an imagined Japanese identity to be an appropriate analogy for elements supposedly inherent to Shakespeare's text.

The Chiten Company's *Coriolanus* at the 2012 Globe to Globe Festival provided a less clear depiction of 'Japan' for audiences at Shakespeare's Globe. As part of the Cultural Olympiad, a series of cultural events across the UK complementing the 2012 London Olympics and Paralympics, such a production might be expected to embody aspects of its national culture. Yet, director Motoi Miura consciously eschewed an overtly Japanese production to avoid what he saw as the potential for 'Orientalism'.[127] Instead, influenced by Tadashi Suzuki's *King Lear*, he believed that theatre is 'an act of presenting something critical'.[128] The result was a performance by Toshiaki Karasawa, playing Coriolanus, and four chorus members.[129] Dressed in loose blue dungarees (and a basket on Karasawa's head), the actors consistently deflated the protagonist's heroism. Karasawa struck numerous ostentatious poses: some were serious; others were awkward and outlandish because he wielded a baguette as a sword, a riding crop and as food. He also varied his speech remarkably, effortlessly shifting from growling anger to diffidence to bizarre moaning. The chorus members, morphing in and out of various characters, repeatedly undermined his dignity and valour, wildly modifying their voices, often creeping or moving stiltedly, and sometimes pointedly ignoring him. At the end, when Coriolanus simply dropped dead, the other actors tried preposterously to carry him off, their failed attempts travestying the funeral procession. These performances can be understood in relation to their context of production. By congregating dozens of overseas companies for a six-week festival, the Globe to Globe supposedly recentred marginal cultures in 'Shakespeare's home',[130] and made English-speaking audiences' understanding of performances reliant on diaspora theatregoers who served as experts when interpreting 'their heritage'.[131] The festival thus became a way to recognize, through intercultural Shakespeare, the value of various diasporas that constituted multicultural Britain. However, English-language response to Chiten's *Coriolanus* did not necessarily conform to this model of reception, as most reviewers admired the vocal acrobatics and playfulness, but were bewildered by what they regarded as the show's experimentalism and were content to speculate that elements of the performance could be vaguely Japanese insofar as they were related to Kabuki, samurai disguises and Buddhist spirituality. This slightly-confused-but-accepting critical reaction is obviously not an enthusiastic endorsement of theatrical interculturalism and multiculturalism. Nevertheless, given that Miura refused to provide an easily graspable and consistent interpretation of *Coriolanus* that overtly signified 'Japan', the fact that reviewers did not lament the lack of a coherent Japanese play-world analogy for Shakespeare's Rome suggests a critical stance tangibly different from that which greeted Ninagawa's Barbican production.

This sort of confusion and critical speculation about vaguely defined cultural identity and the work that Shakespeare might do in a Western multicultural society characterized other recent productions of *Coriolanus* at mainstream theatres. One such production was the RSC's 2017 staging which, in many ways, continued the tradition of textually 'faithful' and 'relevant' Shakespeare. Actors were well-drilled in speaking verse eloquently and with conviction.[132] As in previous RSC stagings, the individual fighting – here between Sope Dirisu's Coriolanus and James Corrigan's Aufidius – was more intensely thrilling than group battles. Hadyn Gwynne's Volumnia was compelling but not manipulative; nor were Martina Laird and Jackie Morrison's tribunes underhanded schemers. Director Angus Jackson regarded the play as politically apt in 2017, a time of a great 'class divide and…messy wars' when 'the population vote[d] for something that is far from in their best interests', apparently referring to Britons' 2016 vote to leave the European Union.[133] Jackson kept his stage quite bare but portrayed the class divide by differentiating the plebeians in scruffy-casual modern street clothes from patricians and tribunes who wore modern formal and business attire. Class politics were complicated by the production's 'diverse' casting: Dirisu is the son of Nigerian immigrants and commented he was conscious of that fact when choosing acting over a career in finance; Jackson cast the traditionally male roles of the tribunes with two women, one of whom, Laird, grew up in Trinidad.[134] Scholars have amply documented that Black, Asian and ethnic minority actors have long been marginalized in Shakespearean performance and those scholars have made persuasive cases for why it is important that actors from marginalized communities be given chances to perform Shakespeare.[135] Yet, precisely what the terms 'diverse' or 'non-traditional' casting mean across a range of Shakespearean theatre is not clear, in part because, as Ayanna Thompson observes, such terms are applied to many types of performance and theatre companies rarely indicate how they intend categories of identity such as race to have significance in any given production.[136] In interview, Dirisu recognized the need to diversify British theatre in terms of both ethnic minorities and casting against gender expectations for roles.[137] Jackson, too, seemed to believe that audiences would sympathize with female tribunes who had to work against the kind of 'privilege' the play's male senators took for granted.[138]

How, then, did Jackson's non-traditional casting affect theatregoers' readings of the production? What did they think of women tribunes planning to banish Coriolanus and stage-managing the people; or of Dirisu roughly grasping Morrison's helpless Sicinius by the neck in 3.1? How did theatregoers regard Dirisu's exceptional composure during most of his encounters with the people, or his anger that finally erupted when rebuking them for his banishment, or his horrific assassination when he defeated a mob of Volsces, but then succumbed to Corrigan's Aufidius who wrapped a chain around Dirisu's neck and pulled repeatedly, while grunting in a sickening, sexual way until his victim went limp? Most audience reaction on the video of the live performance is muted. Reviewers, meanwhile, did not dwell on casting women as the tribunes, though some compared Morrison to Scottish National Party leader Nicola Sturgeon. Other critics asserted this production also invoked contemporary Britain's corrupt populists, perhaps an oblique indictment of these tribunes, but there were no sustained assessments of the performers' gender.

Similarly, reviewers evaluated Dirisu's verse-speaking, athletic heroism and emotional range, approving or disapproving of his performance to varying degrees. Few, however, wrote about race in the production: Geoff Mills compared Dirisu to African-American action-film star Wesley Snipes; Dominic Cavendish believed Dirisu should be more like African-American activist Malcolm X; Neil Allan remarked that the 'significance' of casting a black actor as Coriolanus 'was not made conspicuous' but that certain moments, such as Dirisu's anger at Corrigan calling him '"boy"' had extra 'bite' because of the casting.[139] Allan's comment echoes Thompson's observation about theatre companies not signalling how they intend race to signify in particular performances, and the relative silence about Jackson's 'non-traditional' casting only reinforces Thompson's observation that such silence is common among reviewers.[140] The fact that reviewers overlooked these casting decisions might also suggest that, as Jami Rogers comments, critics assume that 'equality' for performers from marginalized groups 'has been achieved' at large Shakespearean companies which have made high-profile casting choices to diversify their stages, and that issues of race in performance can therefore be ignored by understanding such casting as 'colourblind'.[141]

Comparable circumstances arose when Lepage revamped the scenography for his 2018 *Coriolanus* at Ontario's Stratford Festival and its 2019 French-language transfer to Montréal's Théâtre du Nouveau Monde, though the production's political stakes had changed since the 1990s. Costumes and sets were updates of those from the first show, and the technology employed was more sophisticated than before.[142] Now, the black screen covering the proscenium space opened and closed continuously, apertures appeared to slide across this screen, and Lepage used projections relentlessly. Projections began with Coriolanus's bust coming to life to chastise spectators-as-plebeians, and subsequently depicted corridors, banquets, Roman ruins and baths, a comic text-message exchange and a banishment scene that fragmented and multiplied Coriolanus across numerous screens. Lepage mostly avoided rendering faces invisible, but still achieved intense encounters with this newer technology. For instance, he ended Volumnia's rhetorical victory over Coriolanus in 5.3 by closing the aperture on the defeated hero in a rectilinear iris shot; he did the same after Coriolanus's assassination, closing the aperture on a bereft Aufidius. In both scenes, Lepage echoed cinematic technique to compel spectators to focus on the personal cost of political ruthlessness. Those reviewing the Stratford production wrote positively about Lepage's cinematic effects and its updating of Shakespeare for an era of populism and social media. They also generally praised the actors, concentrating on Lucy Peacock's Volumnia, André Sills's Coriolanus and the homoerotic frisson between Sills's hero and Graham Abbey's Aufidius. If critics regarded Lepage's Stratford debut as a major success for the company, Sills and cast-mate Alexis Gordon (who played Virgilia) understood their performances as black actors in leading Shakespearean roles to be an important advance for the Festival. They discussed the need to make Shakespeare 'relevant' not simply through technologically sophisticated staging, but by instituting training and colour-conscious – rather than colour blind – casting practices that would diversify theatre and institutions like Stratford.[143] Only one critic directly addressed these issues in relation to *Coriolanus*: in an opinion piece in a local publication, Peter Taylor derided the Festival's diverse casting.[144] Québec critics praised the Montréal production in the same terms as those of the Stratford run, though these latter reviewers were evidently more familiar with Lepage's career than were those who reviewed the Festival's version. They were less excited than critics had been in the 1990s about Lepage's fame, and expressed little concern about the relation between Québécois nationalism and either the show or Garneau's text. Although Lepage cast Morocco-born Reda Guerinik as Aufidius, Haiti-born Widemir Normil as Cominius and Louise Bombardier as a female Brutus, Québec reviewers did not focus on such choices. They did, however, read the production in relation to controversies that arose after the start of the Stratford run when Lepage cast *SLAV*, a show about the transatlantic African slave trade, largely with white actors, and planned *Kanata*, a production about the history of Indigenous Peoples in Canada, with virtually no participation from Indigenous Peoples. These controversies make the need for the changes in perspective and practice that Sills and Gordon called for all the more apparent.

Conclusion

This essay has offered one perspective on *Coriolanus*'s performance history by emphasizing the ways that certain theatre artists calibrated, and various communities of theatregoers interpreted, depictions of personal and political relationships in connection with historical contexts that span more than 400 years. This history has necessarily excluded a number of theatrical performances and screen versions of the play, some of which have been accounted for already. Yet, accounting for many others from around the world would reveal much about other contexts of production. Such a study would likely reveal other beliefs about Shakespeare's supposed prestige, the purposes of theatre in various cultures and what broad issues, including ideas about the personal and political, have meant to people from those cultures. What specifics this kind of investigation would reveal is, for now, speculative. Nevertheless, in moving from English productions to European and Japanese ones, and to those touching on multiculturalism within British and Canadian society, this essay has hinted at some of the issues with which that analysis might engage. What seems certain is that the more we know about *Coriolanus*'s global performance history, the more the desire to adopt a 'custodial' approach to Shakespeare's text and inherited meanings – which has not stopped artists from radically adapting *Coriolanus*, but is still fundamental to twenty-first-century Anglo-North-American journalistic writing about Shakespearean performance – seems like a vestige of the past.

3

State of the Art

Graham Holderness

Long before Shakespeare became inescapably 'political', *Coriolanus* could never have been read or performed as anything other than a deeply political play: that is, a historical play about politics, which in some way contained political theories and beliefs of Shakespeare's own time – about monarchy, republicanism, militarism, authority and popular protest – and remains relevant to modern political discourse. It is impossible, in other words, to present *Coriolanus* in terms of 'state of the art' without giving extensive attention to the art of the state. At the same time, because of its focus on individual and family relationships, between men and women, men and men, and parents and children, within the very particularized social context and value system of the Roman Republic, the play has answered readily to psychoanalytic, feminist and gender-focused readings. In addition, partly because the play is so easily manipulated for ideological purposes, and partly because, unlike its companion pieces *Julius Caesar* and *Antony and Cleopatra*, *Coriolanus* is based in a fictional rather than a true history (as its eponymous hero probably never existed), the play has throughout the twentieth century been an attractive source for writers wishing to adapt, rework and otherwise appropriate the play for creative as well as critical reinvention. Taking these three approaches (political, gendered, creative) as those bearing most significantly on interpretation and adaptation of *Coriolanus*, I will examine the origins of each, and show how these approaches have been used to read *Coriolanus*.

Politics, New Historicism, Cultural Materialism

Coriolanus is of course a historical play, one of Shakespeare's four plays dramatizing key moments from Roman history. The historical writing is, as always in Shakespeare, impeccably well sourced, from the great Roman historian Livy and Greek biographer Plutarch, and the portrayal of ancient Rome (despite the notorious anachronisms) is profoundly accurate (even though, in the case of Coriolanus, the history is probably mythical rather than true). Yet the political themes of the play can be transported easily into subsequent historical periods since they concern perennial and unresolved questions about power, authority, representation of the commons, questions that remain active in any democratic society – not least because democratic movements and states have since the nineteenth century so frequently adopted ancient Rome as a kind of 'founding charter'. This makes the play seem permanently contemporary, while at the same time rendering it liable to political appropriation in the furtherance of one political ideology or another.

Modern literary criticism as we know it today has evolved as a consequence of radical changes effected by social, political and cultural movements emanating in the 1970s. Prior to this watershed, mainstream literary criticism concerned itself with the formal analysis of poetic language; with philosophical exercises in the ethical reading of texts; with literary history as a relatively autonomous continuum, taking place against a historical 'background' of social and cultural change; and with textual scholarship. Shakespeare was regarded as the heart of the literary tradition, though naturally critics more interested in the dramatic arts were also concerned to locate the plays in theatre history, thus paving the way for later performance studies.

In the 1980s, modern criticism as it stands today began to develop and consolidate, largely through the emergence of New Historicism in America and Cultural Materialism in Britain, and their convergence with European movements such as post-structuralism. Both New Historicism and Cultural Materialism derived from interdisciplinary work in literature and history, Marxist philosophy and post-structuralist theory. New Historicism, led by American critics such as Stephen Greenblatt, Louis Montrose and Jerome McGann took off from the 'history of ideas', and set out to understand intellectual history through literature, and literature through its cultural context. British Cultural Materialism was closer to traditional Marxist criticism, established by critics such as Terence Hawkes, Jonathan Dollimore and Terry Eagleton, who focused on studying the means and relations of cultural production, and exposing the role of ideology in literature and society. Despite disagreements between them, both methods tended to merge in subsequent critical and theoretical practice. *Coriolanus* became an obvious focus for debates and arguments about the precise historical character of Shakespeare's plays, their political inflection in their own time and their continuing applicability to the politics of the present. In different ways, but united in a common interest in matters of history and politics, leading critics converged on this play as a promising case study.

Such critics, however, tended to disagree about the extent to which Shakespeare's plays reflected or endorsed the dominant power relations of his own society, and were therefore invariably more likely to exert a repressive cultural influence in the present; or alternatively represented a radical critique of Shakespeare's society, and were therefore more likely to support radical cultural and ideological initiatives. This disagreement can be seen in the very different interpretations of *Coriolanus* presented by Michael Bristol and Annabel Patterson. Bristol sees the play in terms of class conflict, and the text of the play as dramatizing 'the legitimation of authority'.[1] In Bristol's analysis, Coriolanus appears as an anomalous figure who disrupts the normal pattern of authority formation within the world of the play, interrupting the expected dialectical rhythms of political engagement, which Bristol compares to the traditional struggle between the principles of Lent and Carnival. Coriolanus, in Bristol's view, prompts a legitimation crisis, provoking a profound divergence over the question of the derivation of authority and the source of social initiative. Bristol maintains that when the threat represented by Coriolanus is finally eliminated in the play, legitimation takes the form of a class compromise by which the party in power is able to re-establish ideological dominance over the popular element. In the process, Bristol suggests the threat of calamity provides the means for incorporating and channelling the energy of popular initiative, whether in republican Rome, Jacobean England or the contemporary world.

These questions are addressed differently by Patterson[2] who seeks in the play for a much stronger sense of radical critique, foreshadowing a futuristic democratic and republican ideology. Patterson defined Shakespeare as 'one of our first cultural critics, in the sense of being capable of profound structural analysis' of his own and historical societies.[3] Patterson sees *Coriolanus* as representing Shakespeare's invitation to his audience 'to contemplate an alternative political system'.[4]

Patterson reads the text directly against its immediate historical background, stressing the importance to the play of the Midlands Rising of 1607. As the rising grew in part out of concern over food shortages, before expanding to take in a greater programme of grievances and desire for reform, Patterson sees a strong link between this agrarian unrest within the early Jacobean state, and the grievances of the plebeians and their struggles with the aristocracy in Shakespeare's Rome. Patterson advances her analysis through a process of detailed, closely observed historical investigation, carefully sifting through royal proclamations, Parliamentary records and contemporary speeches and sermons to establish a body of evidence in support of her claims. She concludes that the fundamental concern of *Coriolanus* lies with conceptions of power, with Coriolanus embodying a militaristic code of power, while the text itself struggles to come to terms with constitutional issues, with 'how it is possible to define and limit such a previously unspeakable concept as common power'.[5]

Although differing from one another in their assessment of the play's political effectiveness, both in the early modern period and in the present, Bristol and Patterson shared historicist methods that became standard in many subsequent readings of *Coriolanus*. For example, in an essay published in 1991, Richard Wilson[6] addressed the relationship between *Coriolanus* and the Midlands Rising by juxtaposing detailed research on the local economy of Stratford-upon-Avon, including economic data on Shakespeare's own business dealings, the ideas of early modern political theorists such as Thomas Hobbes on power and the state, the theories of modern thinkers such as Michel Foucault and Jean Baudrillard, and Marxist ideas about 'exchange' and 'value', in order to 'situate the playwright within the economic and power relations that were transforming his society'[7] from a mediaeval to a modern capitalist economy. Alex Garganigo[8] found in the play's conflicts around authority and power, the clashes between plebeians and patricians, civic and military values, parallels with contemporary political debates concerning the same issues in Britain, specifically in this analysis James I's attempts to unite the kingdoms of England and Scotland.

These critics typically start with history first and work their way toward the play. Steve Hindle[9] argues that the brutal suppression by the authorities in 1607 of social unrest around enclosures provided Shakespeare with the model for his Roman play. In this kind of criticism there is no firm distinction between drama and contemporary historical event: both share in the same 'discourses of hunger, protest, paternalism and punishment associated with the Midland Rising'.[10] Maurice Hunt[11] takes a longer historical view, addressing Jacobean ideas about war and peace in the light of contemporary physiological theories (which were in any case ancient, based in Greek and Roman medicine), and theories about just and unjust wars developed by Augustine and Thomas Aquinas.

Also emerging from the crucible of 1980s criticism, the work of British critic Terence Hawkes took a different approach, focusing on the potentiality of early modern drama for political appropriation.[12] Hawkes's critical method came later to be designated 'presentism' since it tends to be anchored not in the early modern period, but in the continuing 'afterlife' of Shakespeare's plays in subsequent times and societies. Like Bristol, Hawkes sees *Coriolanus* as a play primarily concerned with class politics. Hawkes maps the play's engagement with issues of class confrontation onto one of the major class conflicts of twentieth-century Britain: the General Strike of the mid-1920s. He then goes on to document a particular production of the play planned for Stratford-upon-Avon during the course of the General Strike, which was to take place on 23 April 1926 as part of the Shakespeare's birthday celebrations. Hawkes's presentist focus foregrounds the play's potentiality for ideological mobilization in the interests of a dominant section of society, or of a political party or movement, in this case of an extreme right-wing character.

An interesting recent example of a 'presentist' approach is an essay by Peter Campbell and Richard Jordan[13] claiming Shakespeare as a great strategic thinker ('strategy' here being initially military, but then applied to politics, international relations and human intercourse generally). They begin, as Hawkes often did, at an apparently extreme distance from Shakespeare's play, with the young future US President Dwight D. Eisenhower undertaking a training programme in military strategy which included Shakespeare. The authors then go on to contrast Eisenhower's astounding success as a leader with the career of 'flawed strategist' Coriolanus.

Bristol's analysis draws on the work of Mikhail Bakhtin, Patterson's on traditional historicism and Hawkes's on post-structuralist theory. But the strongest common thread linking them is constituted by a shared recourse to Marxism. More recent criticism tends to deploy similar influences, but proves more eclectic in its handling of theory, and also naturally reflects more contemporary currents of thought. A good example is an essay by Patrick Gray and Maurice Samely on *Coriolanus* and other plays, linking them with the ideas of the 1960s utopian Marxist Henri Lefebvre, with Bakhtin and with the philosophy of Hegel.[14] In the context of French political activism in the 1960s, and of a nostalgia for the utopian dream of the Paris Commune, Lefebvre argued that all inhabitants of an urban space have a 'right to the city' superseding the rights of property owners: the right in other words illegally to occupy, demonstrate, deface buildings and seek to establish collective ownership and management. Gray and Samely link this position with Hegel's ideas on 'the politics of recognition', the view that political protest and dissent are expressions of the need of the people to be acknowledged. This social need is then connected to the theory of alienation as developed in the writings of the early Marx, and to the utopian writings of Rabelais, whose work lies at the core of the work of Bakhtin. Viewing *Coriolanus* in the light of this hybrid theoretical framework Gray and Samely argue that the popular protests that open and drive the play, connected with the parallel food riots of Shakespeare's own time and place, channel this same 'desire for recognition as the engine of political conflict'.[15] States can avoid civil conflict by acknowledging this popular desire. Coriolanus himself has the opportunity of effecting such recognition:

> By petitioning the citizens of Rome for their voices, Coriolanus is obliged to recognise, not merely their role in the political system, but their very existence; their essential worth.[16]

On the other hand, as the authors make clear, Shakespeare's Augustinian conception of a fallen human nature puts him at odds with 'Lefebvre's dreams of a secular utopia'.[17]

We today may be inclined, like Lefebvre, to see working-class riot and rebellion as heroic. For Shakespeare, however, this kind of mob violence is a social ill, akin to civil war.[18]

This essay is typical of good contemporary criticism in its use of a wide and diverse range of theoretical sources – Hegel as well as Marx, Bakhtin and Lefebvre – and its connecting of parallel political movements across time and space, from plebeian unrest in republican Rome to early-seventeenth-century food riots in the English Midlands to the Paris *évènements* of 1968, and on to protest and occupation in modern cities.

More definitively 'presentist' in its approach is an essay by Nicholas Taylor-Collins, drawing parallels between the cities of ancient Rome in Shakespeare and the Belfast of the 'Troubles' in the poetry of Ciaran Carson, especially his collection *Belfast Confetti*.[19] Drawing on ideas from Immanuel Kant, Jacques Derrida and Giorgio Agamben, Taylor-Collins constructs the model of a city engaged in a perpetual civil war, in which the human body stands as a plural signifier that both articulates narratives of conflict and simultaneously exposes the paradoxical problematics of 'hospitality'. 'Hostile bodies', he claims, 'found the modern city.'[20] The argument is not that Carson drew on Shakespeare, though to a limited extent he does, but that both poets were responding to parallel conditions visible in their own cities: Rome is London is Belfast. Taylor-Collins compares how both writers poeticize the fragmentation of the body in political conflict ('anatomized and dissected bodies should signal the sovereign contest undertaken in civil-war cities') and reveal the paradoxes of hospitality in which hostile bodies meeting as host and guest can act out civil conflict, but also encounter one another in a 'neutered zone of indifference' where 'citizens can co-exist harmoniously in acknowledged disharmony'.[21] Taylor-Collins then ingeniously shows how these ideas are activated in the theatre, where hostile bodies take centre stage, and where the stage itself constitutes a space in which hostility and hospitality play out their conflicts. The article concludes with a metacritical gesture that opens a window onto criticism itself as a further space for the enactment of these same paradoxes:

> In this article I welcome *Coriolanus* and *Belfast Confetti* as guests at my table, estranging myself as their host, their terms dictating mine. Of course, the practice of literary criticism is, like culture writ large, hospitable at its core; but as for who is host and who guest – of that we can never be sure.[22]

Some recent critics have sought to recombine studies of history and politics with modern work in linguistics, reminding us that Saussurean linguistics was in the 1980s one of the primary sources for post-structuralist criticism. Thomas Ward[23] examines *Coriolanus* as a play about speech, picking up Peter Holland's observation that the word 'voices' appears more frequently here than in any other Shakespeare play. 'Voice' signifies in this political play on a number of levels: as the primary channel of communication in society, as the means of democratic participation in government (where 'voices' equals 'votes') and as the medium through which actors present themselves to an audience. Ward sees 'voice' in *Coriolanus* as a slippery concept, which purports to be the vehicle of political agency, but ends up being reduced to the powerless cacophony of the theatre.[24] Ward draws on the work of philosopher Jacques Rancière to answer the question: 'to what extent can the physical voice as such be political?' and concludes that *Coriolanus* 'enacts its own anti-politics in the form of deliberately illegitimate noisemaking'.[25] Ward argues that the play offers a view of language akin to that of the Greek Cynic philosophers. The 'actor playing Coriolanus lays bare the powerlessness of theatrical noise', a gesture defined as 'a fundamentally Cynical rejection of politically efficacious speech'.[26]

Other recent critics have combined, in their readings of the play, literary analysis, theatre criticism and political interpretation with considerations of early modern economics and cultural technology. In '"The stamp of Martius"', Harry Newman revalues notions of 'character' and theatrical 'impression' in terms of early modern technologies of 'sealing, coining, medal-making and printing', in all of which 'characters' are 'impressed' or 'imprinted' with legible marks.[27] Conventionally we think of human 'character' as consisting in interiority, and external physical 'characteristics' as legible signs indicating what is within. Newman argues rather that just as 'characters' are printed on paper, so human 'character' is imprinted on the individual by external pressures. This 'technological concept of the imprint ... is integral to the play's metatheatrical self-reflection on the commoditised human transactions involved in commercial theatre'.[28] While Coriolanus, like Hamlet, continually insists he has that within which passes show, in fact his 'characterological value in performance is paradoxically generated by his refusal to participate in forms of imprinting, exchange and transaction that are necessary for his very existence'.[29] Focusing on the 'technology of wounds' and the functions of silence in the play, Newman concludes that

> Coriolanus's impressiveness as a character does not lie in the revelation of his humanity. Rather, it lies in the play's metatheatrical negotiation of our knowledge that he is a creature marked by his cultural production, an artificial entity crafted to make an impression on audiences conditioned to think they are paying to receive 'the stamp of Martius'.[30]

The founding movements of modern criticism took inspiration from interdisciplinary studies, especially between literature and history, literature and drama, literature and cultural, film and media studies. Although there was some limited engagement with economics in Marxist-influenced criticism, virtually all these transactions took place within the humanities. More recent criticism has begun to forge links between literature and the sciences, registering some of the profound changes that have effected paradigm shifts in disciplines such as physics and biology, alongside technological and communication developments arising from the introduction of the internet.[31] In a controversial but fascinating study, Clifford Werier applies influential ideas promoted by evolutionary biologist Richard Dawkins to *Coriolanus* and to Shakespearean drama in general.[32] In *The Selfish Gene* (1976) Dawkins argued that 'memes' are units of cultural transmission analogous to genes, structured by a kind of DNA and capable of independent power of action, and which 'propagate themselves in the meme pool by leaping from brain to brain via a process which, in the broad sense, can be called imitation'.[33]

> Meme theory argues that strong ideas, like genes, possess a selfish momentum which propels them to survive in human minds and associated cultural encodings if the conditions are favourable and mutate and lose their power if the conditions are not.[34]

The meme is likened to a virus that parasitically infects human hosts and competes with other memes in the 'competitive contagion of the memosphere'.[35]

Werier applies this paradigm to *Coriolanus* by arguing that the civil unrest around food shortages that opens and precipitates the action of the play can be defined as a 'more equitable food distribution meme', which spreads from mind to mind in the processes of replication.[36] Correspondingly, the state is shown generating a 'counter-meme' of authority and trust in response to the insurrection. His case is that these memes were active in the England of the 1610s, where riots provoked by the need for food became politicized into demands for reforms in agricultural practice. 'Likewise, the state's response included a counter-memetic strategy that seeded competing memes in the population through print, speech and legal statute.'[37] Versions of the 'more equitable food distribution meme' being active in the minds of his audience,

Shakespeare was able to reactivate them in his depiction of a parallel infection among the plebeians of ancient Rome, and to demonstrate dramatically how the patricians produce counter-memes with the same adaptive tendencies. The play becomes here a kind of scientific thought-experiment:

> Shakespeare is more interested in staging the mechanics of memetic contention – the parasitic power of the meme to find supportive hosts – than in the potentially dangerous ideological charge that the memes hold.[38]

The use of meme theory as a tool of literary criticism is controversial: Werier quotes other critics who call Dawkins's idea 'fanciful and flawed', a mere 'rhetorical device'.[39] It is questionable whether such quasi-scientific analysis produces any more insight than more conventional investigations of political ideas or ideology. Nonetheless, this attempt to synthesize literary with scientific ideas is an important direction of modern criticism.

Feminism, psychoanalysis, masculinity

The second most influential critical methodology that has changed the way in which *Coriolanus* is seen and read is gender-focused criticism, initially feminism – linked with women's movements, and dedicated to exposing narratives of male domination, foregrounding the role of women in literature and celebrating the positive contribution of women in culture and society – and latterly studies of masculinity – examining social constructions of maleness, extending into the more diverse field of 'queer studies'. One of the most important figures in the emergence of this field was Janet Adelman, whose book *Suffocating Mothers*[40] is recognized as a pioneering work in the field of psychoanalytic feminist criticism. Adelman began her studies of Shakespeare's tragedies with *Coriolanus* in a

1978 essay.[41] The psychoanalytic thesis of *Suffocating Mothers* is that Shakespeare's tragedies are preoccupied with 'the nightmare of a femaleness that can weaken and contaminate masculinity'.[42] This includes fantasies of maternal malevolence and the corrupting effect of the maternal body. One of the strong pressures in the tragedies is 'to free the masculine identity of both father and son from its origin in the contaminated maternal body'.[43] Adelman goes on to offer an interpretation of *Coriolanus* in comparison with *Macbeth*, which shows the failure of a man's attempt to deny connection with his mother. *Macbeth* and *Coriolanus* record the attempt to create an autonomous masculinity to ward off vulnerability to the mother. Virulent maternal power unleashed at the beginning of *Macbeth* is contained in the end by eliminating the female: 'mothers no longer threaten because they no longer exist'; however, 'this solution is inherently unstable'.[44] *Coriolanus*, on the other hand, undoes the ending of *Macbeth* by bringing the powerful mother back and by brutally displaying the failure of attempting to sever the maternal connection. With these two plays, 'Shakespeare's tragic art itself seems to have come to an impasse'.[45]

In due course, gender-based criticism rightly evolved to pay equal attention to masculinity, not merely as the hostile binary to femininity, but as a subject requiring analysis in its own right. Coppélia Kahn's 1981 book *Man's Estate: Masculine Identity in Shakespeare*[46] was already broadening the feminist focus to include masculinity. Kahn observes that Coriolanus's masculinity is self-divided, since it reveals his dependency on his mother (he remains in some ways a 'boy') in the very effort at self-individuation:

> Paradoxically his martial supremacy is actually an expression of his extreme dependency, but at the same time an attempt to defend against that very dependency, by achieving godlike superiority that marks him off from any other man.[47]

Responding to this trend, in a later essay 'Shakespeare's Romulus and Remus: Who Does the Wolf Love?',[48] Janet Adelman links her feminist reading of *Coriolanus* to the pervasive legend of Rome's founders, the twins Romulus and Remus, abandoned by their mother, suckled by a she-wolf and doomed to the fratricide permanently associated with the founding of Rome. In Shakespeare's Roman plays, 'male rivalry here repeatedly takes on the metaphorical colouration of fratricide specifically among twins, and murderous impulses play out in a landscape repeatedly associated with wolvish hunger'.[49] Coriolanus's mother Volumnia is of course the she-wolf, fiercely maternal but devoted to violence, the primary source of her son's courage: 'Thy valiantness was mine, thou sucked'st it from me' (3.2.130). Volumnia is both 'the original exiler of her son ... and his wolvish nurturer'.[50] Meanwhile Coriolanus and Aufidius are compared to Romulus and Remus, fiercely bonded together in a murderous destiny of blood.[51]

Recent exercises in gender-based criticism of *Coriolanus* have adroitly combined sexual politics with theatrical criticism and a more detailed and comprehensive knowledge of early modern culture. A good example is an essay by Lisa S. Starks-Estes[52] which brings together a wide range of sources from classical literature and philosophy to Renaissance theology and medicine, all informed by contemporary feminist theory. Her arguments concern conflicts and transitions in thought among different ideas of masculinity and femininity, for instance between ancient medical conceptions of the body as open and porous, to seventeenth-century notions of the body as closed and impermeable; or Catholic representations of the bleeding male body as vulnerable and feminized, contrasted with more Protestant ideas of the male body as self-contained and self-sufficient. She sees Coriolanus himself as engaged in a superhuman effort to maintain the closed body demanded of neo-Stoicism and Roman *virtus*, but compelled in the end to open himself to external influence in a feminized vulnerability. Thus the play enacts discordant models of masculinity inherited from Roman and later Christian traditions, foregrounding the pressures instigated by the emergence of the newly bounded body and commenting on its roots in the discordant strands of humanism, neo-Stoicism and Augustinian philosophy. The concluding image of the bleeding warrior's corpse emphatically punctuates the tragedy's critique of neo-Stoicism and extreme *virtus* in early modern ideals of masculinity.[53]

In a similar way, again collating classical with Renaissance sources, Michela Compagnoni[54] in a study of Shakespeare's Roman women contrasts polarized ideas of motherhood, between the Roman ideal of the patrician mother, and early modern anxieties around the 'suffocating mother' who contaminates masculine virtue with feminising weakness. For Compagnoni, Coriolanus's mother Volumnia is a figure of 'composite motherhood' who 'voices both a Roman and a Renaissance mother'[55] who 'epitomizes the prototype of the respectable Roman mother' and 'also puts on record the paradigm of corrupting maternity haunting early modern literature and culture'.[56] By exercising upon her son the shaping and moulding functions proper to a Roman *mater*, Volumnia simultaneously constitutes a threat to his masculinity:

> [Volumnia] embodies all the fears about monstrous mothers typical of the period, in that she is foregrounded as the matrix of her son's body, in light both of her biological function as *genetrix* and especially of her role as shaper who gives him form, just like a she-bear licking her cubs into shape in the Renaissance imagination.[57]

Another example is 'Acting, Integrity and Gender in Coriolanus' by Kent R. Lehnhof, which reassesses Coriolanus's masculinity in the light of metatheatre, anti-theatrical rhetoric and the presence of boys on the seventeenth-century stage.[58] The hero is convinced he possesses an unshakable masculine integrity ('I play / The man I am' [3.2.16–17]), and that others, by compelling him to act various parts – those of the schoolboy, the harlot, the eunuch and the virgin – risk violating that integrity, since the 'body's action' might 'teach my mind / A most inherent baseness' (3.2.123–4). This of course was the early modern argument against theatre, that the acting of depravity invited inner dissolution. By insisting, in his anti-performative zeal, that his ultra-masculine identity is undermined by the performance of feminine or quasi-feminine roles, Coriolanus reveals that his anti-theatricalism rests on 'a gynophobic foundation':

> However, the play not only exposes this gynophobic foundation but undermines it ... by using the figure of the boy to show that Coriolanus's ostensibly antiperformative manhood is itself a theatrical effect.[59]

In short, Coriolanus's anxious masculinity is fragile enough to be confuted merely by others calling him 'boy'. This ascription of puerility is given a further depth by Lucy Munro, who links it to plays performed by boy companies on the Blackfriars stage, in which heroic manly identities were superimposed onto the bodies of young children.

I will close this section with a recent example of criticism that combines gender studies and theatre history with a presentist approach and, in its concern with appropriation, leads on to my next section. In '"She done *Coriolanus* at the Convent"', Willy Maley revalues a play by Teresa Deevy, performed at the Abbey Theatre in Dublin in 1931.[60] In Deevy's play the heroine Ellie is inspired to escape from the domestic drudgery of her convent life by witnessing a performance of *Coriolanus* in which the hero is played by a woman. Although convent rules prohibit any masculine costume, the actress fully possesses the role and 'carries the house' with face and voice. The fact that the actress subsequently left the convent and took to the stage in London shows Ellie that this theatrical gesture of power, assuming the quintessentially masculine role, adumbrates the possibility of genuine liberation. Maley takes issue with feminist critics who argue that Ellie's nostalgia is for a lost or unfulfilled masculinity. In fact, he claims, 'Ellie's lament is for the loss of one woman. The failure of masculinity is that it fails to live up to the valour she witnessed first-hand in that convent *Coriolanus*', through the gender-troubling performance of a woman.[61] Both women, Maley contends, can be seen to be 'operating beyond a purely masculine paradigm'.[62] He concludes that the solution

> to Ellie's predicament is not a heteronormative hero, or a binary view of gender and morality, but a hybrid vision in which femininity and masculinity are united and transcendent.[63]

Appropriation, creative criticism

Adaptation studies is one of the most successful and influential new developments influencing literary and theatrical criticism today. Beginning in interdisciplinary film studies with a focus on cultural transmission between writing and the screen, adaptation theory and criticism, led by writers such as Linda Hutcheon, Thomas Leitch and Julie Sanders have broadened beyond film studies to offer new ways of reading old texts, and have probably changed the way in which literature is taught and read.[64]

Hitherto critical engagement with *Coriolanus* in terms of new creative writing has taken the form of adaptations, appropriations and 'spin-offs', whether in the theatre, in poetry or in prose fiction. These are usually categorized as moments in the play's stage history, or as symptoms of its continuing 'afterlife'. I have argued elsewhere that 'Shakespeare criticism and scholarship is tending increasingly towards the view that every act of scholarly reproduction, critical interpretation, theatrical performance, stage and screen adaptation or fictional appropriation produces a new and hitherto unconceived Shakespeare'.[65] Hence it is possible to recognize examples of 'creative criticism' in the history of creative responses to the play, whether or not they were intended or thought of as critical interventions. 'Creative criticism' constitutes a relatively new field of 'creative writing that operates as a vehicle for exploring and articulating critical and theoretical ideas.'[66] Scott Maisano and Rob Conkie have defined the methodology as 'creative writing informed by literary criticism'.[67]

The most important creative adaptations of *Coriolanus* are well documented in Peter Holland's edition of the play, where in the section '*Coriolanus* in the 1930s' he discusses liberal theatrical adaptations by William Poel, Henrik Ibsen and René-Louis Piachaud alongside poems by Delmore Schwartz and T. S. Eliot, and some fictional commentary by Charlotte Bronte.[68] T. S. Eliot's handling of *Coriolanus* in his poems 'Triumphal March' and 'Difficulties of a Statesman', published together as *Coriolan,* represent 'creative criticism' at its finest.[69] Eliot was of course both poet and critic, and in the poems, as Holland puts it,

> [t]he one and the many, the sharply separate and the totally undifferentiated constitute a set of antitheses that reflect powerfully on the acute reading of Shakespeare's play that underpins Eliot's fragments.[70]

I would go further and claim that Eliot's poems are not only informed by an acute reading of the play, but offer a new kind of 'reading': a critical-creative intervention designed to stand alongside Shakespeare's play, rather than rank in a position of ancillary hermeneutic service.

In the 1950s Bertolt Brecht worked on an adaptation of *Coriolanus* designed to transform it into a Communist manifesto, though he died before the work was completed or staged. Brecht altered Shakespeare's fickle and unruly mob into an intelligent and determined proletariat, organizing to resist the oppression of the Roman state; and he cast Coriolanus himself as a hero who discovers his own dispensability in the context of popular hegemony. Brecht justified his radical alterations by claiming that Shakespeare would have written the play in this way had he been alive (and presumably living in East Germany): 'I believe he would have taken the spirit of our time into account much as we have done, with less conviction no doubt, but with more talent.'[71] Again the writer makes clear that he is saying something about Shakespeare as well as using Shakespeare's work as raw material for his own vision.

In 1953 a popular uprising against the East German state was brutally suppressed by the Russians. Brecht remained loyal to the Party and to Stalin's Soviet Union, though he later expressed some regret about this stance. After Brecht's death in 1956, Günter Grass reflected on these events in *The Plebeians Rehearse the Uprising*.[72] As Grass depicts it, Brecht is rehearsing his version of *Coriolanus*, the workers burst in and demand he join their revolutionary struggle. Brecht vacillates, unsure of the socialist validity of their cause, and ultimately refuses. Grass was using both Shakespeare and Brecht to express political views about the still-divided Germany, and Brecht's ambiguous role as simultaneously a champion of the workers and a defender of the repressive East German state. But he was also offering, in creative form, critical observations about both his source plays, and about the role of theatre in contemporary politics. As Valerie C. Rudolph observes, Grass's Brecht 'has become curiously close to Shakespeare's *Coriolanus* – the man, who, in Grass's view, ultimately cannot belong to any part simply because he is what he is'.[73]

In 2012 National Theatre Wales staged a conflation of Shakespeare's *Coriolanus* and Brecht's *Coriolan* in an RAF aircraft hangar near Cardiff, using the style of 'promenade theatre' in which the audience is not immobilized in a fixed position, but free to circulate around the space of performance. The method is typical of some types of community theatre, such as the street theatre of the medieval mystery plays, and was adapted onto mainstream stages in the 1980s. As

Penelope Cole[74] describes it, this staging turned the audience into an active and participating element of the performance, becoming in turns a plebeian mob, Roman or Volscian soldiers, bystanders and so on.

> Thus, the audience/viewers were, from the first, cast in the role of the populace of Rome, the body politic, citizens, soldiers, and rioters, to occupy, inhabit, and define the public spaces within and upon which the action takes place.[75]

As Cole indicates, such a participatory theatrical event can bring an audience into much more intimate relationship with the action, engaging their senses and encouraging identification. At the same time the performance works to break down the barriers of separation between theatre and 'real life', very much in the manner of presentist criticism.

At the opposite extreme to Brecht's communist appropriation stands John Osborne's right-wing version, *A Place Calling Itself Rome*, published in 1973 and never professionally performed.[76] Just as Brecht proletarianized Shakespeare's people and caricatured the ruling class, so Osborne consistently depicts the patricians as honourable, and the tribunes as ignoble. Osborne's Coriolanus is a very modern hero, ridden with anxiety, an alcoholic, sexually impotent, emotionally crippled and (like Osborne himself) driven by an insatiable anger against his own age. He bears all the traits, as Cohn puts it, of 'a typical Osborne protagonist'. Osborne shifts the military action to a modern scene of guerrilla warfare, allowing for the archaic presence of single combat: Coriolanus and Aufidius 'are seen to be stalking each other with rifles and/or pistols through street windows and doors and crouching behind rubble and oil cans'.[77]

Although Holland condemns Osborne's right-wing politics as 'venomously reactionary' (though he offers no such critique of Brecht's Communist, even Stalinist, loyalties), his analysis of *A Place Calling Itself Rome* as a critical-creative intervention is astute:

Shakespeare's play operates here as a marker for a space within which the political self can be written and the agony of the private self briefly explored. Osborne's play, for all its theatrical weaknesses, is a brave attempt at a right-wing redefinition of the ways in which *Coriolanus* could come to mean in the 1970s.[78]

With ironic presumption, Günter Grass titled the preface to *The Plebeians Rehearse the Uprising* 'The Prehistory and Posthistory of the Tragedy of *Coriolanus* from Livy and Plutarch to Shakespeare down to Brecht and myself'. In order to represent the full range of critical-creative possibilities afforded by *Coriolanus,* and with far more presumptuousness, I'm obliged to add my own name to that distinguished lineage by referring the reader to *The Lonely Dragon,* a free adaptation of Shakespeare's play into a James Bond-style espionage thriller.[79] Within this narrative genre lies a perfect modern complement to Shakespeare's Roman drama, a medium in which all the themes and preoccupations of the play can be accurately and creatively relocated. Like the Coriolanus of Ralph Fiennes's film, my hero – named Guy Mars, after the Latin Caius Martius – encounters all the experiences that make Shakespeare's hero so memorable and distinctive, but transplanted into a different genre and a different time.

One of the key terms used by practitioners of adaptation studies is 'intertextuality'. At one time even stage and film versions of plays, let alone free adaptations, were treated as extrapolations from the literary text, and compared favourably or otherwise with the 'original'. Modern adaptation studies conceive of a dramatic 'work' like *Coriolanus* rather as a proliferation of different textualities, all responding to and feeding off one another. In turn, when a text undergoes transformation into another medium, it comes under the influence of that medium's own codes and conventions, and this is clearly the case with the film version of *Coriolanus.* L. Monique Pittman,[80] for example, has argued that the two lead actors, Ralph Fiennes and Gerard Butler, both imported into the film influences and associations from other defining film roles, specifically the evil Voldemort in the *Harry Potter* films and King Leonidas the Spartan from *300*. Pittman deploys the argument that *Coriolanus* connects masculinity with the closed, self-sufficient male body, and the feminine with openness and connection, and suggests that these patterns are also to be found in the actor's other film roles. All three filmic texts in her view share mythical narratives and dramatize competing masculinities, showing gendered opposites to be both alike and complementary. Similarly, Catherine Baker[81] claims that the decision to shoot the film in Serbia and Montenegro, and to adumbrate the context of the Balkans wars of the 1990s brings those conflicts and their cultural codes inside the filmic text, thus making the film as much 'about' the former Yugoslavia as it is 'about' ancient Rome.

It would probably be true to say that the holistic way in which criticism is practised today makes it much more difficult to separate historico-political, gender-based and adaptation-focused criticism, since critics tend to draw heterogeneously on all these different critical practices. Since the 1980s many critics across the spectrum have juxtaposed detailed historical research, often archival, into the play's social, political and economic context; discussion of early modern political and economic theory; consideration of subsequent philosophical and theoretical developments, often stretching across several centuries, right up to the present day; and practical critical analysis of the play's language and structure. Such criticism differed from more traditional historicist readings (which distinguished between literary text and 'historical background') by assuming that history permeated the text, and that the text both engages with and reacts upon its contingent history. Later work has continued to be characterized by left-wing ideologies, but became less overtly politically engaged, and therefore often closely resembles more traditional historicist criticism. The exceptions to this norm are those critics who pursue a 'presentist' agenda, and resolutely foreground the relevance and application of contemporary cultural production to the dramatic literature of the past. In a similar way, feminist and gender theories have both permeated mainstream criticism, and deepened their own engagement with history, while retaining a strong political emphasis in engagements with the past. Adaptations studies have also become mainstream, so that most criticism and scholarship today recognize a much wider range of cultural practices as proper to the study of Shakespeare, in particular to a play as rich, complex and critically malleable as *Coriolanus*.

4

New Directions

Putting Tongues in Wounds: The Search for an Honest Body in *Coriolanus*

Anna Kamaralli

When an actor steps onto the stage they submit their body to interpretation by the audience. It is an action that is exposing, vulnerable and risky. In *Coriolanus*, Shakespeare recognizes that anxiety about subjecting one's body to the interpretation of the crowd, and builds his protagonist around it. This work was put together by actors; actors who knew their job was to counterfeit the expression of emotion in both body and word, and who would also have been highly aware of the ethical doubts many people had about the entire nature of such a profession. Shakespeare allows everyone except Martius to argue for the virtue of this activity. Boldly, Martius acts as the resistant body to the job of being an actor (while of course, paradoxically, speaking Shakespeare's lines in representation of a fictionalized version of a semi-legendary, historic figure). He consistently rejects the idea of playing anyone but himself: 'Would you have me / False to my nature? Rather say I play / The man I am' (3.2.15–17). It is the eternal task of the playwright to write the words and actions that elicit an emotional response, and then also to construct that response, presenting both the persuasive case and its counterpoint. In this case the playwright experiments with how persuasively he can write both the argument for and against his own craft.

The body of Martius is the site upon which Shakespeare charts the matrix of emotion, the rhetoric that expresses it and the performance that animates it. This chapter will try to remind us that performance is the thing that draws all these elements together, but is simultaneously the thing that the play paints as least trustworthy, most likely to obscure truth even as it claims to reveal it. Emotional expression in *Coriolanus* is as fervent as in any of Shakespeare's works, but it does not occur in typical places. Much of the play's distinctive character can be traced to the points of entry to its moments of rhetorical passion, that is, the things that cause characters to react and speak emotionally. Characters are frequently drawn to speak out of a passionate desire that a person (usually Martius) be represented correctly, and Shakespeare entwines that with questions about the speaking body as a vessel for communicating emotion. Martius becomes identified with his body, but there is a perpetual anxiety about the potential for that body to be misinterpreted. The positioning of Menenius's famous allegory of the body's rebellious parts at the very start of the play makes the ear receptive to mentions of physical elements carrying representational weight. The opening show of highly charged passions, not in the protagonist but in nameless members of a general rabble, actually makes a point of how it matters what is the prompt to that passion. A citizen wants to make it clear that his call to violent action is born of reasonable cause: 'for the gods know, I speak this in hunger for bread, not in thirst for revenge' (1.1.21–3). His passion's outlet is violent uprising, but his cause comes of reason, and has a physical origin. What prompts expressions of passionate feeling in this play is bodies; bodies and their vulnerability, to injury, but also to misinterpretation.

Nathalie Vienne-Guerrin has explored in rigorous detail the specific role of the tongue here, identifying the Jacobean interest in the effort to rule the tongue, and its capacity to go rogue.[1] The tongue does indeed present as the most significant body part in this play, as well as being unique in being both an organ and a metonym, conventionally representing the act of speech itself. The ingeniousness of this symbolic use of the tongue lies precisely in its role as the overlap between the two sites of questionable authenticity with which Shakespeare confronts the audience: body and rhetoric. Bodies speak, in *Coriolanus*, then people speak to interpret them. The citizens note that it is their duty to do this: 'we are to put our tongues into those wounds and speak for them' (2.3.6–7). This Citizen feels that they have both the authority and the ability to interpret that enables them to do this. Though Stanley Fish believes 'we are not to imagine that they really feel gratitude; rather, they engage in a form of behaviour which counts as an expression of it',[2] these tongues are not the unruly ones that concern Vienne-Guerrin, but tongues marshalled to tradition. Tradition is not enough, however, to reassure Martius about the soundness of their interpretation. He remains convinced that to show his wounds is to risk misinterpretation, because he has no trust in the citizens as interpreters.

The contribution of the actor to animating the meanings Shakespeare lays out is more intrusive here than even in some of his more metatheatrical works. This is because the central body of the play, Martius (who, like Hamlet, Rosalind and many others, does reflect upon himself as an actor) is in a constant state of tension between awareness of all the ways he is a signifier and fury at being called upon to offer meaning to all his audiences – those within the play and by extension those in the auditorium. All Shakespeare's other self-conscious players draw attention to their practice, even to the point of showing off (think how gleefully Richard III forces the audience to notice the art of his performance). Martius is unique in his resistance to his role as actor. When Cynthia Marshall attempts to answer 'what are historic representations, representations of?', she digs into the space between the personage and the actor representing them.³ Yet there is a further division to note functioning within the play: represented persons speaking to express themselves and therefore move the audience of non-playing theatregoers, and the represented persons speaking to persuade and move their onstage companions. The one is an actor performing a part, the other an actor performing a part of someone performing.

Coriolanus makes an extravagant display out of the contrast between two forms of dramatic rhetoric. The more common in most plays is an unmediated form, the first-level form of acting, where the speech is a person in character spontaneously or emotively describing their experience at the time: their goal is to communicate their experience as opposed to being a mechanism of persuasion to move the hearer. But there is also a mediated form, more closely associated with political rhetoric, in that the actor is being asked to represent someone giving a speech, the rhetoric used deliberately persuasively and having been crafted for a purpose. The subject matter of this particular play obviously lends itself to a heavier emphasis on this second, mediated form. I would argue that the counterpoise of these two subtly distinct forms of emotionally charged speech is a particular focus of the playwright. John Plotz, in his essay '*Coriolanus* and the Failure of Performatives', is primarily concerned with the more formal, political use of rhetoric, and so finds the play to be 'filled with characters who deploy language for future gain. For these characters, all language is designed to persuade rather than to represent.'⁴ In order to make his point, Plotz overstates somewhat here. Rather, the play offers us a clever back and forth in language use between the two alternatives. The moments when speech is used without thought of persuasion are highlighted by their rarity and singularity. And it is Martius's moments of using language to represent genuine and immediate emotion that show why he struggles with its other uses.

And yet he is surrounded by allies who seek to persuade him of the morality of playing. Cominius insists on the virtue of speaking a list of Martius's achievements, despite the latter's revulsion at the sound of it. Menenius counsels Martius to 'Repent what you have spoke' (3.2.38); in reply he declares, 'I cannot do it to the gods' (3.2.39). In support of this position, Volumnia is eloquent and persuasive – everything Martius mistrusts.

> Because that now it lies you on to speak
> To th' people, not by your own instruction,
> Nor by th' matter which your heart prompts you,
> But with such words that are but roted in
> Your tongue, though but bastards and syllables
> Of no allowance to your bosom's truth.
> Now, this no more dishonours you at all
> Than to take in a town with gentle words,
> Which else would put you to your fortune and
> The hazard of much blood.
> I would dissemble with my nature where
> My fortunes and my friends at stake required
> I should do so in honour.
>
> (3.2.53–65)

Martius seems to believe that the ability to control or direct emotion renders it false. Volumnia sees no such contradiction, but rather supportive harmony between the body parts of heart, mind and spleen, much as in Menenius's fable.

>   Pray be counselled.
> I have a heart as little apt as yours,
> But yet a brain that leads my use of anger
> To better vantage.
>
> (3.2.29–32)

Emotion given purpose is not inherently false for being controlled. Rather, it is well-directed emotion, and this is a personal goal for the early modern English rhetorician. Martius would not necessarily be seen as right and Volumnia wrong by the play's first audiences.

Being other than his authentic self is humiliating and perceived by Martius as deceptive, but how can an authentic self be established? Speech that arises spontaneously reflects an authentic self. It is in his anger that Martius speaks with wholly his own voice, and it is perhaps this that prompts Peter Kishore Saval to argue that his temper comes from his maturity, not his childishness. As Menenius puts it: 'His heart's his mouth. / What his breast forges that his tongue must vent' (3.1.259–60). It is in his anger that he knows himself to be a man. The irony is that it is only callow, susceptible boys who are led to believe that anger is what makes a man. Eve Sanders pinpoints the relationship Shakespeare establishes between the crisis in masculinity that never really left Martius as he grew from boy to man, and early modern anxieties about the links between boyhood, feminization and acting.[5] She considers Martius's rejection of acting as potentially harmful in relation to the concerns of Shakespeare's contemporaries about what boy players were put through. Consider the surprising invocation by Cominius of Martius as a boy player in battle: 'When he might act the woman in the scene / He proved best man i'th' field' (2.2.94–5). Martius, in Cominius's description, is positioned to be both an apprentice, a boy player, and feminized, retiring in implied fear from battle, but was determined to spurn the phase of life in which that is his allotted part, and seize the role of man. His awareness and hatred of having something to prove clearly began early. As he attained manhood, however, the comparisons between being a public figure (a soldier, a candidate for consul) and being a player proved to be no less humiliating. It is probably a given that Martius was played by Richard Burbage, but it would certainly be interesting if we could establish that the role was given to one of those actors who began as a boy player and grew out of the woman's part to become a full member of the company.

Responding to emotion-eliciting rhetoric is by its nature untrustworthy, the people are easily swayed by speech or crafted words and this is framed as their weakness. The weakness of the populace also permits them to be easily baffled. Performative behaviour can provoke confusing interpretations in those observing it. The citizens seem at first unsure whether or not Martius has shown them his scars. The speech act of promising them has been (briefly) effective in standing in for the bodily event. If the body can be used to persuade in the way speech can be used to persuade then the body is untrustworthy. The body can have ulterior motives, the body can lie or misrepresent or be a tool to the ends of a manipulative person. The body presented in the way demanded of Martius is a body that is not honest. On the battlefield he knows his wounds to be honest, but he does not trust that his wounds are a representation being used honestly in the Forum. Deeds tell the truth, but everything that flows on from them has at least the potential to distort or lie. Recounting deeds, as Cominius does, allows them to be directed toward a desired end, not stand for themselves. Likewise, displaying scars, asking for reward – these things undermine the deeds by putting them to use. Sanders points out that there is no precedent in Plutarch, Shakespeare's key source, for Martius's struggle with showing his wounds to the populace.[6] What prevents Martius from showing his scars? Disgust with performativity or anger at the idea that his word, and report of his action, are not sufficient? 'There's some among you have beheld me fighting' (3.1.225). He naïvely hopes that he can force his mere presence to communicate what he needs, when his right to speak the words he wishes is truncated. His long history on the battlefield has bred him to expect the results he wants will follow automatically from his emotional path. He becomes enraged in battle, acts on that rage, and through that achieves his aim of victory. There is an honesty to the transaction; nothing mediates between the emotion and the desired outcome. The gap between the behaviour that counts as an expression of emotion and the actual experiencing of that emotion is what breaks Martius. Volumnia and Menenius ask him only to engage in behaviour that counts as an expression of humility, 'with such words that are but roted in / Your tongue, though but bastards and syllables / Of no allowance to your bosom's truth' (3.2.56–8), but unable to experience genuinely the matching emotion, Martius cannot bring himself to perform the behaviour adequately. There are many instances in Shakespeare of the question being posed about who can perform behaviour that counts. Can Katherine perform submission convincingly enough to 'count' to Petruccio? Can Iago or Richard III perform concern for those they wish to harm?

If '[t]he price is to ask it kindly' (2.3.74), as the Citizen says, wherein lies the lie in Martius's conduct if he were to comply? He claims that he is not being true to himself when he asks for the favour of the people, that he is playing the wrong part, and yet he does not actually lie or deceive through speech acts. As Saval notes, '[i]t is typical of Coriolanus to care more about the feeling in his words than the formal commitment they produce'.[7] This is true in both positive and negative instances. His inauthenticity of feeling in asking kindly seems to Martius to be more significant than the honest, formal action of following appropriate procedure to become consul. He does not say anything that constitutes a lie: he would be consul. He has scars that he could show. When he presents himself humbly to the people he speaks no lies, but feels his deception in feigned emotion as communicated through his humbled garments and demeanour. He is aware that he is carrying his body as if experiencing feelings counter to the truth of what he feels. His feigned emotional state is the lie. In counterpoint to the citizens who intend to act in gratitude, even if it is not convincing that they feel it, he feels disdain, but behaves as if he is feeling gratitude. He feels high, but acts low. This play shows that deception can exist not only in words, but in affect. The actor uses carefully crafted rhetoric to imitate someone speaking spontaneously without affectation, but the politician is expected to have crafted a speech with a purpose directing it. At what point on this sliding scale of performativity lies an actor playing a politician? What should be the nature of his rhetoric? When Martius speaks to rally the Roman troops in 1.4 his words are chosen to provoke passion in the auditor more than to express passion in himself, demonstrating that even he is not absolutely above the use of persuasive rhetoric.

So, where does the elusive authentic self lie, and why is the struggle to find it so particular to Martius? By all the measures proposed so far, what makes Menenius authentic? He, too, claims a reputation for speaking his truth and saying what comes into his mind without constraint. Menenius claims to share Martius's inability to dissemble and that he is publicly known for a deficiency in ability to mask his true feelings: '[w]hat I think, I utter, and spend my malice in my breath ... if the drink you give me touch my palate adversely, I make a crooked face at it' (2.1.51–4). Yet somehow this has failed to damage his status in Rome, and he is not perceived as dangerous for it. He is looked to as a model for how a man of status should comport himself. The tribunes attempt no coup against him, and in the final time of crisis they expect that his rhetorical power, and his person, will be enough to influence Martius, though he doubts it himself. What of the citizens with their empty bellies? Martius does not believe their bodies; if they were really suffering they would put their bodies more willingly in danger in service of their State, in a position to earn respect and therefore corn.

It is this relationship between speech and action that Martius instinctively registers as what matters in measuring a person, and that therefore generates a platform for the play to investigate that relationship. Fish is perceptive in his observation that this is a play about speech acts.[8] Moreover, it is an ideal play for dissecting the places where speech acts (where words are used to perform actions) and affect theory (where performed action communicates emotion without words), complement each other. Speech acts occur, and the responses from the characters, demonstrations of affect, are then reflected upon in further speech. We know about the affective behaviour from its descriptions by characters watching other characters. The playwright's desire to communicate emotion can lead to speech or to action. Onstage, action can be described through speech, and occasionally prompted with a stage direction. But then, both speech and action can elicit emotion, and the cycle goes around again. Speech acts, however, can be incomplete and therefore signify a personal failing. Both Fish and Saval identify the importance of the moment early in the play where Martius shows a capacity for thoughtfulness, but fails to turn that impulse into action. His recollection of the old man who was his host in Corioles, and his verbalizing of his gratitude and need to offer recompense are inadequate, because he abandons the intention before the action (1.9.85–90). This speech fails to produce an act, and the result is a reflection on Martius's character. Character development is the only reason for the playwright to include such a passage; it is being made clear to the audience that Martius's compassion and duty extend only as far as they involve no effort to take care of others.

To complicate this there is an uncanny preoccupation in *Coriolanus* with the role of the body in these kinds of communication. The body is represented as having the potential to persuade and therefore to mislead or to at least be a mediated speech act. The body, like the politician's rhetoric, is being presented as crafted and with a purpose, that purpose to persuade so the bearer can achieve their ends. The body loses its ability to be unmediated like the actor's speech that does not represent the politician's rhetoric but rather the character's spontaneous representation of their own experience.

Although my concern here is not to record performance choices that have been pursued in the play's stage history, Alun Thomas shows us how crucial the physical dynamic between the actor in this tormented role and his audience is in this play. In the production directed by Mike Pearson and Mike Brooks for the National Theatre Wales, in association with the Royal Shakespeare Company, a promenade staging facilitated encouraging the audience to feel like participants in the group scenes, and therefore blurred the lines between being addressed as audience and as characters. As an audience member, Thomas responded to feeling positioned as an object in relation to Martius's actions and responses: 'In that moment we become the fearful Roman army, repulsed by Coriolanus's absurd level of bravery. His agonized, reproachful stare is directed squarely at us. We have betrayed him.'[9] Such an effective collapsing of the distinction between the actor's speaking to the audience and the character's speaking to other characters shows how theatrical embodiment defeats attempts to find simple categories for performative speech. This is a play that can be mapped by physical bodies in tableaux: Martius entering Corioles as the gates close behind him, him emerging 'as [if] he were flayed' (1.6.22), his presentation before the citizens in humble garb, his drawing of his sword on his own people, his physical embracement by his enemy, his family kneeling and then the dumb show of their return to Rome, and finally, of course, Aufidius standing over, or on, his body.

Sanders fully embraces Shakespeare's consciousness of the fact of the actor, and the multiple available meanings of inscriptions on the body. The struggle of Martius as an actor is that he cannot control the message his body sends: 'assigning a political significance to his scars is an unacceptable distortion of their true meaning'.[10] Sanders believes that Martius grows to learn the techniques of advantageous presentation of an actor: 'The agency Coriolanus discovers as an actor lies not only in the ability to utter performative speech acts but also in the capacity to enact physical gestures and behaviours for strategic ends',[11] but I would argue that he clings to his refusal to accept the legitimacy of such self-shaping right up until the moment of his death, shown in his shock at Aufidius (whom he trusted as an honest body) using rhetorical strategy against him.

Martius has a fixated concern with status, and an absolute certainty that he knows what people's relative status should be. He knows that he should not bow to the people, that his mother should not kneel to him, that he and Aufidius can function as equals when necessary, and that to be called a 'boy' is an utterly unacceptable lowering of his known rank. The concern with the inversion of proper order here is not that of Macbeth, where unearthly portents point toward evil disruption, nor quite that of Ulysses in *Troilus and Cressida* when he gently reminds Achilles of his responsibility to know his place. Rather, Martius takes a large portion of his sense of a secure self from knowing who should defer to whom. This is a strict them-and-us division.

> By mingling them with us, the honoured number,
> Who lack not virtue, no, nor power, but that
> Which they have given to beggars.
>
> (3.1.74–6)

It is noteworthy that Martius continues to speak in verse for almost the entirety of his stage time, but bestows only prose on the proletariat. He speaks in verse to himself, but in prose when begging the approval of the citizens in 2.3. Like Brutus speaking after Caesar's murder, Martius solicits the citizens in prose. Sincere, emotionally prompted speech can certainly result in verse, so his use of prose may be a form of plain speaking, but might also be crafted by the playwright to leave the impression of having the minimal polite response dragged out of him. There are two choices as to what is being communicated by the switch to prose: Martius could be attempting to speak directly in order to reclaim his sense of honest speech. Alternatively, the audience could be receiving an indication that he need not expend the effort of verse on these lowly people.

> Away my disposition and possess me
> Some harlot's spirit! My throat of war be turned,
> Which choired with my drum, into a pipe
> Small as an eunuch or the virgin voice
> That babies lull asleep! The smiles of knaves
> Tent in my cheeks, and schoolboys' tears take up
> The glasses of my sight! A beggar's tongue

> Make motion through my lips and my armed knees
> Who bowed but in my stirrup bend like his
> That hath received an alms! – I will not do't
> Lest I surcease to honour mine own truth
> And by my body's action teach my mind
> A most inherent baseness.
>
> (3.2.112–24)

In this speech Martius makes clear which people he regards as contemptible by virtue of their social status: harlots, eunuchs, the young, knaves, beggars. Anyone, in short, who is dependent on those with more power to grant favours. He indicates a belief that asking for something carries with it the automatic imperative to be manipulative in order to receive it. To ask for something is to lie to his own nature, and the performed action carries the risk of changing him fundamentally: 'And by my body's action teach my mind / A most inherent baseness' (3.2.123–4).

This rock-solid understanding of relative place in his world – that it is acceptable for him to grant to someone asking, but not to ask someone to grant – might be the thing that makes him susceptible to the begging of his family in the final act. He may tell his mother that it is a disruption of order for her to kneel to him, but the rightness would strike him of being returned to a position to grant rather than be the one to beg.

To be unflinching in the face of threat is to claim earned status, to waiver is to lose it, and to seek to match your betters (especially through such paltry means as speech) as he believes the tribunes do, is unforgivable:

> The tongues o'th' common mouth. I do despise them,
> For they do prank them in authority
> Against all noble sufferance.
>
> (3.1.22–4)

Alongside this fear of disruption to the hierarchical order of status runs a concern with inversions in emotional response.

The play is sprinkled with references to inappropriate responses arising from emotional moments:

> Wouldst thou have laughed had I come coffined home,
> That weep'st to see me triumph? Ah, my dear,
> Such eyes the widows in Corioles wear
> And mothers that lack sons.
>
> (2.1.171–4)

More inappropriate responses arise from contrasts set up between what the natural order of things should be and what the reality of the situation demands:

>   thy sight, which should
> Make our eyes flow with joy, hearts dance with comforts,
> Constrains them weep and shake with fear and sorrow.
>
> (5.3.98–100)

These culminate in Martius's abhorrence at seeing his mother kneel to him, an inappropriate response and simultaneously a status inversion powerful enough to unsettle his final resolve:

>   What's this
> Your knees to me? To your corrected son?
> Then let the pebbles on the hungry beach
> Fillip the stars; then let the mutinous winds
> Strike the proud cedars 'gainst the fiery sun.
>
> (5.3.56–60)

Eve Kosofsky Sedgwick's famous work on homosocial bonding emphasizes not just the intimate links sought by men with other men, but the use they make of a woman to activate the transaction.[12] This play lacks an actual woman to use as the currency of exchange between the men (unlike in, for instance, *Troilus and Cressida*), but instead they make do with the pale substitute of their theoretical wives. Both Martius's greeting of Cominius,

> O, let me clip ye
> In arms as sound as when I wooed, in heart
> As merry as when our nuptial day was done
> And tapers burned to bedward.
>
> (1.6.29–32)

and Aufidius's greeting of Martius,

> Know thou first,
> I loved the maid I married; never man
> Sighed truer breath. But that I see thee here,
> Thou noble thing, more dances my rapt heart
> Than when I first my wedded mistress saw
> Bestride my threshold.
>
> (4.5.115–20)

include references to their enthusiasm for their wedding night. Yet despite the apparent dwindling of women into means of expressing passion for male connections, his wife and mother are among the few people Martius unequivocally respects, and this gives theatrical power to their stage presence. Christina Luckyj identifies how strongly the presentation of the actors playing Volumnia and Virgilia will colour audience perceptions of Martius as a character, and of the moral choices of the story.[13] She also gives an excellent overview of the elasticity that crucial moments of silence present to performers, which unsurprisingly is most pertinent to the female characters here. There are times on stage when actors are simply not given lines, and embodied reaction is the only means of communication. Volumnia is given some of the most lengthy and perfectly constructed rhetorical showpieces in this play, but Luckyj is alert to all the places where the primary dramatic effect of a moment emanates from her silence. In the scene of his leaving for exile (4.1), for instance, Martius describes for us the affective impression of Volumnia's response, more than we, or the one acting her, are able to determine her feelings from her lines. It is uncharacteristic for

Volumnia to speak so little in a scene. It is possible she is more perplexed than anything, which is an emotion convincingly rendering a character speechless: she has imagined only two emotional prompts for herself, her son's glory or his disgrace. She has no map for how to verbalize feeling when he is neither dishonoured nor acclaimed. The performance of silent emotion in preference for detailed verbal description of a character's emotional state goes double for Virgilia, whose silence is noted and praised by Martius. Plotz notes the perplexity that Martius feels encountering speech, and his consequent admiration of the way Virgilia maintains her capacity for avoiding it: 'That he calls his wife "my gracious silence" acknowledges that she does not bear the guilt of duplicity that all other Romans do.'[14] Volumnia sets herself up as a contrast to Virgilia through a discourse on what feelings Martius's absence would prompt in her. In Virgilia, worry and retiring. In Volumnia, only hope for glory. 'If my son were my husband, I should freelier rejoice in that absence wherein he won honour than in the embracements of his bed, where he would show most love' (1.3.2–5). But Virgilia is more than merely a foil to show Volumnia in her full dramatic glory. Her presence contributes to the discourse on how bodies should be interpreted, and whether they are trustworthy, because Virgilia's body is indubitably honest. She keeps it contained, and she uses it only in service of husband and dynasty. What provokes Virgilia to passionate exclamation is fear for her husband: 'Oh Jupiter, no blood!' (1.3.40); 'Heavens bless my lord from fell Aufidius!' (1.3.47); 'O, no, no, no' (2.1.117); 'O heavens! O heavens!' (4.1.12). She is allotted no eloquence, just pure reaction, the honest contrast to all the surrounding rhetoric. Her desire to remain within private, domestic space extends to virtual silence whenever she appears in a scene with a public setting, but with one notable exception, when facing the tribunes beside Volumnia: 'What then? / He'd make an end of thy posterity' (4.2.25–6). She can be roused to powerful public voice when given the opportunity to confront her husband's enemies.

Janet Adelman looks for Martius's source of self-definition in his positional relationships with these influential women,[15] but it could be fruitful to expand that approach by examining how he defines himself according to his emotional responses to how others represent him. Martius shows distress when any interaction with another person disrupts his sense of self. Notably, this is not when he is faced with an enemy or a physical threat – this is when he knows himself. The act of putting on garments that he knows to be not his is excruciating to him. Curbing his speech, likewise. He knows whose son he is, and whose husband, and the entire city appears to feel confident about who is his son. When the structures of hierarchical status are removed from around him he is unmoored, hence his need to banish Rome (3.3.122), rather than be banished – he must know himself an actor rather than acted upon. The scene of his exile is an excellent demonstration of affect mediated through the observational speech of another character. It is Martius's speech in 4.1 that is the guide to the affective performance of those around him: Cominius droops, Menenius and Virgilia both weep. More intriguing is the question of what physicality Volumnia is showing that causes him to ask her, 'Nay, mother, / Where is your ancient courage?' (4.1.2–3).

Saval admires Martius's willingness to speak frankly even when this involves risk. Doubting Vienne-Guerrin's assumption that this reflects a lack of ability to control his anger, Saval reads Martius's frank speech as a courageous choice.[16] However, the subject's likely perception of his situation must figure in this interpretation, and it is not at all clear that Martius perceives a risk of bad consequences for himself when he insults those he sees as beneath him. Menenius's assessment is that he, 'being angry, does forget that ever / He heard the name of death' (3.1.261–2). His pride and sense of superiority are such that he (at least in respect to the lines) shows no awareness that the people he looks down on are capable of causing him harm. Rather, he dares them to try, with what appears to be absolute confidence: 'There's some among you have beheld me fighting / Come try upon yourselves what you have seen me'

(3.1.225–6). By the rules of Saval's understanding of speech that carries risk, it is Martius's compassionate, thoughtful yielding, not his confrontational insults, that qualifies. It is only at that moment that he is aware of danger to himself, and chooses to speak anyway.

The play's climax explicitly depicts an emotional response to a question of what to do, rather than a rational one. As at so many crucial points, the play shows a refusal to trust words, but a capitulation to a physical action. Miranda Fay Thomas offers the most eloquent interpretation of the specific thing in his mother's plea that succeeds in turning Martius: not her elegant rhetoric, but her kneeling. After holding fast his position during Volumnia's superbly constructed speeches of supplication,

> seeing his family upon bended knees is what proves ultimately most persuasive. Rather than viewing this as an act of submission, however, it is in fact utilized by Volumnia as a show of strength: it may indicate passivity, but its loaded meaning is passive-aggressive. This gesture of *seeming* humility is anything but: it uses the submissive act of kneeling to shame Coriolanus for forcing his mother into such a position.[17]

The action of kneeling may be the thing that matters to the protagonist, but it would be foolish to therefore discount the speech (5.3.94–182), which will always generate enormous impact on the audience. The kneeling is for Martius, but the rhetoric is for us. In it Volumnia recapitulates all the concerns with voice, body and performance that the play up to this moment has been rehearsing. She speaks first of what their silent bodies would communicate, then goes on to reveal the tension between their familial connection with Martius, and their own, bodily, identification with the Roman State. Coppélia Kahn draws the significance of this out in detail: 'by identifying her womb with Rome, she also evokes the peculiar value of women to Rome as the fertile resource without which the state cannot reproduce itself'.[18] After proposing a resolution that could result in honour for all, she repeatedly begs her son to speak, and then after kneeling returns again to the question of when it is right to speak and when the expressive body must take precedence: 'I am hushed until our city be afire / And then I'll speak a little' (5.3.181–2).

It is the rarest of things in Shakespeare's First Folio (1623) to see a written stage direction for a pause. '[*He*] *holds her by the hand, silent*' (5.3.182 SD) must be recognized as a textual element of extraordinary significance, again prioritizing the visual impact of bodies as vessels of emotional communication.

The affective action Martius performs in turning away with confirmed denial, then almost immediately turning back to take his mother's hand should not be a surprise, as it reflects the rapidity of shifts in emotion that have featured at key points throughout the preceding drama. Anger turns to sorrow, resolve to giving way, stoic restraint to unconstrained fury. Emotion is presented as instantly changeable, and Martius as especially mercurial. In particular, two points of absolute loss of temper mark his journey, first in 3.3, when his attempt at addressing the citizens 'mildly' utterly disintegrates, and later in the final scene, 5.6, when Aufidius turns on him. These are distinct from either his expressions of disdain or his bloodlust-fuelled rallying cries. In both cases being called a traitor is unacceptable to him (despite the accusation coming from two separate nations – surely that must make him a traitor to at least one?).

> O world, thy slippery turns! Friends now fast sworn,
> Whose double bosoms seems to wear one heart,
> Whose hours, whose bed, whose meal and exercise
> Are still together, who twin, as 'twere, in love
> Unseparable, shall within this hour,
> On a dissension of a doit, break out
> To bitterest enmity. So fellest foes,
> Whose passions and whose plots have broke their sleep
> To take the one the other, by some chance,

> Some trick not worth an egg, shall grow dear friends
> And interjoin their issues. So with me.
> My birthplace hate I, and my love's upon
> This enemy town.
>
> (4.4.12–24)

This admission of changeability in loyalty makes no direct mention of Aufidius, but does set up the intensely emotional nature of his decision (double bosoms wear one heart, love, passions, interjoin), as if to deflect from the charge that his justification is cynical sophistry. Once again, Martius shows a need to believe that he is his honest self because his choice arises from his immediate, emotional response.

When Aufidius welcomes Martius with the most erotic speech in the play, his interest in Martius is not as a general, as a man who won the title 'Coriolanus', or as a representative of Rome, but as an unmediated body, a body he knows through pressing his own against it in battle, dreams or welcome:

> I have nightly since
> Dreamt of encounters 'twixt thyself and me –
> We have been down together in my sleep
> Unbuckling helms, fisting each other's throat –
> And waked half dead with nothing.
>
> (4.5.124–8)

It is no wonder that Martius is so easily seduced by exactly what he wants: recognition of his true self through the honesty of his bodily prowess. Earlier, upon hearing that Aufidius has spoken openly about how he hates him, Martius longs to go out and meet him. When he fears being dishonestly dealt with by his own people, it is precisely this kind of truthfulness that he seeks. When Aufidius describes his recurring dream of engaging Martius in a fight they are not shooting arrows at each other nor striking blows with swords but locked body to body. To Martius's ears, would this be what makes it an honest encounter?

This would make it unsurprising that he experiences it as a betrayal when Aufidius deploys rhetoric against him when he makes his accusation in front of the Volscian Lords:

> Read it not, noble lords,
> But tell the traitor in the highest degree
> He hath abused your powers.
> ...
> Ay, 'traitor', Martius.
> ...
> Ay, Martius, Caius Martius. Dost thou think
> I'll grace thee with that robbery, thy stolen name
> 'Coriolanus', in Corioles?
> You lords and heads o'th' state, perfidiously
> He has betrayed your business and given up
> For certain drops of salt, your city Rome –
> I say 'your city' – to his wife and mother,
> Breaking his oath and resolution like
> A twist of rotten silk, never admitting
> Counsel o'th' war. But at his nurse's tears
> He whined and roared away your victory
> That pages blushed at him and men of heart
> Looked wondering each at others.
> ...
> Name not the god, thou boy of tears.
> (5.6.84–6, 88, 90–102, 103)

It is easy to miss that Aufidius's final speech of accusation is not spontaneous, but crafted. His rebuke of Martius's decision to seek peace with Rome comes not as an instantaneous reaction, but is delayed, held over until it is of use to him. Martius reacts with absolute fury at being misrepresented first as a traitor then as a boy. A threat to his masculinity is intolerable, as is being doubted, perceiving himself as performing insincerity, and ultimately being mischaracterised. His final rage at Aufidius comes from hearing his counterpart (as he believes) misrepresent him.

It is perhaps a little sad that Martius finally meets Aufidius not with the kind of joyous respect suggested by their earlier encounters, but with bragging and denigration:

> Your judgments, my grave lords,
> Must give this cur the lie and his own notion –
> Who wears my stripes impressed upon him; that
> Must bear my beating to his grave – shall join
> To thrust the lie unto him.
>
> (5.6.107–11)

The reason for Martius's fury at Aufidius's terms of condemnation, in particular 'traitor' and 'boy' might be that they speak too pointedly to his specific anxieties, but it would be more consistent with the rest of his character representation to take it that he cannot bear being misrepresented. With the same lack of introspection with which Menenius charged the tribunes, Martius here claims, 'Pardon me, lords, 'tis the first time that ever / I was forced to scold' (5.6.106–7). But why does he see his loss of temper at Aufidius's words as both so distinct from his other outbursts, and so justifiable? Aufidius was the one he trusted to interpret his body rightly.

Freed by the success of his rhetorical strategy from the need to represent Martius as diminished, Aufidius can return to that place of trust in deciding what form his legacy will take:

> Though in this city he
> Hath widowed and unchilded many a one,
> Which to this hour bewail the injury,
> Yet he shall have a noble memory.
>
> (5.6.152–5)

By offering to be one of the four to carry his body, Aufidius reinstates their relationship as one of honourable equals. He ensures that the final message to the audience is conveyed not by words, but by the means of bodies engaged in an action of ritual respect. In death, Aufidius does, finally, represent Martius in such a way as he would regard as honest.

5

New Directions

'As if a man were author of himself': Fantasies of Omnipotence and Autonomy

Evelyn Gajowski

'Alone I did it'
– CAIUS MARTIUS CORIOLANUS[1]

'I alone can fix it'
– DONALD TRUMP[2]

Presentism, ecofeminism, trans-corporeality and hyper-separation

Do twenty-first-century US presidential politics illuminate *Coriolanus* in any meaningful way? Conversely, does Shakespeare's tragedy shed light on contemporary US presidential politics? What kinds of new meanings emerge from juxtaposing Caius Martius Coriolanus and Donald

Trump for analysis? How do these two figures resonate with each other, mutually constituting each other? At the outset of the Roman republic in the fifth century BCE, a legendary figure, Coriolanus, with his authoritarian, patrician tendencies, serves as an obstacle to the nascent republic. Conversely, at what may be the end of the US democratic republic, a twenty-first-century figure, Trump, with his authoritarian, autocratic tendencies, facilitates a downward spiral toward totalitarianism. What is to be gained from interrogating the emergence of the Roman republic, on the one hand, and the threat to the fragile experiment known as the US democratic republic, on the other? Questions such as these animate the work of presentism, given its concern with constructing meaning in texts by taking into account our present moment, namely the context of the reader, the audience member and the theatre professional. 'The past takes on new contours and qualities for us', Hugh Grady observes, 'as our thinking shifts in the present.'[3]

Rather than suppressing or repressing the present, as do new historicists, presentism acknowledges our inevitable *situatedness* in the present moment and recognizes that awareness as a theoretical stance. It puts theory into practice, furthermore, by deliberately using that awareness as a starting point for constructing meaning in a text. In other words, presentism performs the fundamentally radical act, as Terence Hawkes puts it, of putting our cards on the table.[4] Elsewhere, I suggest the inherent presentism of feminist, queer, race, postcolonial and ecocritical studies of Shakespeare, based as they are in contemporary political, social and scientific discourses and events. In a similar vein, Sharon O'Dair suggests the inherent presentism of ecocriticism, posing the question, 'Is It Shakespearean Ecocriticism If It Isn't Presentist?'[5] With these theoretical observations in mind, I aim in this chapter to provide a presentist reading of *Coriolanus* within an ecofeminist framework.

In *Shakespeare and Ecofeminist Theory*, Rebecca Laroche and Jennifer Munroe eloquently argue for the value of an ecofeminist approach to Shakespeare's *King Lear* in helping us understand how it engages 'with shifting discourses about knowledge' and the relationship between nonhumans and humans. Rather than a sense of bounded identity, the dramatic text reorients forms of knowledge to stress a reciprocal, mutual embeddedness of nonhuman and human in a common network of life.[6] *King Lear* dramatizes the ways in which the human is corporeally 'intermeshed with the more-than-human world' – co-produced *by* it and *with* it, rather than subject *of* it or *over* it. Stacy Alaimo labels this phenomenon of reciprocal, mutual embeddedness *transcorporeality*. Understanding the extent to which humans are always already intermeshed with the nonhuman world clarifies the extent to which they are ultimately inseparable from 'the environment'. The environment is not located 'somewhere out there', Alaimo notes, but is always 'the very substance of ourselves'.[7] *King Lear* begins with a focus on Lear and land that he privatizes and distributes. But it trades the importance of the individual for the significance of the organism. Nonhuman and human alike are characterized as interconnected components of a collectively comprised whole that revalues women, the poor and the nonhuman as integral agents.[8] Rather than the fall of a monarch or the dissolution of a kingdom or the disintegration of familial bonds, the tragedy that emerges is the destabilization of a fundamental human arrogance that would dominate women, the poor and the nonhuman equally.[9]

In *Feminism and the Mastery of Nature*, Val Plumwood launches a critique of the binaries (self/other, subject/object) that underlie the radical exclusion, or hyper-separation, of humans from other forms of life on earth. Whereas separation stresses difference, she points out, hyper-separation stresses value. Because the 'other' is treated as 'not merely different but inferior, part of a lower, different order of being', she notes, differentiation from it requires 'not merely distinctness but radical exclusion', not merely separation but 'hyperseparation'.[10] In *Environmental Culture: The Ecological*

Crisis of Reason, Plumwood expands her critique of 'Reason' as damaging to life on earth. The problem, she observes, is that contemporary and early modern science are based in a 'monological form of rationality', animated by an impetus to 'hyper-separate ourselves from nature' – an impetus to 'reduce it conceptually in order to justify domination'. Humans do this to other humans, and humans do this to nonhumans; they thereby lose connection, or the ability 'to empathise and to see the non-human sphere in ethical terms'. Humans get a false sense of their species that includes a false sense of autonomy.[11] Yet 'hyper-separation' is a gendered, raced and classed phenomenon, as well. Because women and other 'lesser beings' are enmeshed in 'the base material sphere of daily life', they are thereby constructed as the 'others of reason'. Because elite men transcend this sphere, they thereby construct themselves as having a 'greater share in Reason'.[12] Elite men, therefore, treat women and other 'lesser beings' as not only inferior, but also as their 'province' for exploitation.

Plumwood's theoretical concept of hyper-separation is especially apparent in the fantasies of omnipotence and autonomy of another of Shakespeare's male tragic protagonists – fantasies that resonate with our own contemporary moment. At first glance, Martius and Trump would seem to have nothing in common. One is a supreme warrior unique among the Romans – even for a culture that celebrates valor above all other virtues, as Cominius points out:

> It is held
> That valour is the chiefest virtue and
> Most dignifies the haver. If it be,
> The man I speak of cannot in the world
> Be singly counterpoised.
>
> (2.2.81–5)

The other is a draft-dodger who avoided military service in Vietnam after having been diagnosed with 'bone spurs'. Despite (or because of) Trump's lack of military experience, he does not hesitate to heap indignities upon the US military: he insults the war record of John McCain, who was tortured as a prisoner of war during the US–Vietnam War;[13] he belittles the Muslim Gold Star parents of a fallen US soldier, Humayun Khan, in Iraq;[14] he cuts benefits to Iraq/Afghanistan war veterans;[15] and he dismisses traumatic brain injuries suffered by 109 soldiers during the Iran missile strikes on two US military bases in Iraq on 8 January 2020 as merely 'headaches'.[16] As if to compensate for his lack of military service, he emphasizes the size of his ideal military budget: 'To safeguard American liberty, we have invested a record-breaking 2.2 trillion dollars in the US military.'[17]

Closer scrutiny, however, discloses a number of significant resonances between the Roman military figure and the twenty-first-century US political figure. As a soldier and an entertainer/real estate developer, respectively, neither figure has any experience or expertise in civic life. Both are ill-equipped to take on the challenge. The transition each attempts to make from the military world and the entertainment/real estate world, respectively, to the world of governance and politics results, therefore, in crisis.[18] *Coriolanus* valourizes individual action, as Theodore Kaouk points out, and dramatizes utter disregard for collective organization. Martius's unwillingness or inability 'to partake in civil life' or 'to moderate his excessive individualism for the common good', as Cathy Shrank observes, is integral to Shakespeare's dramatization of civic politics.[19] The same could be said of Trump, who is infamous for his unwillingness or inability to learn the responsibilities of the US presidency. Having brought his life-long authoritarian, autocratic habits into the White House, the implications for the US democratic republic have, likewise, been tragic.

'A long, tall and very powerful wall'

Resistance to various external forces defines both Martius and Trump. For each, the survival of the self depends upon combating these forces. Impenetrable and solitary, the identity formation of each is based on an exaggerated sense of self that is primarily concerned with distinguishing the self from external forces.[20] In the case of Trump, moreover, he projects these traits onto the state, hawking a fantasy that the US not only has the fortune of being protected by the natural borders of the Atlantic Ocean to its east and the Pacific Ocean to its west. Once in control of the power bestowed upon him by the office of the US presidency, he is in the thrall of a fantasy whereby he can wall off the US from its neighboring Latin American nations to its south. As he declared in the 2020 'State of the Union' address, his desire to prohibit free government health care for what he calls 'illegal aliens' will be 'a tremendous boon to our already very strongly guarded southern border, where, as we speak, a long, tall and very powerful wall is being built'.[21] Violence and wrath police the boundaries of the self with the intent of defining the self, constantly, as not 'other' – as patrician, not plebeian; as Roman, not Volscian; as male, not female; as rich, not poor; as US citizen, not 'alien'; as Christian, not Muslim; as Anglo, not Latinx; as white, not black; indeed, as superhuman, not human. In each of these categories, 'others' function as objects of detestation or conquest. Yet, as Janet Adelman points out, 'the very insistence on difference reveals the fear of likeness'; indeed, the dramaturgy of *Coriolanus* as a whole characteristically 'reinforces boundaries, walling in cities and individuals'.[22]

Martius's and Trump's lives are characterized – whether militarily or politically – by solitary combat. Shakespeare emphasizes Martius's isolation at two crucial points in the dramatic action: his entry to Corioles and his exile from Rome. Civic identity is central to *Coriolanus*, as Shrank observes, and Shakespeare dramatizes both crises as Martius's antipathy to the civic body.[23] In Plutarch, on both of these occasions, Martius appears together with other characters. In Shakespeare, however, he appears alone. The military combat between the Romans and the Volscians stresses Martius's isolation: 'He is himself alone / To answer all the city' (1.4.55–6), as one of the soldiers puts it. The military combat between the Romans and the Volscians culminates in solitary combat fueled by mutual, personal hatred between Martius and Aufidius:

MARTIUS
    I'll fight with none but thee, for I do hate thee
    Worse than a promise-breaker.
AUFIDIUS   We hate alike:
    Not Afric owns a serpent I abhor
    More than thy fame and envy.

(1.8.1–4)

When the Herald announces the bestowal of the honorary name, 'Coriolanus', upon Martius, he emphasizes the solitary nature of his military feat:

HERALD
    Know, Rome, that all alone Martius did fight
    Within Corioles' gates, where he hath won
    With fame, a name to 'Martius Caius'; these
    In honour follows 'Coriolanus'.
    Welcome to Rome, renowned Coriolanus.

(2.1.157–61)

Martius's world is a fantasy world of chivalric deeds, as Robin Headlam Wells argues, in which plebeians play no part. When he goes into exile, he views himself as a solitary monster that exists only in the worlds of mythology and romance: 'I go alone, / Like to a lonely dragon' (4.1.29–30).[24]

Rather than a chivalric realm of heroes and deeds, Trump's world is that of sordid international organized crime, run by Russian oligarchs and populated by thugs.[25] Nevertheless, it is also a fantasy world (a bubble, in twenty-first-century parlance) in which he is omniscient (always right, never wrong) – increasingly so, as those advisors who possess experience and expertise that he utterly lacks and that enable them to challenge him end up gone, either by resignation or dismissal,[26] leaving him untethered, surrounded by only a coterie of 'yes men'. Secretary of State Mike Pompeo and Attorney General William Barr are two cases in point. Internationally, regarding US–Iran relations, the hawks defeated the doves in the Trump White House. Pompeo has reportedly been 'itching for war' for so long that, when Trump appointed him as Secretary of State, Ali Khorram, the former Iranian Ambassador to the UN, described Pompeo as 'cowboyish', 'eager to start a war'.[27] Domestically, Barr's abdication of his responsibilities – to represent the people and to defend the US Constitution – and his assumption of the role of Trump's personal attorney constitute a corruption of the office. In placing the US president above the law, Barr violates the rule of law enshrined in the US Constitution – its most significant inheritance from Magna Carta in England in 1215 – and thereby creates a crisis in not only the US Department of Justice but also the nation. As John Brennan, former CIA Director, observes, Trump is using the Department of Justice 'to go after his enemies in any way that he can'.[28]

Vulnerability

Intolerance and rigidity, furthermore, characterize both Martius and Trump. Tolerance of others and sensitivity to others jeopardize their fragile identity formation. Neither figure has a capacity for introspection; neither can afford to reflect on his own motives because doing so may disclose psychological vulnerability and jeopardize fantasies of omnipotence and autonomy that are necessary for survival. When Volumnia, Martius's mother, Virgilia, his wife, and Young Martius, his son, beseech Martius on behalf of Rome, his initial response denies family bonds and fantasizes about his independence and autonomy:

> Let the Volsces
> Plough Rome and harrow Italy, I'll never
> Be such a gosling to obey instinct, but stand

> As if a man were author of himself
> And knew no other kin.
>
> (5.3.33–7)

However, the appeals of his family members, and particularly Volumnia, eventually succeed in breaking down his boundaries and establishing connection with him:

> O, mother, mother!
> What have you done? Behold, the heavens do ope,
> The gods look down and this unnatural scene
> They laugh at. O, my mother, mother! O!
>
> (5.3.182–5)

Martius's fantasy of self-authorship and his attempt to embody omnipotent, god-like power fail, as Adelman points out. This failure leaves him unprotected and devoid of a sense of self. For the first time in the dramatic action, he senses not only vulnerability but also encroaching danger.[29]

> You have won a happy victory to Rome
> But for your son, believe it, O, believe it,
> Most dangerously you have with him prevailed,
> If not most mortal to him.
>
> (5.3.186–9)

If we agree with Adelman that Volumnia has starved Martius of food, as well as affection, equating starvation and masculinity, on the one hand, and hunger and vulnerability, on the other, then in the process Volumnia has created 'a virtual automaton who cannot tolerate his own ordinary human neediness'.[30] Beginning with a recognition that he, like the plebeians he hates, needs food, any acknowledgement of need on his part 'threatens to undermine his masculine autonomy'.[31] In her analysis of the self/other binary that underpins patriarchal hierarchies, Plumwood emphasizes the necessity of an inferiorized 'other' against whom the self defines himself or herself. There must always be a class below whose 'inferiorisation', as she puts it, confers selfhood. 'The more doubtful or insecure the establishment of such an identity is', Plumwood notes, 'the more strongly and vociferously the other's inferiority must be stressed.' Such an identity requires constant reassurance of superiority and hence constant reassertion of hierarchy, a major factor in establishing certain types of masculinity.[32]

In view of Speaker of the House Nancy Pelosi's postponement of Trump's 'State of the Union' address to the US Congress in 2019, Chris Matthews interviewed Tony Schwartz (co-author of the book, *The Art of the Deal*) about Trump's need for theatre, spectacle and drama:

MATTHEWS
> Why is Trump particularly thrilled by the idea of theatre in the round?

SCHWARTZ
> You know, the smaller the human being, the greater the need for big pomp and circumstance. I mean, literally, I think that's what it's about. The more diminished he feels, the more humiliated he feels, the smaller he feels, the more desperate he becomes for any kind of external evidence that he matters.

MATTHEWS
> And when you were co-authoring a book with him, you could feel that smallness next to you, right?

SCHWARTZ
> Could I feel the smallness? I could feel the emptiness at that time. I think he's actually shrunk. So, what I could feel was that there was an absence of any centre. There was an absence of a conscience, of a heart, of a point of view.[33]

'A very stable genius'[34]

Coriolanus, the most political of Shakespeare's dramatic texts, is the only one to open with large-scale rioting in the streets.

The first thing that we learn about Martius is that the plebeians hold him responsible for the grain shortage. The First Citizen blames him for their lot, labelling him 'chief enemy to the people' (1.1.6–7) and declaring 'Let us kill him' (1.1.9). The patricians have utter contempt for the poor, viewing them merely as mouths to feed, and Martius represents his class. And what is his 'modest proposal'? Stephen Greenblatt asks: 'Let the poor starve.'[35] Yet his personal traits of arrogance and pride exacerbate class prejudices. As the First Citizen observes: 'he pays himself with being proud' (1.1.30–1), and 'he did it to please his mother, and to be partly proud – which he is, even to the altitude of his virtue' (1.1.35–7). The tribunes, Sicinius and Brutus, concur:

SICINIUS
Was ever man so proud as is this Martius?
BRUTUS
He has no equal.
...
The present wars devour him! He is grown
Too proud to be so valiant.

(1.1.247–8, 253–4)

In Plutarch, it is Martius's hostility toward the people during the grain shortage that causes his banishment. In Shakespeare, however, it is his failure 'to participate decorously in the electoral rituals', as Shrank puts it, that causes his banishment.[36] Brutus accurately predicts Martius's reluctance to display his war wounds for public consumption, according to time-honored ritual, when he stands for office:

I heard him swear,
Were he to stand for consul, never would he
Appear i'th' market-place nor on him put
The napless vesture of humility,
Nor, showing, as the manner is, his wounds
To th' people, beg their stinking breaths.

(2.1.225–30)

Arrogant, proud, Martius is incapable of donning the 'vesture of humility' – either metaphorically or literally – before the plebeians so as to seek their votes. Shrewd tribune that he is, Brutus knows Martius well. As the dramatic action eventually discloses, Martius is unwilling and unable to comply with custom:

> I do beseech you,
> Let me o'erleap that custom, for I cannot
> Put on the gown, stand naked and entreat them,
> For my wounds' sake, to give their suffrage. Please you
> That I may pass this doing.
> ...
> To brag unto them 'Thus I did, and thus',
> Show them th'unaching scars which I should hide,
> As if I had received them for the hire
> Of their breath only.
>
> (2.2.134–8, 146–9)

Revulsed by the hypocrisy of his fellow patricians and the Machiavellian manipulations of the tribunes, Martius believes that the ritual of displaying his wounds for the plebeians so as to win their votes is an act of dishonesty. It is as though he is muttering to himself: 'Can't they see that I'm covered in blood? Isn't that enough?' Twenty-first-century readers and audiences may well find Martius's characteristic arrogance and pride as difficult to sympathize with as the masculine Roman ideal, *virtus*, in which they are bound up.[37]

Unpresidented[38]

Both Martius and Trump are in the thrall of fantasies of omnipotence and autonomy. The tribunes thereby accuse Martius of not only aiming to be the last man standing but also viewing himself as a tyrant or a god. Similarly, legal scholars, politicians, political pundits and US citizens alike accuse Trump of violating 'the rule of law'[39] that the US founding fathers inherited from Magna Carta and of constructing himself as not only a dictator, or a monarch, but also a god – rather than a president.

Martius's defining trait is his heroic *virtus*, or 'valour' or 'prowess in battle', as Wells points out.[40] In a grotesque inventory, Menenius and Volumnia fetishize Martius's battle wounds, itemizing their location and number:

MENENIUS
Where is he wounded?
VOLUMNIA
I'th' shoulder and i'th' left arm. There will be large cicatrices to show the people when he shall stand for his place. He received in the repulse of Tarquin seven hurts i'th' body.
MENENIUS
One i'th' neck and two i'th' thigh – there's nine that I know.
VOLUMNIA
He had, before this last expedition, twenty-five wounds upon him.
MENENIUS
Now it's twenty-seven; every gash was an enemy's grave.
(2.1.142–52)

The two elders emphasize Martius's nonhuman status. 'It hardly seems like they are describing a human body', as Greenblatt notes: Martius turns himself into 'the inhuman object' that Volumnia wishes him to be.[41] Cominius, too, participates in the construction of Martius as a 'thing', underscoring the gore of Martius's status as a killing machine: 'He was a thing of blood' (2.2.107), as he succinctly puts it.[42]

Fearing Martius's popularity after Corioles and his diminishment of the Senate's political power, the tribunes turn the plebeians against him. Brutus accuses him of speaking as if he were of superhuman status: 'You speak o'th' people as if you were a god / To punish, not a man of their infirmity' (3.1.83–4). Sicinius accuses him of behaving like a tyrant:

> We charge you that you have contrived to take
> From Rome all seasoned office and to wind
> Yourself into a power tyrannical
> For which you are a traitor to the people.
>
> (3.3.62–5)

It is Martius's tyrannical behaviour that Sicinius singles out as grounds for charges of treason against the people of Rome. Brutus declares that Martius is 'banished / As enemy to the people and his country. / It shall be so' (3.3.116–18).[43] As soon as Rome banishes him, Martius turns on Rome, his home nation, with the retort, 'I banish you' (3.3.122). Consumed with anger, he vows to take revenge by joining forces with his nation's sworn enemy: the Volscians. 'My birthplace hate I, and my love's upon / This enemy town' (4.4.23–4), he declares as he enters Antium. As Greenblatt suggests, '[i]t is as if the leader of a political party long identified with hatred of Russia – forever saber-rattling and accusing the rival politicians of treason – should secretly make his way to Moscow and offer his services to the Kremlin.'[44]

Even though the Republicans in the US Senate acquitted Trump of charges of 'abuse of power' and 'obstruction of Congress', he turned on the US, his home nation, vowing, in an hour-long rant on the day after his acquittal, to retaliate against the FBI, the US Senate and the Speaker of the House for his imagined grievances. As Philip Rucker, Robert Costa and Josh Dawsey report:

> President Trump is testing the rule of law one week after his acquittal in his Senate impeachment trial, seeking to bend the executive branch into an instrument for his personal and political vendetta against perceived enemies.
>
> And Trump – simmering with rage, fixated on exacting revenge against those he feels betrayed him and insulated by a compliant Republican Party – is increasingly comfortable doing so to the point of feeling untouchable, according to the president's advisers and allies.[45]

Two days after his acquittal, he fired two witnesses who had testified under subpoena before the US House Intelligence Committee, which had led the impeachment investigation. On Friday 7 February 2020, security guards marched Lieutenant Colonel Alexander Vindman, a decorated Iraq War veteran on the National Security Council staff, out of the White House. The same day, Trump ordered the recall of Gordon Sondland, Ambassador to the European Union. Incapable of letting go of resentment, as Tony Schwartz points out (in another context), Trump is 'the wealthiest and the most powerful aggrieved human being who has ever lived'.[46] Even though the US Senate did not convict and remove Trump from office, he, too, like the banished Martius, nevertheless joins forces with his nation's sworn enemy: the Russians. The difference is that his betrayal of his country occurred years before the Republicans in the US Senate acquitted him of charges of impeachment. Political commentator Bill Maher puts it bluntly: 'The bottom line is, at a certain point, because nobody else would lend Trump money, because he's a fucking deadbeat, the only place he could get money was Russia, and, instead of paying them back, he gave them America.'[47]

Cominius describes Martius in superhuman terms: 'He is their [the Volscians'] god' (4.6.91). Again, his status is more 'thing-like', a product of unnatural forces, than it is human, a product of natural forces:

> He leads them like a thing
> Made by some other deity than nature
> That shapes man better, and they follow him
> Against us brats with no less confidence
> Than boys pursuing summer butterflies
> Or butchers killing flies.
>
> (4.6.91–6)

The descriptions of Martius on the part of Menenius, Volumnia and Cominius bring to mind Donna Haraway's concept of the cyborg, an automaton – in this case, a single-minded killing machine created by forces external to the natural, human world. Toward the end of the dramatic action, Menenius picks up these tropes constructing Martius's nonhuman, god-like, thing-like status:

> The tartness of his face sours ripe grapes. When he walks, he moves like an engine and the ground shrinks before his treading. He is able to pierce a corslet with his eye, talks like a knell and his hum is a battery. He sits in his state as a thing made for Alexander. What he bids be done is finished with his bidding. He wants nothing of a god but eternity and a heaven to throne in.
>
> (5.4.17–24)

Titus Lartius also pays tribute to Martius's god-like powers of destruction:

> Thou wast a soldier
> Even to Cato's wish, not fierce and terrible
> Only in strokes, but with thy grim looks and
> The thunder-like percussion of thy sounds
> Thou mad'st thine enemies shake as if the world
> Were feverous and did tremble.
>
> (1.4.60–5)

Martius is a killing machine whose men follow him because he is a winner – a fantasy of the 'strongman' that Trump desperately thinks that he is, or wishes to be, or wishes to be thought of: hypermasculine, Übermensch, superman. This explains his infatuation with various dictators around the globe in the twenty-first century: Vladimir Putin in Russia, Xi Jinping in China, Kim Jong-un in North Korea, Recep Erdoğan in Turkey, Rodrigo Duterte in the Philippines, Jarosław Kaczyński in Poland, Abdel Fattah el-Sisi in Egypt, Jair Bolsonaro in Brazil and Viktor Orbán in Hungary. Although Trump shirked military duty during the US–Vietnam War, he metaphorically wraps himself in the US flag (or, literally, wraps his body around the US flag)[48] and would clothe himself in the uniforms of those political/military leaders he deems to be 'strongmen' if he could get away with it. He wishes to wield absolute power, as they do – 'I have an Article 2 where I have the right to do whatever I want as president', he claims[49] – a defining characteristic that Brennan understands all too well:

> I've seen this script play out so many times overseas, where you have a power-hungry, narcissistic individual who relies on the ignorance of many people, as well as corrupt politicians and ideologues, in order to continue to solidify his hold on power. And that's what we see with Donald Trump. He is not interested in doing what is right for the country or for the American people. He is interested most in doing what is going to advance his personal interests.[50]

According to *Church and State Magazine*, the notion that Trump is divinely ordained to lead the US is gaining popularity among radical right religious leaders and Republican Party political operatives alike. Franklin Graham and Paula White, two of his most vocal evangelical supporters, are advancing the idea. Brad Parscale, Trump's campaign manager, also promotes the notion: 'There has never been and probably never will be a movement like this again', he tweeted on 30 April 2019; 'only God could deliver such a savior to our nation, and only God could allow me to help. God bless America!'[51]

Nostalgia for the commons

Martius's fantasy of the autonomous male body tropes privatizing enclosure practices that conflict with ecological models of community interrelatedness, such as governance, food and water, as Randall Martin points out.[52] Simultaneous with a preoccupation with boundaries, from a psychological perspective, and borders or walls, from a political perspective, is a less noticed phenomenon: the death of the commons. David Hawkes eloquently describes the effects of the enclosure acts upon those people who had worked the land in the early modern English Midlands. Customary rights to grazing, hunting, fishing and gathering were 'declared inimical to the proper functioning of the "economy", and restricted or abolished wherever possible', Hawkes reminds us. Together with the enclosure of smallholdings, 'this confiscation of communal property drove hundreds of thousands of people into beggary'.[53] Characters such as Tom O'Bedlam in *King Lear*, Autolycus in *The Winter's Tale* and Falstaff's ragtag troops in *2 Henry 4* take on a heightened degree of poignancy when we consider their analogues to historical people displaced by these economic ruptures to early modern Midland life.[54]

In *2 Henry 6*, Jack Cade uses 'the commons' as a rallying cry for class war: 'you that love the commons, follow me' (4.2.173). If the revolt succeeds, Cade tells the beggarly weavers, tanners and butchers, 'henceforward all things shall be in common' (4.7.16), as Hawkes points out. In *The Tempest*, Gonzalo shares this dream; his ideal commonwealth would also have 'All things in common' (2.1.160). Yet these Shakespearean characters do not express 'utopian fantasies of a remote future', as Hawkes puts it; rather, they express 'nostalgia for the recent past'.[55] We can hear the resonances with our present moment. Is the same true of us, in the twenty-first century? Are we currently experiencing nostalgia for the commons – clean air, clean water and clean, living earth? Like early modern England, the US under Trump has experienced an unprecedented shift of wealth from public to private hands, as well as an unprecedented exposure of public lands to private exploitation.

It is not requisite for one to earn a PhD in philosophy, theology, morality or ethics (or English, for that matter) to recognize the intimations of our present moment in early modern England, and in Shakespeare. Desertification and drought conditions drive large numbers of Syrian farmers off their lands into cities, and, eventually, into Europe as refugees. US citizens of Puerto Rico remain devastated several years after the destructive effects of Hurricane Maria and several months after two earthquakes. 'Central America is among the regions most vulnerable to climate change', scientists say. Warming temperatures make it impossible for coffee growers in Guatemala, El Salvador, and Honduras to make a living, driving them to the US southern border in desperation for economic as well as political reasons, seeking refuge from the climate crisis as well as asylum from right-wing military regimes.[56] All of these problems target people of colour, racial and religious minorities – whether African Americans, Muslims, Latinos/Latinas or Indigenous peoples.

The tragedy for nonhuman species and human species on the planet is that 'strongman' leaders and their hyper-separation from life on earth are insufficient to meet the demands of the twenty-first century. When we consider the existential threat to life on earth posed by the contemporary climate crisis, as Katrina Vanden Heuvel puts it, 'strongman' leaders' responses and military solutions are irrelevant.[57] Not only that – they exacerbate the situation. Unfortunately, the implications of 'strongman' leaders and their hyper-separation from life on earth are catastrophic. Bolsonaro deliberately burns down the Amazonian rainforest, the 'lungs of the planet', so as to graze cattle for the meat industry in a factory-farming economy. China, Russia and other economic powers race to develop trade routes and natural resources in the melting Arctic. Trump brags, during the 2020 'State of the Union' address, about the status of the US in unlocking and combusting more of the earth's carbon reserves than any other country: 'Thanks to our bold regulatory reduction campaign, the U.S. has become the number one producer of oil and natural gas anywhere in the world, by far.'[58] This is precisely what climate scientists are admonishing us not to do – arguing instead for allowing carbon reserves to remain sequestered, uncombusted, underground.

At the centre of E. M. Forster's novel, *Howards End*, a motor car in a caravan driven by members of the Wilcox family, the *nouveau riche* capitalists, runs over a cat, killing it. Carousing across the Shropshire countryside in their new-fangled contraption, no member of the Wilcox family gives the incident a second thought – except to arrange for the family insurance company to reimburse the cat's owner for the destruction of property. It falls to a member of the Schlegel family, Margaret, to intervene: 'But stop!' When Charles Wilcox refuses to do so, she jumps out of the moving motor car, believing that a woman needs to deal with the situation. The novel's two value systems are deeply gendered, representing characters and actions associated with cultural constructions of femininity (e.g. the cat, the Schlegel family, the Shropshire countryside, Howards End, art, the ethical life) sympathetically, while simultaneously representing characters and actions associated with cultural constructions of masculinity (e.g. the motor car, the Wilcox family, London, business, capitalism, the vapid life) critically. It is Margaret who attempts to bridge the abyss between the two value systems: 'Only connect.'[59] Even as the motor car in *Howards End* is metonymic of the state of the industrial revolution one hundred years ago, so too is Trump metonymic of the industrial drive over centuries that still cannot comprehend its own catastrophe. Speaking of the wildfires in Australia in 2019, Liam Semler remarks,

> my take on our terrifying fires is that this is the other of the industrial revolution. These growling, exploding, racing, twirling fires are the repressed demon of the industrial revolution (the combustion has escaped the engine) coming back to take its share. Our taming of the explosion, a human tech miracle that goes back to the steam engine, has grown and grown feeding our narcissism and pride and driving our economies and capitalism to this point where its revenge effects are catastrophic.[60]

We are deep in a crucible of our own making, he concludes.

What are the implications of these observations about transcorporeality and hyper-separation in early modern English and twenty-first-century US narratives of the individual – whether Lear, Martius or Trump – for our contemporary moment? Shakespeare's *Coriolanus* dramatizes the transfer of sovereignty from a tyrant to the people, as James Kuzner suggests.[61] Conversely, the Trump presidency threatens to enact the transfer of sovereignty from the people to a tyrant. Fantasies of omnipotence and autonomy become significant not only as a psychiatric disorder of an individual, not only as a threat to the US democratic republic, but also as a threat to life on earth. Plumwood understands this existential truth: to the extent that we 'hyper-separate ourselves from nature and reduce it conceptually in order to justify domination', she observes, we lose the ability 'to empathise and to see the non-human sphere in ethical terms'. We get a 'false sense of our own character and location that includes an illusory sense of autonomy'. She envisages two paths out of the present thicket. Both necessitate fundamental epistemological shifts, or '(re)situatings', as she puts it. The first is (re)situating 'humans in ecological terms'. The second is (re)situating 'non-humans in ethical terms'.[62] Another way to put it, as Alaimo suggests, is to deconstruct gendered binaries – 'nature/culture, body/mind, object/subject, resource/agency' – that denigrate and silence certain groups of humans, as well as nonhuman life. She, too, theorizes an ethics – hers, accountable to a material world that is never merely 'an external place' but is always 'the very substance of our selves and others'.[63] It is a complicated, lengthy road from past to present, from nascent republican Rome to the US democratic republic. The obsessions with boundaries, borders and walls, and the fantasies of omnipotence and autonomy played out by Caius Martius Coriolanus constitute a tragic script the postindustrial world can no longer afford.

6

New Directions

Hegel's Rome and Shakespeare's *Coriolanus*: Grounds for Tragedy

Jennifer Ann Bates

Introduction

In this chapter I offer a philosophical reading of Shakespeare's *Coriolanus*. I draw on G. W. F. Hegel's accounts of ancient Rome in his *Philosophy of History* and *Phenomenology of Spirit* in order to discuss the grounds of this tragedy. This involves Hegel's *speculative* account of ancient Rome in history, as well as his *phenomenological* account of it in terms of what Hegel calls 'Legal Status'.[1]

'Speculative', in Hegel's philosophy, means thinking about something from the standpoint of fully comprehending that thing's (or person's or society's) objective, historical conditions for being. 'Phenomenological' means delving into the experiences of those consciousnesses for whom that something exists. The 'somethings' with which we are concerned are: Coriolanus, and how he and other characters in the play experience and constitute Roman self-mediation.

For Hegel, both speculative and phenomenological kinds of thinking are *dialectical*: each is a back and forth between subject and object, a self-mediation *through otherness*. When not fully comprehended, each gives rise to alienation: an unpleasant, often violent relationship between subject and object, in which speculation can become spectatorship, and phenomenological experience, impossible conflict.

The Hegelian dialectic of alienation, self-mediation and comprehension is apt for exploring *Coriolanus* because the play involves many alienation-producing dual perspectives. For example, the play's language illustrates what Hegel, in his speculative, historical thinking, refers to as the Roman 'duplicate mode of viewing phenomena' (e.g. the stress on first and second names, and the meaning of Coriolanus's wounds). As a result of this duplicate mode, many phrases in the play reveal characters experiencing the essence of things as a secret. This attitude makes Romans, as Hegel claims, both spectators of, and prey to, forms of bad endlessness, or, in Hegel's language, 'spurious infinites'. I deepen this speculative reading of the play using Hegel's phenomenology: I look at *experiences* of spurious infinites in his *Phenomenology of Spirit*; specifically, at how Roman experiences of abstract legalism express a collective 'unhappy consciousness'. I discuss this in terms of contradictory language and counterfeiting behaviour within *Coriolanus*.

At the end of the chapter, I briefly contrast these bad infinites with two Hegelian 'good infinites': 1) 'absolute knowing', which is the experience of dialectical speculative comprehension; and 2) the object of a collective experience of this dialectical knowing, namely, the self-comprehending community. I imply that we can and should try to measure Coriolanus and his Rome (and our own time and experiences) against this Hegelian 'absolute' standpoint.[2]

Another example of why *Coriolanus* and Hegelian dialectic are mutually enlightening concerns the dual perspective involved in figuring out what is wrong with Coriolanus. The effort to determine the grounds of Coriolanus's failings is an interpretative task for the audience, *and* a part of the play itself. Characters muse openly about what those grounds could be: his friend Menenius attributes it to Coriolanus's not knowing how to control his tongue, to his having been 'bred i'th' wars / Since 'a could draw a sword, and is ill-schooled / In bolted language' (3.1.322–4); he 'speaks not like a citizen' (3.3.53); his mother agrees, he was 'bred in broils' (3.2.82). Menenius says that Coriolanus has god-like arrogance:

> His heart's his mouth.
> What his breast forges that his tongue must vent,
> And, being angry, does forget that ever
> He heard the name of death.
>
> (3.1.259–62)

Coriolanus's enemy, Tullus Aufidius, lists several possible grounds: pride, defective judgement, or maybe a natural defect, or immovability (Coriolanus's inability to transition from warrior to consulship) (4.7.37–48). I return to Aufidius's musings at the end of this chapter. The point is that the grounds are a topic for us, and for characters in the play. This dual-perspective puzzling about Coriolanus mirrors our speculative/phenomenological approach.

Now, to begin. The *simplest* speculatively historical, geographical and political Hegelian answer is that during the time of Coriolanus, around 500 BCE, ancient Greek and Roman heroes often just could not succeed without succumbing. Let us look at this briefly before we deepen our analysis of the play by looking at Hegel's speculative account of the transition from ancient Greece to Rome, and his phenomenological account of Rome.

Part one: Hegel's Roman world in the *Philosophy of History* compared with Shakespeare's *Coriolanus*

i) Maybe Coriolanus simply has a Roman hero's destiny?

Hegel describes how, historically, during the fall of the Greek State, its heroes were tragically doomed:

> In the internal condition of the states, which, enervated by selfishness and debauchery, were broken up into factions ... great *individuals* ... appear as great tragic characters, who with their genius and the most intense exertion, are yet unable to extirpate the evils in question; and perish in the struggle ...[3]

According to Hegel, it is in this struggling world of heroes that Rome builds itself and eventually takes over. Shakespeare's Coriolanus lived in the early period of its development. We might conclude that, as a man of his time, Coriolanus was doomed.

Furthermore, Hegel claims that '[t]he Roman State rests geographically, as well as historically, on the element of force':[4]

> [Rome] directly involves the severest discipline, and self-sacrifice to the grand object of the union. A State which had to form itself, and which is based on force, must be held together by force ... The Roman *virtus* is valour, not, however, the merely personal, but that which is essentially connected with a union of associates.[5]

This severity and Roman pride are present throughout Shakespeare's play, most remarkably in Coriolanus's mother's view of her son as a heroic warrior for Rome whose war scars she proudly enumerates (2.1.139–52).[6]

Furthermore, the politics of that time and place play a role: one must 'pay particular attention also to the conduct of the plebs in times of revolt against the patricians'.[7] Menenius warns: 'Proceed by process, / Lest parties – as he is beloved – break out / And sack great Rome with Romans' (3.1.315–18).

Thus far in our Hegelian reading of the play, Coriolanus did not have a chance because of the history, geography and politics of ancient Rome. A more complex picture emerges, however, when we delve into Hegel's account of the transition from ancient Greece to Rome, in his *Philosophy of History* and in the *Phenomenology of Spirit*. There is a remainder of the Greek world in Rome. I think that this remainder is essential for understanding the person Coriolanus.

ii) Transition and remainder: A duplicating modality

a) Transition

Hegel writes:

> of the general character of the Romans we may say that ... in contrast with the beautiful, harmonious poetry and well-balanced freedom of the Spirit among the Greeks – here, among the Romans the *prose* of life makes its appearance – the self-consciousness of finiteness – the abstraction of the Understanding and a rigorous principle of personality.[8]

Coriolanus is prosaically defined as a Roman soldier by the military, the plebs and senators and tribunes, and by his mother. This prosaicism is an advance over Greek attribution of identity because the formal adherence to universal abstract categories like property-owner or soldier frees Coriolanus, and Roman society in general, from what Hegel refers to as the unconscious Greek laws of kinship and character (he cites Sophocles regarding the origin of Greek divine laws: '"where they came from, none of us can tell"'[9]). According to Hegel, the Greek constitution was entirely dependent on morals, disposition 'and sentiment'.[10]

The legal principles of personal rights and property, bound by the common idea of a powerful nation defended by virtuous heroes, seem to make Rome more understandable. However, as in the play, these principles are 'mechanical'; freeing, but deadly. According to Hegel, this is because the Romans' is a 'sterile Understanding', 'abstract' and 'juristic'. The Romans 'were its victims, living beneath its sway'. Nonetheless, 'they thereby secured for others Freedom of Spirit ... that inward Freedom ...'[11]

We here begin to see what is proper to the Roman dialectic, according to Hegel: freedom generating the possibility of persons taking responsibility, and a mechanical understanding that contradicts this freedom. This duality constitutes the form of what I am calling the remainder.

b) Remainder

Coriolanus embodies prosaically what remains of the poetic Greek individual subjectivity of character. He is free from the immediacy of character/ethical roles, but in an abstract way. This prosaic remainder is evident in what Hegel calls the Roman 'duplicate mode of viewing phenomena':

> among the Romans everything exhibits itself as mysterious, duplicate: they saw in the object first itself, and then that which lies concealed in it: their history is pervaded by this duplicate mode of viewing phenomena. The city of Rome had besides its proper name another secret one, known only to a few.[12]

We see this duplicate mode of viewing phenomena in the Roman renaming of the Greek Gods: for example, Dionysus becomes Bacchus. But this duplication, instead of being a quickening, is a deadening. Unlike the Greeks, the Romans give their gods no depth: 'The chief characteristic of Roman Religion is therefore a hard and dry contemplation of certain voluntary aims.'[13]

The duplicate mode of viewing is evident in the Roman practice of giving their heroes a second name, the *agnomen*, derived, for example, from their military virtue. Caius Martius's second name is 'Coriolanus', given to him for conquering Corioli.

The prosaic doubling holds within it a remainder: for example, the secret meaning of a person's or city's name. This remainder is a sought-for meaning to which one can never return. The secret is a surface of contending meanings, forces contending to be more; it is prosaic, without poetry, or subjective point. For the Romans, custom is essentially *alienation*. Explaining this is largely what the rest of my chapter is about.

The nature of this secret is important to understanding Shakespeare's Coriolanus (as character and play). To dig deeper, let us switch from Hegel's speculative, historical description of the Roman world to look at the Roman world from the point of view of social experience, as Hegel recounts it in his *Phenomenology of Spirit*.

Part two: Hegel's Roman 'Legal Status' in the *Phenomenology of Spirit* compared with Shakespeare's *Coriolanus*

i) The *Phenomenology of Spirit*

This book is Hegel's 'science of the *experience of consciousness*':[14] it exhibits increasingly comprehensive forms of individual and social phenomena, each of which is a dialectical comprehension of previous contradictions *and* a new set of contradictions to be comprehended. (The process is called 'sublation' [*die Aufhebung*].) It is Hegel's manual for learning how to fully comprehend experience.

Phenomenological moments are not the same as historical moments. They are shapes of experience, drawn from memory. Like dramas, they can play out on different (historical/geographical/political) stages. Thus, like many Shakespearean plays, Hegel's *Phenomenology* draws non-linearly from history for events that exemplify phenomenological moments, and it is therefore anachronistic. However, as in the plays, the connections between moments make sense.

At the end of Hegel's book, the moments are recollected in a 'gallery of images'[15] which the 'absolute knower' enjoys reflecting upon, even recognizing in real time, knowing that these moments are never *equivalent* to historical events, because they are *phenomenological*. That is, the absolute knower knows that there is always something *more* to experience, whether viewed as phenomenological moment, or as historical, because neither is reducible to the other absolutely (that is part of the import of knowing 'absolutely').[16]

By the end of the book, history is not a fixed linear sequence of facts. It is *comprehended*. The phenomenological and the historical, when known absolutely, are *each* 'duplicate modes of viewing phenomena' *which must be comprehended together*. To begin to explain this, let us look at what Hegel takes to be ancient Rome's phenomenological achievements and shortcomings.

Consistent with the *Philosophy of History*, Roman 'Legal Status' is the *phenomenological* solution to the decline of ancient Greek character consciousness. The more abstract, Roman law of atomic individual rights extricates individuals from dispositional and kinship responsibilities. The individual is no longer a character in a theatrically unconscious social drama (performative of a role he/she does not view as a role), but rather a *person*: an understood, legal unit; an individual who is *self-conscious* of his/her social role.

'Legal Status' fails in turn, because its self-certainty about personhood is in truth a kind of self-alienation: persons and the state are said to have entitlements and integrity, but these are shallow and contradictory. Rome's truth 'is directly the perversion of the self ...; it is the loss of its essence. The actuality of the self that did not exist in the ethical world [ancient Greece] has been won by its return into the "person"; what in the former was harmoniously one now emerges in a developed form, but as alienated from itself.'[17] According to the *Philosophy of History*, Roman persons are 'secretive', 'prosaic'; according to Hegel's *Phenomenology*, Roman experience gives birth to 'Self-Alienated Spirit: Culture'.[18]

The *Phenomenology* is described as a 'way of despair'[19] because the cure only comes at the end, and every cure on the way is just another, more complexly structured disease. What is the particular disease of Coriolanus's Rome and what is its ostensible cure?

ii) The phenomenological disease of *Coriolanus's* Roman spirit

We are told at the start of Shakespeare's play that it is a disease of the body politic, as the argument between the Citizens (plebeians) and the senator Menenius makes clear in the opening scene of the play. It is a disease not of the Roman individual alone, but of the social spirit or *Geist*, of Roman society. In Hegel's 'Legal Status' and in Shakespeare's *Coriolanus*, Rome, not the individual, is the dialectical ground and path of despair. Let me explain.

Coriolanus appears on the scene just mentioned in which the body politic is evoked, as a force against the plebs, whom he calls 'dissentious rogues' (1.1.159), and *for* the senators. But his speech also evokes how the multiple forces at work in Rome, especially public tongues, turn things into their opposites. He refers to them as having a sick man's appetite:

CORIOLANUS
                               Who deserves greatness
Deserves your hate, and your affections are
A sick man's appetite, who desires most that
Which would increase his evil. He that depends
Upon your favours swims with fins of lead
And hews down oaks with rushes. Hang ye! Trust ye?
With every minute you do change a mind,
And call him noble that was now your hate,
Him vile that was your garland.

(1.1.171–9)

Each group thinks the other forces are the disease,[20] but Coriolanus gives the prognosis: left unchecked, this disease will turn everything into its opposite. This proves true.

What are the dialectical contradictions at work? They are the parts of the body politic – for example, Romans with bellies to fill – and, simultaneously, the general struggle between freedom and power. Thus, in the play, as in Hegel's 'Legal Status', the dialectical problems stem both from the claims of each social unit's rights – to property and freedom – and, the threat that these claims pose; for example, that one free unit or person will claim ownership of all the grain and all the power: the threat of tyranny.[21]

The plebs and their tribunes are angry not just at Coriolanus's proud dismissal of their hunger: they fear Coriolanus might gain the power of the consul and thereby become tyrannical. Leading up to Coriolanus's exile, Brutus advises his fellow tribune: 'In this point charge him home: that he affects / Tyrannical power' (3.3.1–2). After Coriolanus's exile, Brutus reflects upon him as 'A worthy officer i'th' war, but insolent, / O'ercome with pride, ambitious past all thinking, / Self-loving' (4.6.30–2). His fellow tribune Sicinius adds: 'And affecting one sole throne / Without assistance' (4.6.32–3); 'We should by this, to all our lamentation / If he had gone forth consul found it so' (4.6.34–5).

Historically, tyrannical leaders of Rome arise only centuries later, with the Roman emperors (27 BCE until the fall of Rome in the fifth century AD).[22] Nonetheless, these forces are at work in the Rome of *Coriolanus*: we are told that Rome had only just expelled the last of the Roman Kings, the Tarquins. We see the tribunes' fear of consular power, and at the end of the play, Aufidius successfully scheming into power in Rome.

Thus, generally speaking, the disease-making contradictions in Hegel's 'Legal Status' match those in Shakespeare's play. But we have only scratched the surface. Let us therefore examine Hegel's phenomenological account of Roman social consciousness more deeply, and then discuss it in relation to the play. This is where things get most interesting.

iii) 'Legal Status' as the second-round, Roman city version of the unhappy consciousness

Hegel claims that the Roman Spirit recycles the earlier movements in the *Phenomenology* of what Hegel calls 'the unhappy consciousness'. Any unhappy consciousness is a unity of stoicism and scepticism (explained below). The first unhappy consciousness is an experience of a single individual; the second, *Roman* version of the unhappy consciousness, is the experience of the State.

The first unhappy consciousness is sometimes characterized as a medieval monk trying to unify with the Divine through ascetic self-denial.[23] His problem is the unification of his changeable self with an unchangeable ideal. (I tell my students that any perfectionist who becomes self-deprecatingly ill as a result of their perfectionism pretty well captures this condition.)

The background is that the pure *thought* into which this individual had stoically retreated, became a reified, 'Unchangeable' ideal. That ideal presented a real problem: the stoic could not bring the ideal into his life's beliefs and customs, because beliefs and customs are, by the stoic's own account, *changeable*; none of them could express the Unchangeable. Enter the sceptic: he laughed at the stoic for not being able to realize his Unchangeable ideal. The sceptic, however, experienced the pain of constant change. Enter the unhappy consciousness: he accepts both stoic and sceptic conclusions, and becomes mortally ill attempting to unify them in experience.

The resolution of that first unhappy consciousness occurs through the intercession of a mediator who takes on the responsibility of interpreting how the Unchangeable is to be thought in the changeable world (in the medieval version, the Priest). This triangulation disengages self-consciousness from its perfectionism, and gives birth to 'Reason'. Reason is the rational individual who is now able to go about his business in an (ostensibly) conflict-free way. He can do so because his dis-eased efforts to actualize truth in time, to 'customise' truth (uniting the Unchangeable ideal in a changeable self), have been cured by accepting the instructions of the mediator, who takes upon himself the problem of incorporating freedom. Mediation is the secret of the mediator.

Hegel's chapter on Reason shows the successes of Reason as the new phenomenological moment. But it also shows the contradictions (and social diseases) to which it gives rise. These arise because the individual accepted a mediator's intercession without questioning the nature of the mediator, and without taking up the question of what social responsibility for mediation is. As a result, Reason is one-sidedly objective. It produces theories about the individual that are reductive, like the science of phrenology, in which a man's skull bone and its bumps are taken as indicative of his subjective disposition.[24] Reason's path of despair shows why the mediations of a society's *Spirit* in the production of objectivity and subjectivity alike, need to be thought through.

Reason's eventual recognition of its need to understand *mediation* begins the development of its insight into the ways in which its self, its 'I', is a We, and its We, is an I. As is usual in the *Phenomenology*, the new moment begins with a new immediacy: the 'immediacy' of Spirit is the 'Ethical World' of ancient Greece and of Sophocles' *Antigone*. That collapses into Roman 'Legal Status', which collapses into 'Self-Alienated Spirit: Culture'. Eventually, through the failures of 'Self-Alienated Spirit: Culture' and then of 'Morality', Spirit develops into self-mediating 'Absolute' Spirit.

What matters for our reading of *Coriolanus*, is that a *second* unhappy consciousness occurs in 'Legal Status'. It is the Roman abstract idea of persons with rights. Despite being a form of independence, this is a return, at a more developed level, to the unhappy consciousness. This new unhappy consciousness is a formalistic, *social* stoicism, and its contradiction is likewise a *social* version of scepticism about customizing those abstractions.[25]

This second, *social* unhappy consciousness is shaped by what I earlier called the secret: it is the shape of an emerging alienated custom. Rome is the ground for something more than mere tribal, family-based custom, and more than mere proprietary power. But what is this 'more'?

The resolution of the first unhappy consciousness came through a mediator. In this second, social version of the unhappy consciousness of Rome, the mediator can no longer be only an individual: he must appear as Spirit, that is, a societally defined *person*. Coriolanus is a failed version of a societal mediator, because he embodies the unhappy consciousness that Rome is.[26]

However, for Hegel, Rome is, historically and phenomenologically, the place of the appearance of *another social mediator*: the Roman world is the ground for Christianity.[27] We can see this in the duplicate mode of *that* mediator's *two* names: Jesus and Christ. The next form of Spirit in Hegel's book, and in the Holy Roman Empire, is the self-alienated Spirit of Christian European culture trying to work out this social self-mediation. This takes place over many centuries. According to Hegel, this unhappy consciousness is only resolved at the *end* of Hegel's book.

I am not presenting a *Christian*–Hegelian reading of the play. Nonetheless, religion must be involved. First, the dialectic throughout Hegel's *Phenomenology* concerns incarnating truth by bringing the divine down to human consciousness and human consciousness up to it:[28] that self-comprehending incarnation was the goal of Spirit over time, and revealing its necessity, the goal of his book. Second, at the end of his book, the question *remains* as to whether philosophy, phenomenologically, treats Christianity as one of its historical instances, or whether Hegel's philosophy is finally *Christian*. (This is the difference between a fully comprehending philosophy as a phenomenological moment instantiable in other religious histories, or its being the revelation and culmination *of only* Christian history.) In my view, and thus in my application of Hegel to Shakespeare, Hegel's goal is achieved in post-protestant *philosophy*: philosophy hovers over Christianity; and, other religious histories (both past and to come) do and can instantiate 'Revealed Religion'.[29] Third, in Hegel's speculative history of Europe, Rome is the *ground* of Christianity and its subsequent phenomenological history; my application of Hegel to Shakespeare involves that story. It is the story of the unhappy consciousness of Rome, which gives birth to the trajectory of Europe involving a religion characterized by freedom of responsibility, anxieties about power and the constraints of a spiritual (socialized) mediation.[30]

iv) Roman unhappy consciousness: Coriolanus

In the first unhappy consciousness, contradictions were played out within the subjectivity of the individual. In the Roman unhappy consciousness, contradictions play out socially via the *person*. These are contra-*dictions*, generated by being a person in (*Coriolanus*'s) Rome.

Throughout the play, speeches are most often made to others, in public places. There are few soliloquies.[31] Rather than an individual's perfectionist intolerance and self-destruction of embodiment, the conflicts are between factions who argue, banish and kill each other. It is force against force (Coriolanus vs Plebs and Tribunes, Tribunes vs Senate and Patricians, Rome vs Volces, Coriolanus vs Aufidius). Brutus warns the citizens that they will be in *self-conflict* if they let Coriolanus have power: 'your voices might / Be curses to yourselves' (2.3.181–2). The tribunes count on Coriolanus being (in) contradiction, in order to set him up for exile: 'Put him to choler straight. He hath been used / Ever to conquer and to have his worth / Of contradiction' (3.3.25–7).

In the first unhappy consciousness, the individual's body is ascetically reduced to nothing. In the Roman unhappy consciousness, the body is violently opened by others' swords to public interpretation: the people's tongues are put in the wounds. ('For, if he show us his wounds and tell us his deeds, we are to put our tongues into those wounds and speak for them' [2.3.5–7].) A Roman's task is to interpret what the political body means: to understand its secret. Coriolanus's body is emblematic of the afflicted city. His wounds are mouths of the body politic.[32]

As in our discussion of Hegel's Roman world, the ground of these warring forces is the secret meaning of what a warrior is, what Rome is, what someone's name, or Rome's name, is and means. The Roman dialectic is driven by the desire for a ground; but this society's tongues can only speak a secret that cannot be known.[33]

Coriolanus seems to contradict this desire for meaning when he says, 'I had rather have my wounds to heal again / Than hear say how I got them' (2.2.67–8); he adds, 'I had rather have one scratch my head i'th' sun / When the alarum were struck than idly sit / To hear my nothings monstered' (2.2.73–4). He would rather submit to more assaults than have the meaning of his wounds determined. Coriolanus's free self is *more*, more than words, more than history. But neither he nor we can be satisfied with the idea of repetitions of the traumatic self-sacrifice, any more than with letting others 'nothing on' about what that sacrifice means. Hegel is right that we are driven to make things meaningful and to be responsible for that meaning as the '*Self's* own *act*'.[34] Coriolanus's Rome presents the *problem* of the social birthplace of meaning-making as social self-mediation. Rome's secret – its essential problem – is *social media*. The Roman unhappy consciousness plays out as the social media of rhetoric, but also as social media of other kinds.

Robert Lepage's 2018 production of Shakespeare's *Coriolanus* at Stratford, Ontario, Canada, got this *media* aspect right.[35] Media of all kinds were used on stage: television, speakers, radio microphones, web-cams, phones, texting and even emojis. This brought the play into our time. It also picked up (inadvertently) on what I am claiming Hegel would say about this play, namely, that Rome's unhappy consciousness is the dis-function of the body politic; it is a dysfunction embodied in its media – in the warring words and actions that make up that political body – and emblematized by Coriolanus's body. Contradiction in Coriolanus's Rome is self-contra-*diction* in social media (a Citizen says to Coriolanus: 'You have deserved nobly of your country, and you have not deserved nobly' [2.3.86–7]).[36]

The contradictions of this unhappy, duplicate mode of viewing phenomena, with its undiscoverable secrets, are present in the Roman practice of giving first and second names.

v) Roman names

A person's name matters in this play, and names frequently advance the plot. For example: Coriolanus is banished 'I'th' people's name' (3.3.103); Aufidius greets exiled Coriolanus, repeating 'What is thy name?' (4.5.59, 64, 66); Menenius tries to get an audience with Coriolanus on the grounds that Coriolanus will recognize his name (5.2.12–58); Coriolanus expresses his capitulation (to make peace with Rome instead of attacking it) uttering, 'O, mother, mother!' (5.3.182); he seeks Aufidius's approval uttering his name 'three times in four lines' as noted by Holland (5.3.190–3n); Aufidius chastises Coriolanus, renaming him: 'Name not the god of war, thou boy of tears' (5.6.103), Coriolanus is incensed, shouting: '"Boy?"' (I discuss another pivotal moment ['O Martius, Martius!'] below.) This play is a tragedy of media, and symptomatically, of names.

Caius Martius's *agnomen* is given to him for his heroism in war. Coriolanus, this second name, is not the name of his *character*, like 'Antigone' in the Greek Sophoclean play. She has only one name and her duty is inscribed by it: she must perform her kinship rites and obey the laws of her family by burying her brother. Unlike her, Coriolanus's *agnomen* is imported from outside him: he is the Roman soldier who conquered a city – Corioli – for Rome. His second name is that city's name. This second name is that through which he is constrained to speak: it is his *per-sonare*.

But when Coriolanus speaks through that second name, he has little success. The Roman unhappy consciousness is a disease of the body politic, the alienation of/from custom. A second name is always already alienated. Hegel writes: 'Consciousness of right, ... in the very fact of being recognized as having validity, experiences rather the loss of its reality and its complete inessentiality; and to describe an individual as a "person" is an expression of contempt.'[37]

This is the ground of the tragedy. This social unhappiness, expressed in that which should mediate – the medium of meaning, media contra-*dictions* – is the spirit that Coriolanus embodies. In Hegel's *Phenomenology*, with the demise of ethical individuality 'the individual ... withdraws into the certainty of his own self; he is that substance as the *positive* universal, but his actuality consists in his being a *negative* universal self. ... [T]hat very necessity of blank Destiny, is nothing else but the "I" of self-consciousness'.[38]

The Roman social order and its members, especially its heroes, are caught up in Destiny. For Hegel, Destiny results from the Roman phenomenological one-sidedness of atomic legal personality. Greece had rich character individualities who were attuned to their gods;[39] Destiny is the duality of freedom and necessity.

Destiny gives the Roman individual his *persona*: his second name, his *agnomen*. But the truth about Destiny is that it is a secret that is unknowable. The person's second name comes after the fact (conquering a city, for a city) and yet is more than the fact (more than conquering, more than for Rome). There is no self-equivalence. The person's name expresses that the self's own act can never be the self's own act.

Antigone, despite her tragic fate, was not an unhappy consciousness of the first or second kind. The 'Immediate Spirit' she embodied was tragic because its members did not mediate social identity. Rather, they acted according to customary prescription. Rome's spirit fails for a different reason. Although the Romans know how to reason about social unity and can assign socially generated names *to* themselves, the meaning of such names is not worked out. This is evident in Coriolanus's case: he is given the name of a *conquered* city, not the name of a *free* city (at that time – possibly still – no such city exists). 'Coriolanus' circumscribes the free man.

Coriolanus's problem in the play is explaining the secret of his names: Caius Martius and Coriolanus. But the grounds for their unity, their meaning, is essentially contradictory because of the Roman formal duplicate mode of viewing identity. Nor is this problem solved by preferring one name over the other, despite how it seems to be thus solved in 5.5. Let me explain.

Coriolanus's first, given name – Caius Martius – is most potently used by his enemy Aufidius, in the scene in which exiled Coriolanus offers him his alliance against Rome. In their conversation, Caius Martius's first name and his speech through it, are *effective*. This is in marked contrast with Coriolanus's earlier speech as a soldier (even before he gets his *agnomen*, as hero of Rome, he was wary of speech: 'oft / When blows have made me stay I fled from words' [2.2.69–70]). When he joins Aufidius, Aufidius calls him by his first name, repeating it many times, meaningfully. 'O Martius, Martius!' (4.5.103).

Rather than being swayed by Martius's sword, Aufidius is swayed by his words. In this scene, Caius Martius is the name of an individual who, now, successfully wields words. He self-mediates.

This suggests that the first name reaches the heart of the secret. Aufidius appears to truly see Martius, neither a Roman nor a Volscian, but as he is, essentially.

However, by the end of the play, Aufidius kills Martius. Thus, this first-name exchange was all along subject to the same contra-*dictions* as the second name. Indeed, the only time in the entire play in which the most intimate name 'Caius' is used is by Aufidius when he plots Caius's death (4.7.56). The most intimate name means death, the contradiction of *being* (a Roman).

Thus, the secret, the self, for Romans, is a 'more than Roman', a more that can never be. That 'more' is how alienation is expressed in Rome.[40] Aufidius eventually makes this 'more' actionable. He figures out that the power of this secret can be used to drive out power. I'll come back to this.

My point here is that there is no complete self inside either first or second names. *The Roman secret is the doomed man, the man whose name is not knowable.* That is the unhappy spirit running through the whole play.

Recall that the scene in which Coriolanus gets his second name is the scene in which Coriolanus cannot remember the name of the man who was kind to him and should be spared (1.9.89–90). That man whose name is unknown represents the Roman secret, the heart, the mercy of Rome.[41] In this imperfect duplicate mode of perception, the good man remains a mystery, both public and hidden, tragically missed, unfound, unfindable, destined to die.

In Hegel's *Phenomenology of Spirit*, the unnamed mediating individual returns, in different incarnations, until s/he is comprehensively self-mediated/mediating. That occurs when the mediating individual is recollected and restored as 'absolute spirit': as the philosopher's self-mediating comprehension of 'absolute knowing'. Using religious language, Hegel expresses this final incarnation of the doomed man as 'the Calvary of Absolute Spirit'. With this, the unhappy consciousness finally finds truth in time.[42]

The grounds of this tragedy are socio-political, and *ontological*. This is evident in the Hegel passage from which I cited earlier:

> The Romans ... remained satisfied with a dull, stupid subjectivity; consequently, the external was only an Object – something alien, something hidden. The Roman spirit which thus remained involved in subjectivity, came into a relation of constraint and dependence, to which the origin of the word 'religio' (lig-are) points. The Roman had always to do with something *secret*; in everything he believed in and sought for something *concealed*; and while in the Greek religion everything is open and clear, present to sense and contemplation – not pertaining to a future world, but something friendly, and of this world – among the Romans everything exhibits itself as mysterious, duplicate: they saw in the object first itself, and then that which lies concealed in it: their history is pervaded by this duplicate mode of viewing phenomena. The city of Rome had besides its proper name another secret one, known only to a few ... [etc.].[43]

The doomed merciful man, whose name is not known, is also the ground of this play in another sense. He prefigures Coriolanus's tragic end: like that man, Caius Martius Coriolanus does not have a name by which he can be saved. Destiny swallows both men.

What kind of name, we might ask, *would* save him? That is the question to which Rome gives (a) birth, and which Christianity (ostensibly) answers. It becomes the secret with which the body politic of Christian Europe then spends two millennia trying to come to grips. Thus, Hegel's grasp – his *Begriff* – his resolution of this second unhappy consciousness, takes us well beyond 'Legal Status', and well beyond the historical life of the mediator who ostensibly saves Rome.[44]

For both Hegel and Shakespeare's *Coriolanus*, Rome is the ground of a tragedy, the solution for which had not yet come (and in some sense, is always to come). The ground of the tragedy is Rome's secret, its unhappy spirit. That spirit undoes Coriolanus. In Rome, the tongue in the wound becomes an acratic mouth, a mouth that cannot speak coherently, because the meaning of the wound is the secret heart, but the secret heart has no *known* name (yet), and so cannot be saved. Though equivalences are sought, there is never a match: in *Coriolanus*, there is always 'more'. Rome therefore generates a theatre for spurious infinites, rather than speculatively comprehending thinkers.

Part three: Duplicate vs dialectical: Roman spectator logic vs Hegelian speculative logic

i) Roman spectator logic

In Shakespeare's *Coriolanus*, people desire to get even, but just produce 'more'. There's always 'something odd' (2.3.81). Coriolanus reflects: 'Purpose so barred, it follows / Nothing is done to purpose' (3.1.149–50). Romans watch conflicts unfold destinies. The most violent are spectacles of bloodbath, like the public games. Hegel writes that '[i]n these the Romans were, properly speaking, only spectators. The mimetic and theatrical representation, the dancing, foot-racing and wrestling, they left to manumitted slaves, gladiators, or criminals condemned to death.'[45] In the play, Coriolanus's bloody battles are spectacles. The enumeration of his wounds makes *him* a spectacle.

In 2.3, Coriolanus speculates *about having to be this spectacle* when he must show his wounds in order to get votes: 'I will practise the insinuating nod and be off to them most counterfeitly; that is, sir, I will counterfeit the bewitchment of some popular man and give it bountiful to the desirers. Therefore, beseech you I may be consul' (2.3.97–101). But his purpose is barred when he reflects more deeply:

> What custom wills in all things, should we do't,
> The dust on antique time would lie unswept,
> And mountainous error be too highly heaped
> For truth to o'erpeer.
>
> (2.3.116–19)

He concludes, abjectly: 'Rather than fool it so / Let the high office and the honour go / To one that would do thus' (2.3.119–21). This is his spectacle: in Rome, any attempt to act on the ground of *custom* makes time dusted over with meaningless, counterfeited acts; custom is heaps of alienated essences.

As with the first and second names, this *suggests* that there is a true, secret, essential time, and an essential way to be in time; a way of properly relating to time, of dusting it off, being with it neatly, cleanly, properly, so that custom's dust never gathers on it. This way of being would be to relocate as time, with time, rather than to be dislocated from time and thus remain on the same spot, collecting dust.

Likewise, there is the supposition that there is a real truth, that there is or was or will be a way to be in truth, such that one would not make errors, or at least could peer over them. But, as we have noted, the way back to an immediate (Greek) time is barred for Romans (and according to Hegel, for Europe's 'Romantic' spirit from then on). And that inability to return is costly: not remembering a man's name can be deadly.

Coriolanus is stuck between Greece's immediate spirit and the Roman secret. He experiences constraint and dependence: *religare*, religion. The trajectory of time has thus changed from linear to linear and transcendental, with mystery at the cross. One might think of this cross in explicitly religious terms as prefiguring the Cross of Christ in Rome. But Coriolanus's world is not yet Christian Rome: it is a Roman person's crisis of trying to make sense of time, the crossing of the (horizontal, social, historical) diachronic time with the (vertical, self's transcendent) synchronic moment, when that person rises above their timeline in order to try to see themselves in time in an attempt to give their moment (and time itself) meaning. It is a crisis of self-mediation.

This Roman incarnation of Spirit is spurious. The Roman secret constrains without liberating: move in any direction along its axes and one unhappily piles up falsehoods. No choices are good: move backwards in time and one lives an inauthentic immediacy of the Greeks; move forward in time and one lives in counterfeited mediation; dig in, and one ends in violent contradiction; transcend, and one reflects on alienated time below from an empty, impotent heaven.

It is from that higher vantage point that Coriolanus speaks about the dust on time. Below he sees only socially mediated, alienated custom, meaninglessly piling up, dust on time, and a mountain of errors which the individual on the ground finds too high to see over. We do not learn from him or the play, what time is, or what that truth is that would peer over.

Coriolanus does not move forward out of this unhappiness. He does not see hope in the secret, in the idea that there is a proper time or seeing of truth. He just accepts more, and so goes on counterfeiting: he decides to pretend to be the man that 'would do thus. I am half through; / The one part suffered, the other will I do' (2.3.121–2). There is no merit in doing what is customary, just a dishonest pragmatism; he gives *up* at the same time that he gives *in to* purpose, a purpose with facetious logic.

Later, Coriolanus tries moving past measure, but Brutus shouts 'Enough, with over-measure', to which he replies 'No, take more' (3.1.141–2).[46] Coriolanus embodies the secret, the *more*: as a serviceman says, 'He had, sir, a kind of face, methought – I cannot tell how to term it.' To which another replies: 'He had so, looking, as it were – would I were hanged but I thought there was more in him than I could think' (4.5.157–61). But Coriolanus's more is always barred.

Aufidius appears to actualize the 'more'. He pushes this unhappy, Roman dialectic toward the Imperial. He understands the structure of this spurious secret, and how it will undo Coriolanus: he claims that to the 'vulgar eye' Coriolanus

> bears all things fairly
> And shows good husbandry for the Volscian state,
> Fights dragon-like and does achieve as soon
> As draw his sword, yet he hath left undone
> That which shall break his neck or hazard mine
> Whene'er we come to our account.
>
> (4.7.21–6)

In Aufidius's musings about the ground of Coriolanus's failure, he shifts to a meta-analysis about interpretation being 'of the time', and how there is no 'chair' or 'tomb' in which to place power such that it be understood (4.7.49–53). Aufidius knows that the secret of Roman power is that it works *as* a secret.

He uses this insight to his advantage. Earlier, when second in command after Coriolanus, in the Volscian attack on Rome, Aufidius is referred to by his soldiers as '[t]he second name of men' (4.6.128). We eventually learn that he was in fact counterfeiting this name, using this persona to accomplish his plot.

At the end of his musings about Coriolanus, Aufidius shifts from meta-analysis, into a rhyming, oracular pronouncement about how (he thinks) things change:

> One fire drives out one fire, one nail one nail,
> Rights by rights falter, strengths by strengths do fail.
> Come, let's away. When, Caius, Rome is thine,
> Thou art poor'st of all; then shortly art thou mine.
>
> (4.7.54–7)

One Aufidius for one Caius: this was almost Caius's desire, expressed early in the play: 'were I any thing but what I am, / I would wish me only he [Aufidius]' (1.1.226–7). But Caius's wish expressed unachievable equivalence. Aufidius's wish expresses achievable substitution: he wishes to be (one) more than Caius. Aufidius moves forward along the temporal axis of becoming, as if his being (one) more – the next – were good; Aufidius is oblivious to the alienation he carries forward. He does not see that his plan to drive one fire out with one fire, is a spurious infinite. We sense Aufidius's doom, that Coriolanus was wiser about the shape of Roman personal destiny. Neither escapes the spectator logic of this duplicate mode of viewing phenomena.

ii) Hegel's happy speculative logic

For Hegel, dialectic has to be thorough-going mediation: 'The *goal*, Absolute Knowing, or the Spirit that knows itself as Spirit has for its path the recollection of the Spirits as they are in themselves and as they accomplish the organization of their realm.'[47] The city of Rome was not able to be an enlightened organization of Spirit's realm because it was a social form of unhappy consciousness. By contrast, Hegel's final shape of a city of God is a realm of free, social persons. These are persons who, like ancient Romans, can regard their embeddedness as a history – that 'side of their free existence appearing in the form of contingency'. But unlike Romans, they can also regard themselves *phenomenologically* – as acting socially defined members, and self-critical *re-memberings*, of the city. Hegel describes this *final*, speculative duplicate mode of viewing as the 'philosophically comprehended organization … the science of knowing in the sphere of appearance'. These two together – history and phenomenology – make the city into something that reflects on itself absolutely, a 'comprehended history'.[48] This is a city which Hegel describes in Christian metaphors, but which we comprehend philosophically as being a city whose secrets are deep, yet in principle *knowable*. For Hegel, ancient Rome was the origin of modernity's free *form* of *religare*: that is, the origin of our dependence and restraint with regard to social *media*tion.

At the end of Hegel's book, rather than unhappy time dusted over with alienations of custom, absolute spirit happily drinks what 'foams forth' from the chalice of memory.[49] This might be another unchangeable ideal of an unhappy consciousness frothing spurious infinites. But I believe that our city can be happy. Either way, the grounds of tragedy in Shakespeare's *Coriolanus* are relevant to us: if we do not want to end up like Coriolanus, responsible freedom constrains us (*ligare*) to think our media through very carefully. That, for us, is the secret, the remainder, of *Coriolanus*'s Rome.

7

New Directions

Coriolanus and the Datasphere

Hugh Craig

The study of a play like *Coriolanus* generally starts with meanings. Commentators offer their interpretations of the actions and language of the play, its world, its characters, and its striking local expressions and interactions, and these in turn prompt other responses. More broadly, the play is put in wider contexts of purposeful human effort like the theatrical tradition, the book trade of the time, a longer reception history and so on. There is another possible approach, however, which starts from the play as a series of words, regarded simply as signs, cut off from what they signify, or more radically as a series of letters, punctuation marks and spaces beginning with a title and ending with whatever the person transmitting the text chose as the concluding content. These words or other formal elements can be sorted into sequences – speeches, say, or scenes, or the play as an entirety, to be compared to others – and the occurrences of formal elements within these sequences can be counted and tabulated as a means of recovering characteristics of the work. This approach is possible with printed books, but is vastly quicker with digital text, and it is the availability of digital text and computing resources to count and analyse digital text that has led to this approach becoming established as an active field, stylometry, with affiliations both to literary studies and to what is known as the digital humanities.

It may be hard at first to see why anyone would take this extreme step of discarding meaning at the outset. The most obvious benefits are in authorship attribution, where the mechanical accumulation of large amounts of raw data offers objectivity and repeatability, but there is a case to be made in relation to stylistics as well, where patterns otherwise hidden can emerge. Practitioners of stylometry are few compared to the number of mainstream students of Shakespeare's work, but they have become more noticeable in recent years. One example of this increased prominence is the *New Oxford Shakespeare* (2016–present).[1] This edition offers a challenge to traditional views of the Shakespeare canon, based on quantitative attribution work. It is the first Collected Works to put computer-assisted stylometry at the centre of its presentation of the plays and poems.

Stylometry is the focus of the current chapter. We will think of *Coriolanus* not as a dramatic action rich in meaning but as a verbal universe subject to all sorts of measurements. We move from concerns with textuality and ideology to numbers. We thereby escape some kinds of arbitrariness and subjectivity and encounter others. In statistics, no number stands on its own. Numbers only signify in relation to other numbers, and the choice of that comparison is always a matter of judgement and of available resources. Numbers are unanchored and irresponsible. Unadorned arithmetic counts may well be answers to questions no-one has asked. Once made, they may or may not engage with literary interpretation. Statistics is at the same time impoverished – blind to the obvious, and relentlessly reductive – and endlessly and disablingly productive. There is no end to the numbers we could collect, no surety that we have collected all the important numbers, and no ultimate confidence that any of the numbers are important. On the other hand, some of the observations we routinely make about plays are already quantitative, involving frequencies of features of various kinds, and numbers do have the virtue of being explicit and fixed once we agree on the terms. They offer a way to describe a complex system like the language of a play in relation to other comparable specimens, with precision and economy and effortless expansion of scale.

We make a first venture into the datasphere using a map from a previous expedition. In *Style, Computers, and Early Modern Drama: Beyond Authorship* (2017) the present author and Brett Greatley-Hirsch examine the patterns of language in 531 larger character parts in 197 plays which were performed between 1580 and 1619, including *Coriolanus*.[2] That play has four characters which satisfy the operating criterion of speaking 2,000 words or more in total, namely Coriolanus, Menenius, Volumnia and Aufidius.

The analysis starts with counts of 100 very common words in the character parts, expressed as percentages of the character parts as wholes. We then use a statistical procedure, Principal Component Analysis (PCA), to seek out latent factors underlying the apparently random variation from character to character.[3] These factors are mathematically defined as a set of coefficients, or weightings, for the words – for example, *the* positively weighted, *you* negatively weighted, *are* very lightly or neutrally weighted, and so on for all the words included.

Once the weightings are identified, we can work out a score for each sample (in our case, each character part) on each Principal Component. We multiply the proportional count for the first word in the particular character part by the appropriate weighting, add this to the count for the second word multiplied by its weighting, and so on for all the words.

If you imagine the values for each of the words for each of the character texts as a cloud of points, the First Principal Component would be the straight line making the best fit through this cloud, that is, the line with the smallest average distance from the points. In more technical terms, PCA finds a set of weightings that make a vector that accounts for most of the variance in the whole set of proportions, and then the set of weightings for a vector that accounts for the second largest independent amount, and so on. In the book and below we look simply at the first two of these vectors.

There are two ways to visualize the results of the PCA, one by plotting the weightings for the word-variables on the first two Components, and the other by plotting the scores for the samples on the same two Components. The charts can then be read together. A word which is heavily weighted in one direction on one axis is likely to be unusually frequent in a character part which appears at the extreme in the same direction on the same axis in the character-part plot. Figure 7.1 shows the weightings for the word-variables on the first two Components, labelling those with highest and lowest weightings.[4]

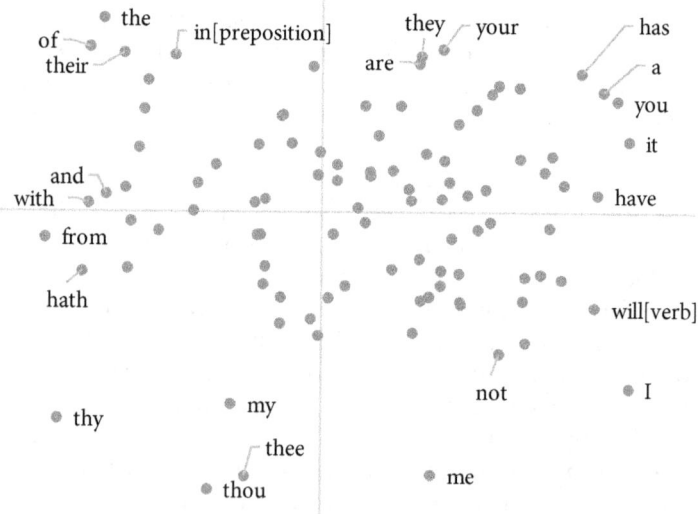

FIGURE 7.1 *Word-variable weightings for a Principal Component Analysis of 100 very common words in 531 character parts each of 2,000 words or more. X axis: First Principal Component; Y axis: Second Principal Component.*

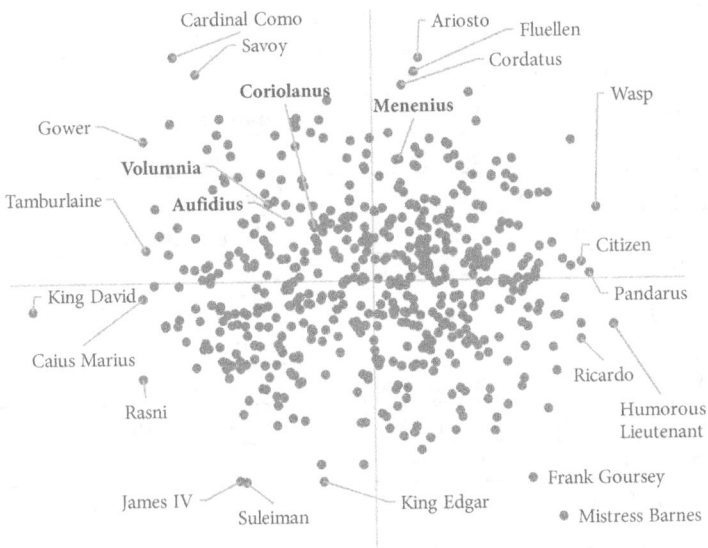

FIGURE 7.2 *Character scores for a Principal Component Analysis of 100 very common words in 531 characters each speaking 2,000 words or more. X axis: First Principal Component; Y axis: Second Principal Component.*

Figure 7.2 shows the four Coriolanus characters and the characters at the extremes of the two Components. The First Principal Component is along the horizontal axis. Looking at the word-variables at either end, we can see contrasts in pronouns: *their* and *thy* at the left-hand, negative end, and *I*, *you* and *it* at the right-hand, positive end. There are outgoing forms, *thy* and *hath*, at the left-hand end and incoming ones, *has* and *you*, at the right-hand end. There is a lone conjunction, *and*, at the left-hand end, and more auxiliaries, *have* and *will* as well as *has*, at the right-hand end. The definite article *the* is at the left-hand end and the indefinite article *a* at the

Table 7.1 *Identification of labels in Figure 7.2*

Character label	Author	Play
Ariosto	Webster	*Devil's Law Case*
Aufidius	Shakespeare	*Coriolanus*
Caius Marius	Lodge	*Wounds of Civil War*
Cardinal Como	Dekker	*Whore of Babylon*
Citizen	Beaumont	*Knight of the Burning Pestle*
Cordatus	Jonson	*Every Man out of His Humour*
Coriolanus	Shakespeare	*Coriolanus*
Duke of Savoy	Chapman	*Byron's Conspiracy*
Fluellen	Shakespeare	*Henry V*
Frank Goursey	Porter	*Two Angry Women of Abingdon*
Gower	Shakespeare and Wilkins	*Pericles*
Humorous Lieutenant	Fletcher	*Humorous Lieutenant*
James IV	Greene	*James IV*
King David	Peele	*Love of King David and Fair Bathsheba*
King Edgar	Uncertain	*Knack to Know a Knave*
Menenius	Shakespeare	*Coriolanus*
Mistress Barnes	Porter	*Two Angry Women*
Pandarus	Shakespeare	*Troilus and Cressida*
Rasni	Lodge and Greene	*Looking Glass for London and England*
Ricardo	Middleton	*Widow*
Suleiman	Kyd	*Suleiman and Perseda*
Tamburlaine	Marlowe	*2 Tamburlaine*
Volumnia	Shakespeare	*Coriolanus*
Wasp	Jonson	*Bartholomew Fair*

right-hand end. Two higher level factors seem to be at play: old-fashioned versus modern, and impersonal disquisitions versus an interlocutory discourse.

The characters contrasted on the same Component are (as Craig and Greatley-Hirsch put it) 'kings and choric figures on the one hand and fussy busybodies on the other'.[5] The speeches of King David from George Peele's *The Love of King David and Fair Bathsheba* are 'well-turned and replete with stately, elaborate poetic illustration' while the Humorous Lieutenant from John Fletcher's play of the same name is much more staccato in discourse, focused on immediate sensations and interactions with other characters, and 'entirely caught up in the moment'.[6]

The Second Component, on the vertical axis, contrasts *thou, thee, thy, I* and *my* in the pronouns (lower end) to *they, their* and *your* (higher end). There is the particle *not* at the lower end and the prepositions *of* and *in* at the higher end. We have characters 'caught up in an action which is focused on personal relations (domestic or intimate)' at the lower end and 'characters whose role is to dissect some aspect of the play-world' at the higher end.[7] Domestic combatants (Mistress Barnes, Frank Goursey) and despotic or besotted lovers (James IV, King Edgar) are contrasted with pundits (Cardinal Como, Ariosto, Fluellen and Savoy).

Three of the *Coriolanus* characters are clustered in the top-left quadrant and one (Menenius) sits apart in the top-right quadrant. The first trio are classified as speech-makers and pundits, more like Cardinal Como and Savoy than like Goursey or Barnes. Menenius is also a pundit but more like the humours characters and more involved in immediate interactions. None of the four engage with others in a domestic or intimate way. The discourse styles of Coriolanus, Volumnia and Aufidius are broadly similar in terms of the two main dynamics identified by the analysis, more declamatory and generalizing, and less humorous and intimate. The opposition in styles within the play is not between members of this trio but between them as a group and Menenius.

In the PCA we allow the characters of *Coriolanus* to fall where they may in a larger map of characters from the drama of the time. We can also take a more directed approach and search out where the play is unusual. One aspect of this is its vocabulary, which provides clues to its distinctive preoccupations and the ways they are framed. For this we need standards of comparison. I assembled four sets of plays for this purpose. One is a large collection of plays of the time, 274 in all. Another consists of other plays either written by Shakespeare, or to which he very likely contributed. A third is a set of tragedies and a romance by Shakespeare and others set in the Roman world. The fourth is a set of plays first performed 1606–11. The dates are chosen so as to have about as many plays from the years before 1608, the date for *Coriolanus*, as from the years after, given the composition of our corpus.[8]

I looked for words which are common in *Coriolanus* and rare in the other sets, and vice versa. I divided all the plays into 2,000-word segments, with any residue incorporated into the last segment. I then counted how many segments had an instance of a given word. For words relatively common in *Coriolanus*, I took the proportion of *Coriolanus* segments with one or more instance, and added that to the proportion of the other set of segments with no instance. The extreme case would be a word that appeared in every *Coriolanus* segment but in no segment of the other set, giving a score of one plus one (i.e. two). For words relatively rare in the play, I did the reverse, adding the proportion of *Coriolanus* segments with no instance to the proportion of segments in the other plays with one or more instance.[9]

This method gives full value to regularity rather than sheer quantity. If there is a cluster of instances in one segment for some local reason, that still only counts as a single occupied segment for the purposes of calculating the index. Dividing the plays into segments introduces a finer-grain consideration of repeated use. Having said all that, there would be arguments for different parameters and they might bring slightly different outcomes.

Table 7.2 shows the ten words with the most contrasting distributions between the play and the comparison sets. The

Table 7.2 *The ten highest and lowest scoring words in comparisons of regularity and rarity between* Coriolanus *and four sets of plays. Words appearing in all four top-ten sets are in bold*

	Words more common in *Coriolanus*	**Words rarer in** *Coriolanus*
Coriolanus compared to 274 other plays	general city people enemies heard wars **gates** worthy action beseech	her [personal pronoun] master marry **soul** she mistress young alas just pleasure
Coriolanus compared to 39 other plays written wholly or partly by Shakespeare	city **general** country people worthy has lose deserved action **gates**	her [personal pronoun] marry our [royal plural] master young we [royal plural] grace dead **soul** brother

Coriolanus compared to fourteen other non-comic plays set in the Roman world	city heard has beseech **gates** **general** request home market sworn	her [personal pronoun] dead fear **soul** high just ill thoughts who[interrogative] brother
Coriolanus compared to 49 other plays with first performances 1606–11	**general** city people wars enemies **gates** heard noble beseech sword	her [personal pronoun] master marry she **soul** light mistress none next just

algorithm identifies *general* as the word with the most extreme contrast in regularity and rarity between *Coriolanus* segments and segments of the full set of available plays. There are just over 2,500 of the latter, and *general* appears in about one in five of them, whereas we find it in twelve of the thirteen *Coriolanus* segments. A similar contrast persists in the smaller, more focused comparison sets. Roman plays, for instance, frequently deal with war and armies but their characters do not keep referring to a *general* as persistently as do their counterparts in *Coriolanus*.

Coriolanus is also unusual in that the word *city* keeps reappearing in dialogue. One or more instance occurs in all but one of its segments, but only in one in four segments of the large comparison set of plays. This reminds us that two cities dominate the play, Rome and Corioles. There is an unusual focus on these cities as collective entities and bounded locations which characters leave, invade and re-enter. The word *city* appears in twelve out of thirteen segments of *Coriolanus*, but only in one in four segments of the large set of plays, which perhaps is not surprising, and in only between one in four and one in three segments of the Roman plays, which is more so.

On the other hand while *her* as an object pronoun (as in 'Let her alone') does occur in the play, it is only at odd moments, while it is a constant in the comparison sets. Here *Coriolanus*'s dialogue looks lopsided – constantly invoking the two cities of Rome and Corioles; and, though furnished with one powerful woman character, Volumnia, paying little attention for most of the action to women in general. The difference persists in all four comparisons.

The table also tells us that the word *soul* is surprisingly rare in *Coriolanus*. The figures lying behind Table 7.2 indicate that this word is reasonably common in the other three sets. In each of them it appears at a very steady rate, that is, in between a half and three-fifths of all segments. It does appear in *Coriolanus*, but in only two of the thirteen segments. Playgoers, we might say, would expect to hear the word regularly, whether in plays in general, Shakespeare plays or Roman plays, but *Coriolanus* breaks the pattern and characters use it very sparingly. *Soul* is used by the playwrights for added solemnity, and to elevate and add complexity to a sense of the self (as in 'O my prophetic soul!', or 'between her and her fighting soul', *Hamlet* 1.5.40, 3.4.109). In *Coriolanus* Shakespeare does less of this than we expect in plays of the same era, in his other plays in general, in Roman plays in general and in early modern English plays in general. Perhaps the self projected in the play does not have the usual theological undergirding. It is more secular and difficult to conjure up with any confidence. (Readers might like to imagine, or even carry out, an experiment which would extend this observation, for example by compiling a list of words associated with the numinous and with existential speculation, and comparing the rate of occurrence in *Coriolanus* with that in a reference sample of plays.[10])

Has was the incoming form replacing *hath* in the period. This word appears more regularly in *Coriolanus* than in the comparison sets of Shakespeare plays or Roman plays, though the word does not appear in the top ten words for the other two comparisons.[11] This raises the question of where the dialogue in *Coriolanus* stands in relation to some of the language changes happening in English at the time.[12] In general, *-s* endings for verbs were replacing *-th* endings, with very common auxiliaries like *hath* and *doth* as well as with full lexical verbs like *giveth* and *maketh*. *Thou* as an alternative form of the second person pronoun was becoming less common and being replaced by *you* even for singular uses, though it still was available to signal intimacy or – in some cases – a lack of respect. We calculated four ratios to cover these developments: the ratio of *has* to *hath*, the ratio of *does* to *doth*, the ratio of *you* forms to *thou* forms (*you*, *your* and *yours* versus *thou*, *thee*, *thy* and *thine*), and the ratio of instances of 180 verbs with *-s* or *-es* endings to instances of the same 180 verbs with *-th* or *-eth* endings.[13]

We then calculated these ratios for *Coriolanus* and for other plays in the four sets. Figure 7.3 is a box-and-whisker plot of *has:hath* ratios for our four comparison sets, with the *Coriolanus* score for reference. Box and whisker plots show the four quartiles, the lowest as a vertical line with a bottom marker, the middle two as a central box divided by a line representing the median and the highest as a vertical line with a top marker. The average is shown as a cross, and outliers are given separate datapoints.

Within the full set, the *Coriolanus* score is in the third quartile, above the average and the median for the full set. It is in the top quartile for Shakespearean plays, only exceeded by *Othello* (1604) and *The Winter's Tale* (1611) of the unaided Shakespeare plays, as we can tell from a more detailed look at the scores. The outlier in this set, marked with a circle, is *The Two Noble Kinsmen* (1613), a collaboration between Shakespeare and John Fletcher. Within the 1606–11 set, however, *Coriolanus* is right on the median. It is surprising that even at this relatively late date three of the fifty plays

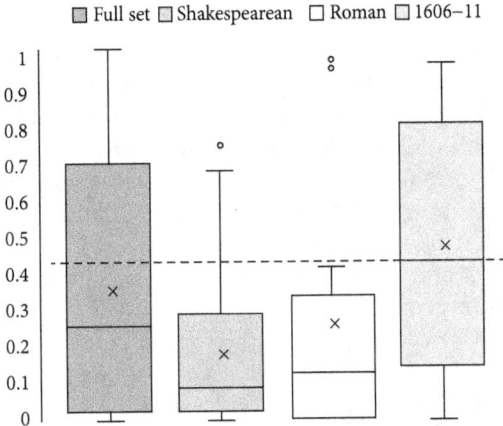

FIGURE 7.3 *Proportions of* has *to* hath (has/(has+hath)) *in four sets of plays. The dashed line represents the* Coriolanus *proportion (0.41).*

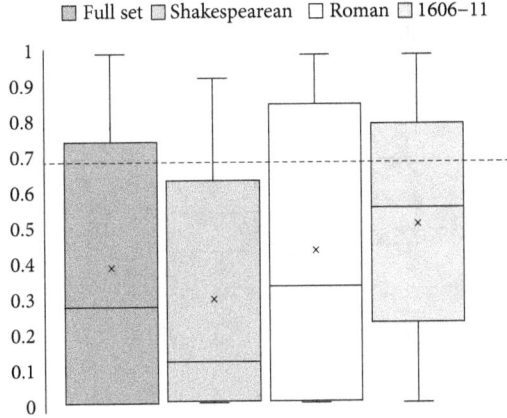

FIGURE 7.4 *Proportions of* does *to* doth (does/(does+doth)) *in four sets of plays. The dashed line represents the* Coriolanus *proportion (0.68).*

have ratios of zero, i.e. all *hath* and no *has*. These are John Mason, *The Turk* (1607), George Chapman, *The Tragedy of Biron* (1608) and Thomas Heywood, *The Fair Maid of the West* (1610). The highest ratio of the 1606–11 plays is 0.96, for Thomas Middleton, *The Second Maiden's Tragedy* (1611).

Generally, Shakespeare is a traditionalist rather than an innovator in terms of language changes[14] and the *has* data indicates that *Coriolanus* is 'modern' for a Shakespeare play, but not for a play of its time. Figure 7.4 shows the picture for the *does:doth* proportion.

Here the *Coriolanus* proportion is again high for Shakespeare, but not exceptional elsewhere. We can also compare the proportions of *you* forms to *thou* forms (Figure 7.5).

Coriolanus has the highest proportion of the *you* forms among the Roman plays. It is in the top quartile for the full set. (The low outlier is George Peele, *The Love of King David and Fair Bathsheba* [1590] at 0.16.) It is also in the top quartile for the 1606–11 plays, where the low outlier is John Fletcher, *The Faithful Shepherdess* (1608) at 0.27.

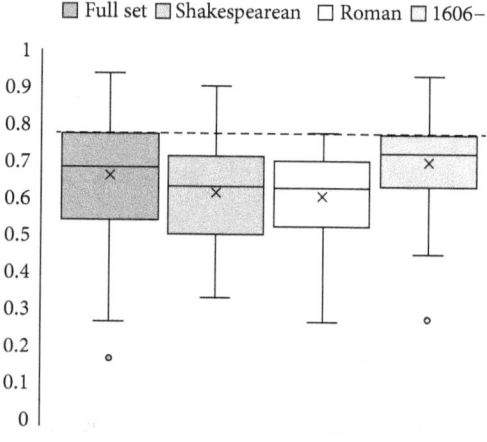

FIGURE 7.5 *Proportions of* you *forms to* thou *forms* (you+your+yours)/((you+your+yours)+(thou+thee+thy+thine)) *in four sets of plays. The dashed line represents the* Coriolanus *proportion (0.78).*

Our final set of incoming and outgoing forms is the wider set of *-th* and *-s* endings beyond *has* and *does* (Figure 7.6). Most plays have predominantly *-s* endings. The lowest of the low outliers in the full set is Nicholas Udall, *Ralph Roister Doister* (1552), with a proportion of 0.21. The low outlier for Shakespeare is *Henry VI, Part 1* (1592), 0.88. The low outlier for the Roman set is Samuel Brandon, *Virtuous Octavia* (1598), 0.79. It is possible that audiences at the time might have detected an archaic flavour in these plays because of their use of the *-th* endings. *Coriolanus* has 100 per cent of *-s* endings, as do forty-seven other plays in the full set, six others in the Shakespearean set, three others in the Roman set, and eight others in the 1606–11 set. This comparison puts *Coriolanus* comfortably among the most modern plays in these terms, including among the plays of its own time.

One approach to Shakespearean drama which has been quantitative from the beginning is prosody. Marina Tarlinskaja and George T. Wright published books on Shakespeare's

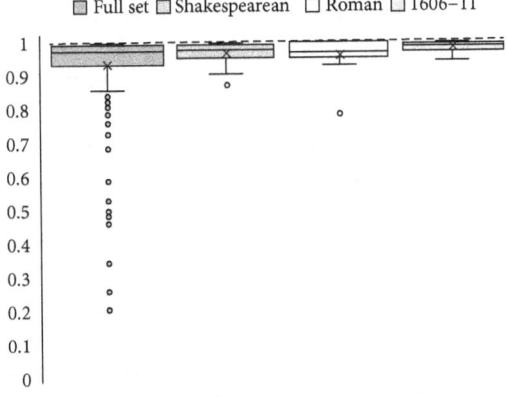

FIGURE 7.6 *Proportions of verb forms ending in* -s *to verb forms ending in* -th *for a set of 180 verbs (*-s *forms/(*-s *forms+*-th *forms)) in four sets of plays. The dashed line represents the* Coriolanus *proportion (1.0).*

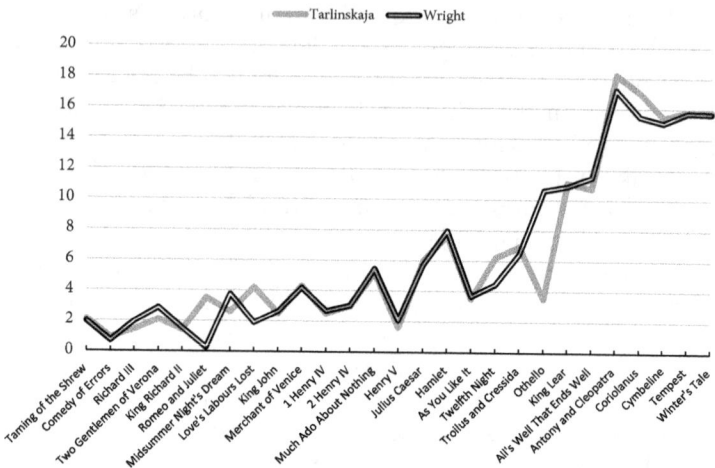

FIGURE 7.7 *Percentage of verse lines which are shared between characters in twenty-seven Shakespeare plays arranged in order of date of first performance.*[16]

versification in 1987 and 1988 respectively. They both noticed that lines shared between speakers – where part of the line is spoken by the first speaker, and part spoken by a second or even a third – were rare in Shakespeare's earliest plays, making up 2 per cent or so of the total, but became more common in his middle period, and commoner still at the end, with the last plays averaging over 15 per cent.[15] There are some discrepancies between their two counts, but they agree on the overall pattern (Figure 7.7).

Wright offers an attractive explanation for Shakespeare's practice here. Lines shared between characters 'suggest the casualness of natural conversation' and Shakespeare included more as time went on from a 'wish to present credible and credibly various language on the stage'.[17] *Coriolanus* has 15.5 per cent (Wright) or 17 per cent (Tarlinskaja) of its lines shared between speakers. Either way, it fits comfortably in the group of late Shakespeare plays with very high scores.

Shared lines may come at the beginning or end of a long speech, but they also may be free-standing, and result in full speeches shorter than a complete pentameter. The variation in the number of shared lines belongs with a larger story of change in the length of speeches. Most important here is a collective move around the turn of the century to shorter speeches.[18] This is clearest if we look at the commonest speech length in plays, that is, the length that accounts for the highest number of speeches. In statistical terms this is the 'mode'. The mode for earlier plays was nine words, surprisingly short, given the overwhelming focus of commentary on the plays on longer speeches. Then there was an abrupt change to become even shorter, so that four words is the normal mode for plays after 1602 or so, not only for Shakespeare but also for early modern English drama generally. The Russian scholar Boris Yarkho proposed the ratio of the number of utterances in a play to its overall length as a 'liveliness index',[19] and the move from a mode of nine words to a mode of four corresponds to a shortening of the average speech, and thus a move to more lively drama in Yarkho's terms. *Coriolanus* has many shared lines, as we have seen, and also follows a collective move to short speeches, with its mode of speech length being four words (Figure 7.8).

Ninety-six out of 1,102 or 8.7 per cent of the speeches in the play are four words long. This corresponds to a half-line of verse. These numerical observations do not mark *Coriolanus* as exceptional, but rather place it along a continuum and with other plays with similar characteristics. It is a modern play and a play of conversational suppleness relative to the longer tradition of Shakespearean drama. (The longest speech in the play, at 439 words, is Volumnia's final appeal to Coriolanus at 5.3.131–82.)

A sample of language is a succession of different words. As it continues it inevitably starts to repeat some of the different words, while under normal circumstances it continues to add new ones as well. Some samples have a lot of repetition, while others are more various in their vocabulary relative to their size. Claude Shannon in the 1940s introduced a measure

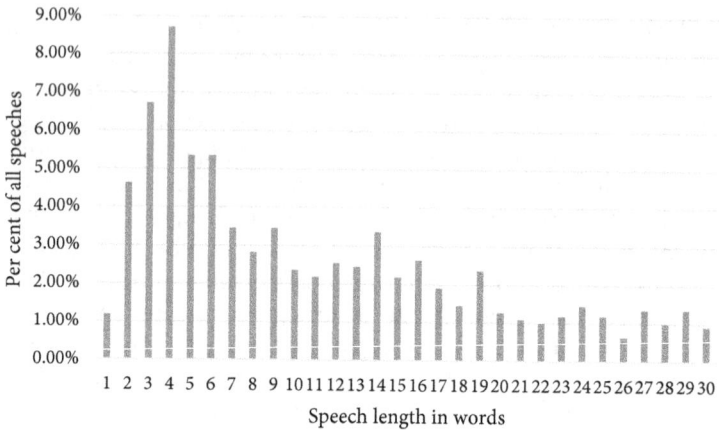

FIGURE 7.8 *Percentage of speeches in* Coriolanus *consisting of one word, two words, three words etc., up to thirty words. (NB speeches with more than thirty words account for the remaining 22.5 per cent of speeches.)*

of this repetitiveness, now known as Information Entropy, with the symbol H. To calculate Information Entropy for language we find the proportion of all instances accounted for by instances of the first word and multiply this proportion by its logarithm, and then change to sign to make a positive quantity. We then do the same for all the words and add up all the products of proportions and logs. A low value indicates that a few words with many repetitions make up most of the total, and correspondingly a high value indicates that the total of instances is divided among numerous different words. If we have a sample of four words, 'one two three four', then we have four words each with a proportion of one-quarter or 0.25. The natural logarithm of 0.25 is −1.3862 so we have

$$H = -((0.25 \times -1.3862) + (0.25 \times -1.3862) + (0.25 \times -1.3862) + (0.25 \times -1.3862)) = 1.386$$

On the other hand if our sample is 'one two one two' then H is lower,

$$H=-((0.5 \times -0.69315) + (0.5 \times -0.69315)) = 0.693$$

And lowest of all would be a sample with one word repeated, as in 'one one one one':

$$H=-(1 \times 0)=0$$

H is related to type-token ratio (TTR), i.e. the number of word types or different words, divided by the number of word tokens or the running total of words. For our three samples the TTR would be 0.25, 0.5 and 1. I prefer to use Information Entropy because it is more responsive to the distribution of word types. The TTR for 'one one one two' is the same as for 'one two one two', 0.5, whereas H is lower for the first (0.562 compared to 0.693).

Repetitiveness is a useful measure because it relates to the dramatist's contrasting purposes in writing dialogue. One scene of a play may have very little repetition because characters are elaborating a narrative or an argument. Rendering a situation or environment in speech for an audience unfamiliar with them requires the use of an extensive vocabulary for precision and to convey detail. On the other hand, where characters are focusing on objects and people which are within sight or part of shared knowledge they can make extensive use of pronouns for reference and so will be more repetitive.

To explore how Information Entropy varies within the dialogue of *Coriolanus* we divide its 26,953 words into 500-word segments. These are long enough to iron out some very local variation, and short enough so that where there are sustained patches of difference, they are not unduly masked. Information Entropy, like all repetitiveness measures in their raw form, is sensitive to sample size – it tends to be lower as samples get longer – so we discard the last, slightly shorter sample of 453 words and concentrate on the remaining fifty-three samples of exactly 500 words.

Two segments are markedly lower than the rest, no. 21 and no. 40. The segment with the highest H value is no. 9. To gauge where these values fit in the general span of the drama of the time, we place them in the context of our usual comparison sets and *Coriolanus* itself. We find the rank orders of these values within the sets, and the centile in which they fall. For each of the comparison sets we find H values for complete 500-word segments, discarding any last portion which is not exactly 500 words long.

The twenty-first segment spans 2.3.47 to 2.3.112. This segment is in the first centile in each of the comparison sets, i.e. 99 per cent or more of the values are higher. It has the second lowest score among the 629 segments of the non-comic Roman plays and the sixth lowest score among the 2,052 segments of the 1606–11 plays (Table 7.3). We can confidently say that this is a low H value and that this segment is therefore a stand-out in terms of repetitiveness among comparable short passages.

Table 7.3 *The Information Entropy scores of three 500-word segments of* Coriolanus, *placed in rank order and centile of the Information Entropy of 500-word segment arrays of various comparison sets*

	Coriolanus	Full set	Shakespearean plays	Roman plays	1606–11 plays
N of plays	1	275	40	15	50
N of segments	53	10,506	1,728	629	2,052
#9 H value	5.303	5.303	5.303	5.303	5.303
#9 rank order	53	9,684	1,617	531	1,874
#9 centile	99th	93rd	94th	91st	91st
#21 H value	4.824	4.824	4.824	4.824	4.824
#21 rank order	1	38	11	2	6
#21 centile	1st	1st	1st	1st	1st
#40 H value	4.880	4.880	4.880	4.880	4.880
#40 rank order	2	128	27	3	18
#40 centile	1st	2nd	2nd	1st	1st

The Information Entropy analysis tells us nothing about the reasons for the low score of the segment. It simply highlights the fact that by this measure this is an unusually repetitive sample from among thousands of comparable samples. We need to examine the passage itself and try to understand the stylistics of a low H score in this case.

In one part of this passage Coriolanus has the task of soliciting votes from the citizens, but refuses to follow the convention by which the candidate expresses his humility to individual voters in turn. There are awkward exchanges in which the artificiality of the transaction is exposed through repetition:

Enter three of the Citizens.

CORIOLANUS
Bid them wash their faces
And keep their teeth clean. So, here comes a brace.
You know the cause, sir, of my standing here.

3 CITIZEN
We do, sir. Tell us what hath brought you to't.

CORIOLANUS
Mine own desert.

2 CITIZEN
Your own desert.

CORIOLANUS
Ay, but not mine own desire.

3 CITIZEN
How not your own desire?

CORIOLANUS
No, sir, 'twas never my desire yet to trouble
the poor with begging.

3 CITIZEN
You must think, if we give you anything, we
hope to gain by you.

CORIOLANUS
Well then, I pray, your price o'th'
consulship?

1 CITIZEN
The price is to ask it kindly.
CORIOLANUS
Kindly, sir, I pray let me ha't: I have wounds
to show you which shall be yours in private. [*to 2
Citizen*] Your good voice, sir. What say you?
2 CITIZEN
You shall ha'it, worthy sir.

(2.3.59 SD–78)

Communication Accommodation Theory tells us that there is a natural tendency for speakers to modify what they say to demonstrate that they are taking in what they are hearing. They adopt a common vocabulary, for example.[20] In this passage from *Coriolanus* one speaker's echoing of another's vocabulary and phrasing is done to such an extent that it registers the opposite, i.e. a sense that there is an intractable degree of cross-purposes in this conversation. At its end the third Citizen understandably comments, 'But this is something odd' (2.3.81).

The fortieth segment has the second lowest H score in the play. It belongs to the second centile in the comparison with the 'Shakespearean' plays and the full set (Table 7.3), so is low, but joins a larger group of segments in Shakespeare and beyond with a similar degree of repetitiveness. Nevertheless, it is worth a little attention in terms of dramatic craft. It covers lines 158 to 221 of Act 4, Scene 5. Various servingmen in Antium are discussing the recent arrival of Coriolanus and the new alliance of their master Aufidius and Coriolanus against Rome:

3 SERVINGMAN
O slaves, I can tell you news, news, you
rascals.
1, 2 SERVINGMEN
What, what, what? Let's partake.

3 SERVINGMAN
> I would not be a Roman of all nations. I
> had as lief be a condemned man.

1, 2 SERVINGMEN
> Wherefore? wherefore?

3 SERVINGMAN
> Why, here's he that was wont to thwack
> our general, Caius Martius.

1 SERVINGMAN
> Why do you say 'thwack our general'?

3 SERVINGMAN
> I do not say 'thwack our general'; but he
> was always good enough for him.

2 SERVINGMAN
> Come, we are fellows and friends. He was
> ever too hard for him. I have heard him say so himself.

1 SERVINGMAN
> He was too hard for him directly, to say
> the truth on't. Before Corioles he scotched him and
> notched him like a carbonado.

(4.5.175–90)

Repetition reflects the speakers' excitement and their underlying unease about the superiority of Coriolanus's prowess to Aufidius's. One speaker says that Coriolanus used to 'thwack' Aufidius in battle, but this is questioned and then withdrawn, and then they settle on the more cautious formulation that Coriolanus was 'too hard' for Aufidius, an idea which can be tolerated among 'fellows and friends'. The three servingmen compare notes, and advance and retreat to settle on a common view and common terminology for the situation, all of which means unusual repetition in the very common words like *he* and *him* and in the more unusual ones like *thwack*.

The segment with the highest Information Entropy score in *Coriolanus* is no. 9 (1.5.5 to 1.6.38). This passage covers part of the battle for Corioles. The battle is created for the audience through the animated action on stage and through a running commentary shared between characters.

Coriolanus's blood is up and he rants in high dramatic mode:

> See here these movers that do prize their hours
> At a cracked drachma! Cushions, leaden spoons,
> Irons of a doit, doublets that hangmen would
> Bury with those that wore them, these base slaves,
> Ere yet the fight be done, pack up.
>
> (1.5.4–8)

This is language which might excite the interest of Pistol ('What! shall we have incision? shall we imbrue?' [2 *Henry IV*, 2.4.195–6]). It keeps adding new vocabulary. With its volleys of particularized, fanciful description it would score highly on an index of rare and unexpected terms as well.

Segment no. 9 does not always remain at this level of declamatory intensity but it does unroll steadily, introducing new vocabulary all the time, and rarely turns back on itself. In the following section, which completes and in fact slightly overflows the segment, there is repetition – Coriolanus has two successive sentences with the same four-word sequence, for instance, examples of the four-word speech discussed earlier – but there is also a series of new conceits, which bring with them an expanding variety of vocabulary:

> *Enter* MARTIUS
> COMINIUS   Who's yonder
> That does appear as he were flayed? O gods,
> He has the stamp of Martius, and I have
> Beforetime seen him thus.
> MARTIUS
>   Come I too late?

COMINIUS
> The shepherd knows not thunder from a tabor
> More than I know the sound of Martius' tongue
> From every meaner man.

MARTIUS
> Come I too late?

COMINIUS
> Ay, if you come not in the blood of others,
> But mantled in your own.

COMINIUS
> Oh! let me clip ye
> In arms as sound as when I wooed, in heart
> As merry as when our nuptial day was done
> And tapers burned to bedward. [*They embrace.*]

COMINIUS
> Flower of warriors, how is't with Titus Lartius?

MARTIUS
> As with a man busied about decrees,
> Condemning some to death and some to exile,
> Ransoming him or pitying, threatening th'other;
> Holding Corioles in the name of Rome,
> Even like a fawning greyhound in the leash,
> To let him slip at will.

> > (1.6.21 SD–39)

The high Information Entropy score of the segment helps us see that this is a peak for the play in terms of depicting the hurried movement of bodies onward through space and time, a moment when the dramatic action comes closest to epic. The commentary is shared between speakers, but the common current flows swiftly, with rich language full of unexpected conceits and exotic vocabulary depicting a single action. For once there is little hesitation, introspection or closely engaged conversation.

Coriolanus is not an exceptional play on any of the general measures trialled here, though if we look for the unusual, as with vocabulary, we find it. The numbers tell us that

Coriolanus is an up-to-date play in terms of early modern English and that it shares in a collective movement in early modern English drama toward shorter speeches. It has three more formal speechmaking main characters and a fourth who has something of a humorous bent; it has one remarkably repetitive passage reflecting Coriolanus's deep unease with his role as a candidate; it has a special focus on the city and on gates; and in its discourse there is remarkably little focus on women once they are not on stage. None of these observations are surprising in any lasting way, though if asked prior to seeing the analysis what is the commonest speech length in the play, or who is the odd one out stylistically among the four main characters, I doubt that many would give the same answer as offered above.

The basis in numbers for these findings is unarguable in its own terms, but this very explicitness means that it leaves open further avenues. The terms can themselves be challenged, and the starkness of the proposals invite other students of the play to supplement them, or supplant them by new approaches, or ignore them entirely. *Coriolanus*, like any entity with material aspects, participates in the datasphere, but, as a product of the human imagination, and the starting point of a vast and evolving reception, it is by no means confined to it. A digital-humanities method like stylometry stands or falls by its capacity to contribute to our understanding of literary works. It is only fair to note that not everyone is convinced that it can. Many would argue that it is disabled from the start by its disjunction from meaning. The disagreement is an important one at this moment in Shakespeare studies and every student of Shakespeare, whether beginning, experienced or in the middle, has the privilege or otherwise of working out their own position.

8

'Teach my mind': Approaches and Resources for the *Coriolanus* Classroom

Claire Hansen

> I will not do't,
> Lest I surcease to honour mine own truth
> And by my body's action teach my mind
> A most inherent baseness.
> (*Coriolanus*, 3.2.121–4)

Teaching is an act at times resisted by Coriolanus, and Shakespeare's *Coriolanus* can be considered a resistant text with a challenging protagonist. But it is also an enormously rewarding play to explore in the classroom. This chapter will provide a range of theoretical and practical approaches to teaching *Coriolanus*, including introductory activities centred on the belly fable, a theoretical framework to encourage students to highlight the play's connections and turbulence, suggestions for tackling historical and presentist approaches, an overview of key themes and ways to use digital technologies and film in your *Coriolanus* classroom.

There is no shortage of resources responding to the challenges of Shakespeare pedagogy. These challenges are articulated by Brian Vickers in his discussion of teaching *Coriolanus*, in which he voices his 'dissatisfaction' with teaching Shakespeare at university.[1] Ralph Alan Cohen also reviews common challenges in the Shakespeare classroom, including the 'psychological blocking' he refers to as 'ShakesFear'. His book offers teaching activities for *Coriolanus*.[2]

If educators sometimes find Shakespeare to be a hard sell in the classroom, one of his most challenging plays may be *Coriolanus*. Vickers describes it as 'a long and complex play' and 'the most misjudged of the major tragedies'.[3] Graham Holderness observes that it is generally considered the most 'difficult and intractable' of Shakespeare's Roman plays.[4] Peter Holland writes of the ease with which we can collapse the challenges of the play and its eponymous protagonist:

> Intransigent, intractable, often difficult to love, sometimes difficult to like – it is striking how often words and phrases that might aptly describe Coriolanus also fit *Coriolanus*. There are times when the play can feel as contemptuous of its audiences as Caius Martius does of the citizens in Rome.[5]

These sentiments are reiterated by Cohen, for whom the 'otherness' of *Coriolanus* exceeds all of Shakespeare's plays:

> *Coriolanus* is not a lovable play, largely because Coriolanus (first Caius Martius) is not a lovable man. ... But even beyond its proudly unpopular title character, the play itself resists the affection of an audience, as though an audience senses – as it should – that Coriolanus's contempt for the people extends to them.[6]

The challenges of *Coriolanus* in a pedagogical context are also echoed in responses to its inclusion as a prescribed text in the 2016 South African Independent Examinations Board curriculum. Sarah Roberts notes that, on the surface, it appears 'austerely inaccessible and remote' from the learners' context.[7] For Tanya van der Walt, while *Coriolanus* offers 'learning opportunities' and parallels to contemporary South African politics, it is 'by no means an easy play, and in many ways it defies definition or categorisation'.[8]

If *Coriolanus* is such a challenging play, then where do we start? How might we approach this resistant text in our classrooms?

Editions and productions

Editions

The Arden Third Series, the Oxford World's Classics, the New Cambridge Shakespeare and the Penguin Classics Shakespeare Series offer accessible, scholarly and relatively inexpensive editions for undergraduate study. *The New Oxford Shakespeare* and *The Norton Shakespeare* provide newly edited versions of *Coriolanus* and valuable editorial content in their respective Complete Works. For open-access digital versions: the Folger Shakespeare Library edition is downloadable and offers a synopsis, textual introduction, quick-jump and search functionality; Internet Shakespeare Editions provides an original-spelling transcription of the 1623 First Folio text; and Spark Notes's 'No Fear Shakespeare' gives side-by-side original text and modern translation. Various audio versions of the play are available via Audible.

Productions

In addition to accessing a DVD or Blu-ray copy of the 2011 film, Ralph Fiennes's *Coriolanus* is available to rent or buy on YouTube and Google Play Movies. The Royal

Shakespeare Company's 2017 production (directed by Angus Jackson) is available on DVD, with some open-access resources available online via the RSC website. Shakespeare's Globe does not at present offer a recording of an English language production, but the Globe Player website includes a Japanese production (directed by Motoi Miura) which was performed at the Globe in 2012 as part of the Globe to Globe Festival. You can rent a recording of Stephen Berkoff's 1997 production of *Coriolanus* through Digital Theatre. The 1984 BBC Shakespeare version of *Coriolanus* (directed by Elijah Moshinsky) is available on DVD. In 1963 the BBC broadcast a nine-part television series, *The Spread of the Eagle*, which incorporated *Coriolanus*, *Julius Caesar* and *Antony and Cleopatra*.[9] The 2013 Donmar Warehouse production, directed by Josie Rourke and starring Tom Hiddleston, was broadcast by National Theatre (NT) Live in 2014. Currently on YouTube you can access a trailer and unofficial paratextual material. Peter Kirwan's review and Michael D. Friedman's 2016 article are useful resources on the Rourke production. Some *Coriolanus* performances are available on the Norton Shakespeare YouTube channel.

Enter via the belly

A good starting point for teaching *Coriolanus* is the 'pretty tale' (1.1.85) known as the 'Fable of the Belly' (1.1.91–158). This exchange encapsulates many of the play's – and the period's – central concerns, showcasing how '*Coriolanus* teems with the language of the body politic'.[10] An initial discussion of the belly fable can bring to the fore the centrality of the body politic, the representation of bodies onstage, and the play's socio-political structure. A staged reading of this exchange – with its extended metaphor, the characterization of the citizens, the tone of Menenius and the entry of Coriolanus – sets up a useful map of the political landscape which students can use to navigate the play.

When staging this scene in a first lesson with undergraduate students, discussion may include the following topics.

1. Analysis of the opening scene's stage directions. Ask students to determine how many citizens are needed onstage and coordinate the details of their representation.

2. Consider whether the First Citizen represents the voice of all citizens onstage; are they a 'hive mind' or a group of individuals? Ask students to locate precise points where we can observe the effect of Menenius's words on the citizens. Consider how the other citizens react to Menenius's 'great toe' insult (1.1.150); this may be a moment when the 'many' are divided into parts by Menenius's rhetoric.

3. The staging of Menenius's physical position in relation to the citizens raises questions about shifts in power dynamics and the representation of these shifts through the movement of bodies onstage. While staging can appear simple when discussed hypothetically, it quickly becomes complex when enacted. My students decided to demonstrate the power of Menenius's rhetoric over the citizens by having them move closer to him as he spoke. However, the effect of this when staged was quite the reverse – the citizens seemed menacing, and Menenius appeared vulnerable and outnumbered. This reminded students that staging can powerfully alter the audience's perception of a scene, and that language and staging have a complex relationship which needs thoughtful articulation through play and experimentation.

4. Discuss the play's interest in representations of the body. As Holland writes, 'no Shakespeare play since *Richard III* had so insistently brought the title-character's body into view'.[11] You may like to raise Zvi Jagendorf's question with your students, and consider: 'Why is the presence of the body and the impression of the body's

language so prominent in this play?'[12] This encourages students to identify how bodies are represented onstage, and to find references to the body in the play's language. Students could be asked to create categories of 'body language' references in the text. This would enable you to shift the discussion from the body politic to Volumnia and Virgilia's discussion of the warrior's body (1.3.1–44), and Coriolanus's reluctance to reveal his wounds (2.2.135–49; 2.3.75–6, 104–8). Students can look for moments where the language shifts between literal and figurative references to the body and its belly (for example, Menenius advises the citizens to 'digest things rightly' [1.1.145]). This is useful for identifying Shakespeare's sophisticated play with metaphor. You may like to ask students to consider how, in Simon Palfrey's words, Shakespeare's metaphors 'do far more than dress an already apparent world. Without them, there is no world'.[13] For Palfrey, metaphors operate as 'little stages' containing their own stories.

5. Staging the entry of Coriolanus and his spatial positioning in relation to Menenius and the citizens stimulates rich discussion. A close reading of Coriolanus's language in his opening speech (1.1.162–83) offers an interesting comparison to the previous dialogue and enables consideration of the relationship between the tone, imagery and meaning of Coriolanus's language. The metaphorically dense speech features a catalogue of rich, paradoxical images, such as the chiasmic 'the coal of fire upon the ice, / Or hailstone in the sun' (1.1.168–9). Students could isolate Coriolanus's metaphors in this passage and consider their relevance to the citizens.

6. The belly fable can be historicized by comparing Shakespeare's text with his sources.[14] Historical discussion may also illuminate what Andrew Gurr calls the 'anomalies' and 'unfitness of the body-politic concept' for early modern England under King James.[15]

7 Students could be asked to map out the socio-political world of *Coriolanus* using the metaphor of the body. How would they divide up Shakespeare's Rome using this image? Does this metaphorical map need to change during the course of the play? Stimulus questions might include the following. Is the body politic gendered? Where does Coriolanus sit in the body politic metaphor? How are Aufidius and the Volscians incorporated? Is the body healthy, and where do we see references to disease and injury? What should become apparent is that the map alters depending on perspective; for Coriolanus, the citizens are less likely to be imagined as a part (even a toe), and more likely to be identified as a disease plaguing the Roman body. For Sicinius and Brutus, Coriolanus himself is the diseased limb to be amputated from the body or a contagion-bearer to be contained (3.1.296–312).

By entering the play via the Fable of the Belly, students will be able to grasp the key relationships and tensions that drive the narrative, as well as core thematic interests (the one and the many; the body politic; tropes of plague and disease; the space of the city; political rhetoric; the politics of early modern England).

For helpful analyses of the belly fable, readers should consult works by Andrew Gurr (1975), Nate Eastman, Alex Garganigo and Arthur Riss in the Bibliography. Useful primary resources like 'The belly fable in Camden's *Remains Concerning Britain* (1605)' can be found online through the British Library's Discovering Literature pages.

Complex *Coriolanus*: pedagogy and complexity theory

Menenius's belly fable presents Rome's socio-political system as a biological system. We could call this a systems-based approach to political rhetoric. The belly fable and the teaching of *Coriolanus* itself can be viewed through the lens of a systems theory which is increasingly prominent in pedagogy: complexity theory.

Complexivist approaches to pedagogy can enhance teaching and learning practice generally and offer novel ways to engage with *Coriolanus* in the classroom. As Deborah Osberg and Gert Biesta observe, '[m]any educationalists have found complexity theory helpful for describing, characterizing and understanding the dynamics of education differently'.[16] For examples of its use in pedagogy, see Brent Davis and Dennis Sumara's book and Mark Mason's edited collection in the Bibliography.

Complexity theory is increasingly utilized in fields including economics, physical and social sciences, politics and health.[17] The theory examines complex systems which do not have leaders; they are created, sustained and managed by the interaction of many parts. The human body is an example of a complex system, comprising nested parts which include other systems (like the human brain). Because of this self-organizing structure, no single part can control or even completely grasp the whole system.[18] A complex system is

> a *distributed knowledge* system, in which knowledge is not centrally located in a command-and-control centre or the property of a limited set of agents (e.g. senior managers); rather it is dispersed, shared and circulated throughout the organisation and its members.[19]

Through this theoretical lens, Menenius's claims become incompatible with the reality of the human body. The human body and the Roman socio-political system are not seamlessly managed by a 'command-and-control centre'. As Darcy Wudel notes, Rome's ruling class 'is not always capable of acting in a coordinated fashion'; despite espousing a top-down, linear model of leadership and control, the Rome of Shakespeare's *Coriolanus* actually functions in a more complex manner.[20] But Menenius asserts that only the belly has a complete view of the body; the other body parts 'cannot / See what I do deliver out to each' (1.1.137–8). The belly knows best, and it will decide when and where food will be distributed 'through the rivers of your blood', from the heart to the 'small inferior veins' (1.1.130–3).

Menenius's understanding of top-down control is shared by our educational systems, which often reduce complexity to minimize unpredictability and enhance controllability.[21] But complexity theory takes a different approach to understanding relationships between system parts: it focuses on the generative nature of self-organizing interactions. Complexivist approaches to learning aim to enhance dynamism, unpredictability and creativity. In order to encourage complexity within educational processes, Liam Semler proposes the creation of 'ardenspaces', which are pedagogical scenarios or experiments designed to provoke more creative and generative learning experiences than rigid educational systems might normally allow.[22] The following complexivist approach to teaching *Coriolanus* is designed to encourage students to identify connections and perturbations in the text, as both can lead to pedagogically fertile 'ardenspaces'.

Connections and perturbations in *Coriolanus*

Complexity theory's emphasis on the importance of interactions can direct our approach to teaching *Coriolanus*. A key trait of complex systems is connectedness.[23] Coriolanus, however, refuses to support the connections that maintain his socio-political system. He resists the 'internal communication and connectedness'[24] embodied in rituals like asking for the people's voice. Even in battle he is 'alone', a word that 'resonates throughout Shakespeare's play' because 'the key word for Coriolanus is isolation'.[25] According to Catherine Lisak, '[c]ritics regularly bring to our notice the many ways in which *Coriolanus* sets out to isolate its hero, even from his own sense of humanity'.[26] Coriolanus's struggle with connection is evident even at a linguistic level. Robert N. Watson writes that Coriolanus 'uses language to break rather than build connections' and Cathy Shrank notes that he 'fails to connect semantically with those around him'.[27]

A complexivist approach to *Coriolanus* encourages students to focus on mapping these connections and disconnections across the course of the play. This might include investigations of the ways in which Coriolanus and other characters sustain or resist connections and interactions among their social, familial, political, civic and martial structures and communities. One example is what Holland calls the play's 'interconnection of the thinking of mother and son'.[28] The deep, psychophysical, bilateral interconnectivity of Coriolanus and Aufidius is also central to the play. Students should note how their intimate enmity builds well before their first onstage encounter (1.1.223–31; 1.2.34–6). Crucial scenes for examining the connection between Coriolanus and Aufidius include their first staged fight (1.8) – although we know from Aufidius that this is not their first encounter (1.10.7–8) – and Coriolanus's meeting with Aufidius in Antium (4.5.52–149). A third key connection is Coriolanus's relationship with representatives of the patrician class, such as Menenius. Students could compare the first and last interactions between Coriolanus and Menenius: both of which begin with 'What's the matter?' (1.1.159; 5.2.59). Students can also investigate the connections and disconnections between Coriolanus and his soldiers. A rich contrast is provided by looking at two of Caius Martius's speeches to the Roman soldiers: his curse of Roman cowardice before he enters Corioles (1.4.31–46), and his invitation for Cominius's men to 'follow Martius' (1.6.75) into battle against Aufidius (1.6.66–84). There is, of course, another group who interact critically with Coriolanus: the citizens. Tracing the interactions between the plebeians and Coriolanus is central to interpreting the play's interest in complex connections. Shakespeare's Coriolanus attempts to remove the necessity of interacting with the people (2.2.134–8), and after failing to do so, the play tracks the unstable and volatile relationship between Coriolanus and the people from the 'custom' (2.2.141) of asking for the people's voices to Coriolanus's banishment (3.3.106). To investigate the turbulent, dynamic interactions between Coriolanus, the tribunes and the citizens, students should carefully follow the action across five scenes: 2.2 (the appointment of Coriolanus as consul by the senate); 2.3 (the custom of asking for the people's voices and Coriolanus's admittance as consul by the people, followed by Sicinius's and Brutus's reversal of that decision); 3.1 (the conflict between Coriolanus and the tribunes, which leads to a physical altercation); 3.2 (Coriolanus is persuaded to 'return and mend' his relationship with the citizens [3.2.27]); and 3.3 (which repeats the pattern of Coriolanus's failure to connect with the citizens, leading to his banishment). Focusing on these patterns of interactions should illustrate the precariousness and volatility of the relationships.

In examining these series of connections and disconnections between Coriolanus and those around him, students may detect a paradoxical pattern of acceptance and rejection, intimacy and alienation, stability and volatility. This is crucial for a complexivist approach to the play, because in addition to prioritizing interactions over a focus on individual parts, complexity theory also recognizes the value of turbulence. In a complex system, disorder and perturbations generate vital change, moving systems into new modes of interactions.[29] Identifying moments when specific interactions generate instabilities and change in *Coriolanus*'s socio-political systems can be a valuable way of analysing the play. When examining the lead-up to Coriolanus's banishment (2.2–3.3), ask students to consider which agents are stabilizing influences and which are generating perturbations or turbulence (and further, consider the benefits and limitations of promoting stability or turbulence). Look for stabilizing and destabilizing characters, events, moments and even words. The naming of Coriolanus as a 'traitor' (3.3.65-6) shows how a single word generates a disproportionately significant reaction; the word is a catalyst for Coriolanus's final banishment. Tracking these moments of perturbations may also reveal to students the play's unusual 'architecture'; *Coriolanus* 'inverts' the normal structure of histories and tragedies that feature stage combat, by placing 'the big battle and the kinetic energy' at the start of the play.[30]

In order to foster ardenspaces of 'creative interactivity' in our *Coriolanus* classrooms, students could also reimagine alternative connections or disconnections within the world of *Coriolanus*. For example, how might one imagine a meeting between Virgilia and Aufidius? What would change if Brutus and Sicinius were no longer in alliance? How might Volumnia respond to the Roman soldiers at Corioles? Hypothetical interconnections or disconnections may develop students' understanding of the characterization and complex interactions at work in the play.

Students could also visually map the interactions between the complex parts of *Coriolanus* using digital tools (see 'Digital technologies' section below). This focus encourages students to identify the stable and chaotic interactions that shape the domestic, political and military systems of *Coriolanus*'s world.

Historicist and presentist approaches

Using history in the classroom

The importance of turbulence for system development is also pertinent to historicist approaches to *Coriolanus*. There are plenty of early modern socio-political perturbations whose effects can be detected in *Coriolanus*, including:

> the earl of Essex and Sir Walter Ralegh, the Midlands Grain Riots, abstract constitutional debates about king, Parliament, and Parliamentary selection, London city politics, the plantation of Ireland, and Prince Henry's militant Protestantism.[31]

To incorporate discussion of Shakespeare's historical sources for *Coriolanus* into your classes, you may wish to use Thomas North's translation of Plutarch's *Lives of the Noble Greeks and Romans*. Cohen provides a teaching activity comparing Shakespeare with this key source.[32] If you do not have institutional access to Early English Books Online (EEBO), you can access North's translation freely via the Online Library of Liberty (extracts are also provided in R. B. Parker's Oxford World's Classics edition).

You may wish to consider an alternative way of historicizing *Coriolanus*, as Andrew Hadfield does in disrupting 'the perceived need to read the plays in terms of familiar generic types' by removing *Coriolanus* from its traditional clustering among the 'Roman plays'.[33]

To assist students in understanding the possible connotations of the name 'Coriolanus' for an early modern audience, it is useful to incorporate William Barlow's 1601 *Sermon* preached after the Earl of Essex's execution. This sermon makes clear what Holland describes as a perceived 'parallel' between Coriolanus and the Earl of Essex.[34] Ask students to draw out and interrogate possible correlations between the two figures and consider what shared traits may be highlighted (or omitted) in the play-text.

To make tangible and real the language of famine, dearth, riot and revolt in *Coriolanus*, it is useful to share with students the context of the 1607 Midlands Revolt (or Rising). Students could be divided into groups to examine primary materials such as the 'Declaration of the Diggers of Warwickshire', the letter from the Earl of Shrewsbury to his brother, the depiction of the Revolt in Stow's *Annals* and the 1607 Royal Proclamation concerning the Revolt (all available online through the British Library's Discovering Literature *Coriolanus* page). In groups, ask students to identify the objective of the writer/s, to pull out keywords and phrases and to identify tone and any perceived bias. Then, as a class, compare the vocabularies, tones and objectives of the documents. What are the similarities and discrepancies? Educators may wish to parallel this discussion with a presentist exercise where students are asked to collect different sources of information (official government announcements, media articles, personal commentaries) on a specific recent event or issue. This may assist students to understand the complexities of the sources for the Midlands Revolt.

Plague is always a crowd pleaser in the classroom, and although the play does not include an actual instance of plague, it features repeatedly in *Coriolanus*'s rhetoric of disease. In his insightful chapter on *Coriolanus* and plague literature in early modern London, Ian Munro writes of 'the hidden plague of *Coriolanus*'.[35] As a disease fostered by crowds, the play's plague discourse is importantly connected to its representation of the city and its people.[36] Thus the play 'is full of the horror of the urban body, in both its particular and collective forms'.[37] Plague also functions as 'one of the most shocking metaphors for political crisis'.[38] Incorporating plague writers like Thomas Dekker into classroom discussions of *Coriolanus* can draw attention to the play's disease imagery (1.1.160–1; 1.4.31–5) and construction of the public, while deepening students' knowledge of early-seventeenth-century London. Dekker and Middleton's *News from Gravesend* (1604) and James I's *Plague Orders* (1603) are useful parallel texts.

Finally, the estimated date of composition and first performance for *Coriolanus* makes pertinent an important development for Shakespeare's company: the use of the private, indoor, Blackfriars Theatre, 'the first-purpose-built (or refitted) indoor theatre in the English-speaking world and the most profitable early modern theatre during England's biggest boom in playmaking'.[39] For a play explicitly concerned with the conflict between the private individual and vocal public, there are important connections to be made with the possibilities of staging *Coriolanus* at Blackfriars, which the King's Men started to utilize from 1608.[40] As an indoor playhouse, Blackfriars was significantly smaller than outdoor stages like the Globe (Gurr gives Blackfriars's interior dimensions as 66 feet or 20.1 metres by 46 feet or 14 metres).[41] Unlike the Globe, the most expensive seats were closest to the stage. The stage was most likely smaller and busier than outdoor playhouses, in part because spectators could pay to occupy stools on the stage, making the acting space 'cramped' and producing 'an intimacy that the open-air stages never enjoyed'.[42] This is significant for a play whose protagonist struggles so much in social situations. Of course, one of the other notable differences in indoor theatres is the use of artificial lighting.

> Taken together the distinguishing characteristics of the second Blackfriars – its historic and royal associations, its tiered and crowded volume, its mixture of real light and candlelight, its interludes with their alternative entertainments, its intermingling on stage of actors and audience, its narrowed demographic – made for an unprecedented interpenetration of the fictive and the social worlds.[43]

Consideration of the practicalities of *Coriolanus*'s theatrical context could prove illuminating. Students could be asked to stage a scene such as Caius Martius's storming of Corioles (1.4.23–66) in both an indoor and outdoor early modern theatre space. This scene requires students to think carefully about audience location (at Blackfriars, some spectators will sit onstage), representing large bodies of people (such as '*the army of the Volsces*' – 1.4.23 SD), music and sound effects (there are multiple 'alarums'), props and costuming (Martius re-enters '*bleeding*' at 1.4.65 SD), and managing entries and exits ('*the gates*' must be opened and closed – 1.4.43, 46, 48 SD). For advice on turning the classroom into an Elizabethan theatre, see Cohen.[44]

Using the present in the classroom

Holderness believes that *Coriolanus* is 'very much a play for today'.[45] Kate Wilkinson writes that '[t]opical allusions to politics at the time of production have been a key aspect of the performance history of *Coriolanus* since its inception'.⁴⁶ A presentist approach to the study of *Coriolanus* encourages educators and students to recognize that, as Hugh Grady and Terence Hawkes articulate, 'the questions we ask' of the play will 'inevitably be shaped by our own concerns'.⁴⁷ Wilkinson explores the play's 'engagement with the social and political contexts of the time of production', most notably through a comparison with the 2011 Occupy movement.⁴⁸ The challenge with such presentist approaches is that they can become quickly dated: when I used the Occupy movement as a presentist parallel in my *Coriolanus* classroom in 2019, it was necessary first to introduce my students to the movement itself. The more recent Extinction Rebellion (XR) movement may offer a timelier parallel. This movement's UK base makes three demands to government: to 'tell the truth' by declaring a climate emergency; to act now to halt 'biodiversity loss' and reduce greenhouse gas emissions to zero by 2025; and to move 'beyond politics' by creating a 'Citizens' Assembly'.⁴⁹ The third demand in particular echoes the citizens' concerns in *Coriolanus* via XR's concerns about potential food shortages due to climate change, as well as its advocacy for the 'Citizens' Assembly' which 'will bring together ordinary people to investigate, discuss and make recommendations on how to respond to the climate emergency'.⁵⁰ Students could investigate and discuss the structure of the XR movement and its conceptualization of 'citizens', comparing the representation of the citizens in *Coriolanus* and in contemporary public discourse around climate change. Another presentist example is Chris Thurman's 'Shakespeare and the ANC [African National Congress]' module which mapped the ANC's intellectual history 'through the Shakespearean engagements of various key figures in the movement', including past president Thabo Mbeki and *Coriolanus*.⁵¹ Discussion considered the question: 'Can Coriolanus be black?'⁵² For Thurman, this approach raised questions about 'the apparent incompatibility of an approach to Shakespeare that is politically progressive ... and one that is pedagogically practical'.⁵³ For students less familiar with Shakespeare, 'a basic understanding of the plays' may be needed before framing the texts through a political and ideological lens.[54]

Themes

Politics

Robin Headlam Wells argues that '*Coriolanus* is Shakespeare's most political play'.[55] Alongside language, Shrank identifies politics as one of 'two recurrent concerns of criticism on *Coriolanus*'.[56] Stephen Greenblatt describes the play's machinations as 'a lesson in bare-knuckles politics, as Shakespeare understood it'.[57] For Jagendorf, '[a]lthough Coriolanus may be one of Shakespeare's most politically naïve characters, he is the protagonist of a play that is hugely, indeed grotesquely, political'.[58] This umbrella term, 'politics', is almost too broad to be useful, comprising anything from early modern politics to the politicizing of Shakespeare 'as a cultural currency'.[59] Further, *Coriolanus* is well recognized for its protean ability to operate as ideological support for conflicting political views. Holderness sums this up neatly:

> The clash of political philosophies within the play – despotic and democratic, authoritarian and libertarian, aristocratic and republican – has strongly attracted adaptors from both extremes of the political spectrum. In the 1930s, German, French, and Italian fascists mined the play for its anti-democratic tendencies, its apparent contempt for liberal democracy, its celebration of the martial heroism of a fearless leader. A German school text of the 1930s drew an admiring parallel between Coriolanus and Hitler. But the play was equally attractive to communists such as Bertolt Brecht, who adapted the play as a model for popular revolt against military dictatorship and political corruption.[60]

The concept of leadership offers a way to centre a political reading of *Coriolanus*. Roberts suggests that '[o]ne strategy for pursuing the contemporary resonance of Shakespeare's play for young readers and scholars is to pursue the motif of dispersed leadership'.[61] John O. Whitney and Tina Packer discuss *Coriolanus* in relationship to business, leadership and shifting power.[62] Students could investigate models of political leadership in private spheres, domestic and international politics. Students can also be invited to problematize differentiations between the concepts of the 'leader' and the 'hero'.[63] Cominius's public acknowledgement of 'the deeds of Coriolanus' (2.2.80–120) is an ideal passage to explore representations of leadership and heroism. The dense 'report' (2.2.42) of Coriolanus's military achievements builds to the image of the warrior as 'a thing of blood' (2.2.107).

The teacher, bringing *Coriolanus* into the classroom, may at times feel that they are the 'one' against the 'many'. Munro writes that *Coriolanus* is famously a play about the one and the many and Watson observes that 'the word "one" appears more often in *Coriolanus* than in any of Shakespeare's earlier plays'.[64]

There are many ways of interpreting this trope within *Coriolanus*. Most clearly, it embodies the play's 'two protagonists': Coriolanus and the 'hydra'-like public (3.1.94).[65] Studying *Coriolanus*, according to Roberts, almost 'compels' a 'formative engagement with individual and collective positions and responsibilities'.[66] This raises related topics around individual subjectivity, self and identity, and representations of social groups. For Marjorie Garber, 'the play continually returns to this problematic term, "self"'.[67]

Thinking about the world of the play through the lens of this concept of the 'one and the many' also highlights the ways in which *Coriolanus* is fascinated by fragmentation.[68] This includes the multifaceted or fragmented nature of Coriolanus's characterization. Vickers identifies 'four main images of Coriolanus' as part of his 'multifocal' teaching approach: the patricians' image; the people's image; Volumnia's image; and Aufidius's image. He uses these four images as the basis for an in-class activity:

This is an exercise which can be fruitfully done by dividing a class up into groups and having them place themselves in each perspective. I have sometimes found it necessary to have a central group not involved in this project who can detect when the others begin to identify with their perspective, thus losing the self-awareness needed to criticize it.[69]

This activity enables students to recognize that identifying the 'one' as opposed to the 'many' is entirely a question of perspective.

Language

Coriolanus has a 'problematic attitude' to speech and language.[70] Shrank notes that the play itself is sometimes understood to contain 'a "crisis", "failure", "revolt", or "disturbance" of language'.[71]

When discussing the rhetoric of *Coriolanus*, students can consider the effectiveness of language in terms of achieving the perceived goals of the characters. How is language used to achieve character objectives, and when does it succeed and fail? I divide my tutorial into groups, giving each group a character and asking them to discuss the following questions and present their answers to the class:

(a) what does your character want?
(b) what are some notable features of their language?
(c) how would you direct an actor playing your character?

It becomes clear that character objectives are more complex than first assumed, and for some characters may alter across the course of the play.

To introduce students to the language of *Coriolanus*, there are several useful general resources. Jeremy Lopez's *Introduction to Reading Shakespeare* highlights important moments like the 'vivid original stage direction', '*Holds her by the hand, silent*' (5.3.182 SD). Lopez analyses Shakespeare's plays by segmenting the language into structural units; from stage directions to first words. Useful (although brief) attention is paid to the 'first words' of Coriolanus; the strangely abrupt 'Thanks' (1.1.159) tends to draw students' attention and even awkward laughter.[72] Students could also examine the first and last words of other characters in the play.

For an activity that encourages students to connect language and staging, focus on the play's 'visual language' and its preoccupation with clothing, which for Jean MacIntyre 'becomes part of the "plot", not just part of the "thought"'.[73] How might students imagine and depict the hat and the '*gown of humility*' (2.3.38 SD)? Learning activities could include a comparison of production costuming choices and the creation of students' own designs.

For other general introductions to Shakespeare's language, useful texts include Adamson et al.'s *Reading Shakespeare's Dramatic Language* – which offers a brief discussion of grammar in *Coriolanus* in relation to 'may' and 'shall' – and Palfrey's *Doing Shakespeare*. For a specific example connecting grammar and political intent, see Margaret Sinclair's article in the Bibliography.

Gender and queer theory

John Garrison writes that '[s]cholars have found Shakespeare's *Coriolanus* (1608) to be highly generative of a variety of queer readings'.[74] Friedman puts it more succinctly: '*Coriolanus* is queer.'[75] For readings on *Coriolanus* and queer theory, see the works by Friedman and Menon in the Bibliography. For an introduction to gender studies and queer theory, see Lisa Hopkins.

I have found that students can be quick to turn on Volumnia. To deepen and enrich their evaluations of Coriolanus's mother, Coppélia Kahn's chapter on Volumnia is an essential starting point.[76] Especially useful is Kahn's historicized account of Roman mothers. For close reading, Volumnia and Virgilia's encounter with the tribunes (4.2.8–53) situates the women in a fascinating public confrontation and raises questions about what constitutes 'mankind' (4.2.16).

Representations of masculinity can be explored through resources including Joo Young Dittmann's examination of how *Coriolanus*, through the eponymous character's fall, 'subjects the early modern ideal of masculinity to intense critical scrutiny'.[77] Kent R. Lehnhof explores the 'links between Coriolanus's antiperformative zeal and his ultra-masculine identity'.[78]

Emily Griffiths Jones highlights the remarkable under-acknowledgement of what she terms 'striking correspondences between psychosexual and political or economic approaches' to the play, arguing that 'scholarship on *Coriolanus* has done little to contend with the pervasive interweaving of socioeconomic and sexual discourses, both throughout the play and in Shakespeare's England'.[79]

Digital technologies in the *Coriolanus* classroom

The incorporation of digital technologies and resources into the *Coriolanus* classroom is commonplace at a time when many students are 'digital natives' and we are faced with an 'immense number of competing electronic resources'.[80] However, this is not to ignore the 'global digital divide': Chris Thurman writes that in 2017 only 10 per cent of South African households had home internet access.[81]

Christie Carson and Peter Kirwan argue that 'Shakespeare studies in the digital age is significantly and specifically different to its previous incarnations'.[82] When pondering a digital humanities approach, Jeremy Ehrlich advises that we should start by 'thinking of the desired learning we hope to see in our students' and then identify appropriate digital 'tools' (which he privileges for facilitating active participation over digital 'materials' that risk 'user passivity').[83] The following resources are divided into 'tools' and 'materials'.

Tools for close reading and collaboration

Close reading is 'one of the deepest (and most rewarding) relationships between the text and the reader', according to Ayanna Thompson and Laura Turchi.[84] Not only is this skill essential for Shakespeare studies, it is 'necessary in most fields and careers'.[85] They argue that many of our 'twenty-first-century learners' are already practising close reading skills in 'informal learning communities', including 'virtual landscapes'.[86] If students are more adept at close reading their virtual landscapes, then adopting a virtual tool for close reading a play like *Coriolanus* may enhance their Shakespeare analyses. One way to combine digital technologies and close reading is through an annotation tool like Hypothesis. The website offers quick-start guides and suggestions for using digital annotation in English classes.[87] Using this, students could close read by identifying what Palfrey refers to as the 'quick sense' of *Coriolanus* as well as its 'denser' material or 'latent layering'.[88] He analyses Coriolanus's banishment speech (3.3.119–34). Other suitable passages for analysis include Coriolanus's soliloquy upon his entry into Antium (4.4.12–26), his speech to Aufidius (4.5.67–103) and Aufidius's response (4.5.103–37), Aufidius's fears about Coriolanus (4.7.28–57), and Volumnia's final persuasion of her son (5.3.94–182). In addition to close reading, students can use digital tools like StoryMap or Visual Understanding Environment (VUE) to map character interactions in the play.[89]

A second important skill for *Coriolanus* students is effective communication and collaboration with peers. With the use of digital tools like Padlet and videoconferencing technology, educators can create international collaborative classrooms. An innovative and unique example of videoconferencing pedagogy is the *Coriolanus* Online project, a 'virtual mobility project' co-run by Coventry University (UK) and the University of Tampere (Finland).[90] Using H.323 videoconferencing technology, rear projection screens so participants 'had the impression of a shared space', as well as Facebook and Adobe Connect, the project created a shared 'virtual rehearsal space' at both universities where students could work on *Coriolanus* in English and Finnish.[91]

> The scene chosen [3.3] from *Coriolanus* also allowed the opportunity to investigate the concept of the citizen in the 'mobile' age, the relationship between politicians and the people and their ability to engage in meaningful political dialogue through computer-mediated exchanges.[92]

After initially asking students to pretend they were occupying the same physical space, the *Coriolanus* Online project learned to embrace the presence of the cameras and microphones. Students became 'their own camera operators' and were encouraged to proceed as if 'Coriolanus and Cominius were communicating with the senate and the Roman mob via videoconferencing'.[93]

For the creators of the *Coriolanus* Online project, a videoconferencing pedagogic model 'opens up the possibility of new modes of learning, not just learning mediated by teachers, but also through peers in collaborative online theatre workshops conducted across the globe'.[94] The project investigated digital citizenship, developed students' 'intercultural competences and digital skills' and fostered international collaboration.[95] Sheila Cavanagh identifies similar benefits in her videoconferencing project, which connects international students in North America and India.[96]

Social media can also be incorporated within the *Coriolanus* classroom. Peter Kirwan uses Twitter in his teaching practice:

> On my advanced module, Screen Shakespeares, I teach the course partially through Twitter. Using the hashtag

#shaxfilm, students are invited to tweet their responses to the set film for the week, to share links with one another to further resources and websites and to pass around reactions. More excitingly, however, the students are surprised and delighted to discover a virtual community of other Shakespeare film enthusiasts wanting to engage with the debates being carried out in the live classes.[97]

In this module, students are assigned specific topics and contribute resources to an online 'Knowledge Hub'.[98] Through this approach, the research phase is transformed into a collaborative, crowd-sourced exercise.[99] Kirwan observes that '[c]areful deployment of digital media in this way can enhance collegiality across all ages of the pedagogic process', a sentiment echoed by Ehrlich in his identification of blogs as a tool which 'creates community'.[100] For more on social media and Shakespeare, see the 'Shakespeare and Social Media' special issue of *Borrowers and Lenders*.[101]

Digital materials

The British Library Discovering Literature web page has an extensive array of open-access materials relevant to *Coriolanus*, including Michael Dobson's introduction, Andrew Dickson's discussion of Roman values in Shakespeare's plays, and Henry Irving's annotated playscript. The RSC offers a *Coriolanus* Teacher Pack for KS3–4 students based on its 2017 production, directed by Angus Jackson. The Folger's open-access *Coriolanus* resources include an online edition of the text and an image gallery, and general teaching resources. Stratford Festival offers a digital study guide, Shakespeare Theatre provides a teacher and student resource guide (with a handy 'who's who' and hierarchical structure of Roman politics, activities and discussion questions), and you can access a downloadable TES lesson plan for the play.

Coriolanus *on film*

The 2011 film *Coriolanus* is the first film adaptation of the play.[102] There are limited options for sourcing other recorded adaptations (see 'Editions and productions' above), so it is likely that Fiennes's film will be the most accessible for educators and students (with online teaching guides from Film Education and Shakespeare on Film available). As an alternative, incorporating theatre reviews is a rich, illuminating means by which to bring a sense of the theatricality of the play into the classroom. Asking students to source and compare reviews of specific productions (such as Josie Rourke's 2013 Donmar Warehouse production) makes for a productive learning activity.

If incorporating the Fiennes film into your class, you may like to point your students' attention to its many textual changes. First, Fiennes makes Caius Martius 'a military commander who seems nominally in charge of the police' rather than 'a warrior patrician whose role is that of taking on external enemies, not policing internal domestic politics'.[103] Second, students will quickly pick up on the altered fate of Menenius; his suicide in the 2011 film means that Coriolanus is no longer the only character to die in the play. Third, the film makes significant use of modern media technologies: discussion could centre on the use of news media in the narrative, and the 'mixture of television and film techniques of representation, such as the handheld camera'.[104] A fourth important textual change is the film's ending. In the text, Coriolanus is killed by '*conspirators*' on Aufidius's orders (5.6.131 SD). In the film, while the Volscian men do attack Coriolanus, it is Aufidius who 'delivers the oh-so-tender death blow with his dagger, in total silence. There is no "Kill! Kill!" as in the text, and there is no further dialogue.'[105] For Fiennes's alternative ending to the film, which gives far more prominence to Volumnia, see Friedman.[106]

A study of the 2011 film alongside other contemporary films featuring what Holderness calls 'the Coriolanus myth' makes for an engaging presentist pedagogical approach. Two films which are also invested in 'the Coriolanus myth' – a 'contemporary realisation of the classic man of war' – are *The Hurt Locker* (2008) and *Skyfall* (2012).[107] Students could compare these films and look for other examples of the myth in popular culture (for example, a recent article compares the play to *The Hunger Games*).[108]

NOTES

Introduction

1 All quotations from *Coriolanus* in this book are from Peter Holland's edition for the Arden Shakespeare, Third Series (London: Bloomsbury, 2013). References to other Shakespeare plays are to the Arden Shakespeare editions unless otherwise indicated. I thank William Walker and Beverley Sherry for their guidance as I wrote this Introduction.

2 In terms of word length, *Coriolanus* falls well short of Shakespeare's longest plays *Hamlet* (in Q2 or Folio) and *Richard III* (Folio) (which are first and second, respectively), just short of *Cymbeline* (Folio) (third) and just ahead of *Othello* (Folio) (fifth). I thank Hugh Craig for running the numbers for me.

3 T. S. Eliot, 'Hamlet', in *Selected Essays*, 3rd edn (London: Faber and Faber, 1951, 1961), 144.

4 Harley Granville-Barker, 'Verse and Speech in *Coriolanus*', *Review of English Studies* 23, no. 89 (1947): 9, 5.

5 Kenneth Burke, '*Coriolanus* – and the Delights of Faction', *The Hudson Review* 19, no. 2 (1966): 190.

6 Ibid., 190.

7 Ibid., 187.

8 Brian Vickers, 'Teaching *Coriolanus*: The Importance of Perspective', in *Teaching Shakespeare*, ed. Walter Edens et al. (Princeton: Princeton University Press, 1977; repr. 2015), 247. For the account of each perspective, see 247–62.

9 Ibid., 247.

10 The best account of the play's sources is found in the Introduction to Holland's edition, 25–49. Plutarch's text and other sources are reproduced in *Narrative and Dramatic*

Sources of Shakespeare, Vol. 5: The Roman Plays, ed. Geoffrey Bullough (London: Routledge and Kegan Paul, 1964; repr. 1966), 453–563. On the importance of Livy and Averell, see respectively: Anne Barton, 'Livy, Machiavelli and Shakespeare's *Coriolanus*', *Shakespeare Survey* 38 (1985): 115–29 and Kenneth Muir, 'Menenius's Fable', *Notes & Queries* 198 (1953): 240–2. On Coriolanus's debatable historicity, see Tim Cornell, 'Coriolanus: Myth, History and Performance', in *Myth, History and Culture in republican Rome: Studies in Honour of T. P. Wiseman*, ed. David Braund and Christopher Gill (Exeter: University of Exeter Press, 2003), 73–97.

11 Cynthia Marshall, 'Shakespeare, Crossing the Rubicon', *Shakespeare Survey* 53 (2000): 74–5, 80–8.

12 *Coriolanus*, ed. Holland, 33.

13 Kenneth Muir, *The Sources of Shakespeare's Plays* (New Haven: Yale University Press, 1977, 1978), 246–51.

14 See, for example: Janet Adelman, *Suffocating Mothers: Fantasies of Maternal Origin in Shakespeare's Plays, Hamlet to The Tempest* (New York: Routledge, 1992), 130–64; Stanley Cavell, '"Who does the Wolf Love?" Reading *Coriolanus*', *Representations* 3 (1983): 1–20; and Coppélia Kahn, *Roman Shakespeare: Warriors, Wounds and Women* (London and New York: Routledge, 1997), 144–59.

15 David George, 'Plutarch, Insurrection and Dearth in *Coriolanus*', *Shakespeare Survey* 53 (2000): 61.

16 Richard Wilson, 'Against the Grain: Representing the Market in *Coriolanus*', *The Seventeenth Century* 6 (1991): 111–48.

17 On these issues, see George, 'Plutarch, Insurrection'; *Coriolanus*, ed. Holland, 56–77; and Steve Hindle, 'Imagining Insurrection in Seventeenth-Century England: Representations of the Midland Rising of 1607', *History Workshop Journal* 66 (2008): 21–61.

18 Gordon Braden, 'Shakespeare's Roman Tragedies', in *A Companion to Shakespeare's Works, Volume 1: The Tragedies*, ed. Richard Dutton and Jean E. Howard (Oxford: Blackwell Publishing, 2003), 204. In addition to the scholarship noted in this paragraph, Robert S. Miola's *Shakespeare's Rome*

(Cambridge: Cambridge University Press, 1983), 164–205, provides an excellent analysis of the play.

19 Braden, 'Shakespeare's Roman Tragedies', 205–6, summarizing the view of J. L. Simmons, *Shakespeare's Pagan World: The Roman Tragedies* (Charlottesville: University of Virginia Press, 1973).

20 Braden, 'Shakespeare's Roman Tragedies', 206, summarizing and quoting the view of Geoffrey Miles, *Shakespeare and the Constant Romans* (Oxford: Clarendon, 1996).

21 Braden, 'Shakespeare's Roman Tragedies', 207, summarizing and quoting the view of Paul A. Cantor, *Shakespeare's Rome: Republic and Empire* (Ithaca, NY: Cornell University Press, 1976).

22 Braden, 'Shakespeare's Roman Tragedies', 207.

23 Ibid., 209.

24 Ibid., quoting Cantor, *Shakespeare's Rome*, 207.

25 For a survey of critical response to Coriolanus's (in)articulateness, see David George, with Thomas Clayton, Niels Herold, Megan-Marie Johnson and Ashley Spriggs (eds), *A New Variorum Edition of Shakespeare: Coriolanus*, 2 vols ed. (Accurance, 2019), 2.257–9.

26 Shakespeare, *Julius Caesar*, 3.2.74.

27 See John Porter Houston, 'Syndeton and Asyndeton in *Coriolanus*', in *Shakespearean Sentences: A Study in Style and Syntax* (Baton Rouge, LA and London: Louisiana State University Press, 1988), 159–78; Page DuBois, 'A Disturbance of Syntax at the Gates of Rome', *Stanford Literature Review* 2 (1985): 185–208; and Russ McDonald, 'The Idioms of the Late Tragedies', in *Shakespeare's Late Style* (Cambridge: Cambridge University Press, 2006, 2009), 52–66.

28 Wilbur Sanders, 'An Impossible Person: Caius Martius Coriolanus', in Wilbur Sanders and Howard Jacobson, *Shakespeare's Magnanimity: Four Tragic Heroes, Their Friends and Families* (London: Chatto and Windus, 1978), 141, 153. Silence is also a gender issue in the play as Christina Luckyj has adeptly shown in 'Volumnia's Silence', *Studies in English Literature 1500–1900* 31, no. 2 (1991): 327–42.

29 The language of the play has attracted a mass of scholarship that may be entered by consulting: Stanley Fish, *Is There a Text in this Class? The Authority of Interpretive Communities* (Cambridge, MA: Harvard University Press, 1980), 200–45; DuBois, 'A Disturbance of Syntax'; Houston, 'Syndeton and Asyndeton'; John Plotz, '*Coriolanus* and the Failure of Performatives', *ELH* 63, no. 4 (1996): 809–32; and Michael West and Myron Silberstein, 'The Controversial Eloquence of Shakespeare's Coriolanus – An Anti-Ciceronian Orator?', *Modern Philology* 102, no. 3 (2005): 307–31.

30 Plotz, 'Failure of Performatives', 816, 814.

31 Cynthia Marshall, '*Coriolanus* and the Politics of Theatrical Pleasure', in *A Companion to Shakespeare's Works, Volume 1: The Tragedies*, ed. Richard Dutton and Jean E. Howard, 464.

32 Muir, *The Sources of Shakespeare's Plays*, 251; Bullough, *Narrative and Dramatic Sources*, vol. 5, 540–1.

33 James Holstun, 'Tragic Superfluity in *Coriolanus*', *ELH* 50.3 (1983): 493, 497, 498.

34 Ibid., 504.

35 David Scott Kastan, '"A rarity most beloved": Shakespeare and the Idea of Tragedy', in *A Companion to Shakespeare's Works, Volume 1: The Tragedies*, ed. Richard Dutton and Jean E. Howard, 19.

36 Ibid., 19–20.

37 Ibid., 20

38 The astonishing range of interpretation over about 400 years is captured in David George et al.'s magisterial *A New Variorum Edition of Shakespeare:* Coriolanus.

Chapter 1

1 See Stanley D. Mackenzie on the generation of 'confusion and perplexity' that takes place in the final scene of the play, and Emma Smith on the way that the play's 'attempts to get to know Coriolanus' are continually 'rebuffed'. Stanley

D. Mackenzie, '"Unshout the noise that banish'd Martius": Structural Paradox and Dissembling in *Coriolanus*', *Shakespeare Studies* 18 (1986): 192; Emma Smith, *This is Shakespeare* (Harmondsworth: Penguin, 2019), 192.

2. Elizabeth Ann Inchbald, 'Remarks' [on *Coriolanus*], in *The British Theatre, or Collection of Plays Which Are Acted at the Theatres Royal, Drury Lane, Covent Garden, and Haymarket*, vol. 5 (London, 1808), 5. For more on Kemble's importance in the play's history, see Chapter 2, 'Performance History', by Robert Ormsby.

3. Smith, *This is Shakespeare*, 192.

4. William Hazlitt, *Characters of Shakespear's Plays*, in *The Complete Works of William Hazlitt in Twenty-One Volumes*, vol. 4, ed. P. P. Howe (London and Toronto: J.M. Dent and Sons, 1930), 217.

5. Inchbald, 'Remarks', 3–4.

6. Duncan Wu, *William Hazlitt: The First Modern Man* (Oxford: Oxford University Press, 2008), 212.

7. Hazlitt, *Characters of Shakespear's Plays*, 214.

8. Percy Bysshe Shelley, *Poetical Works*, ed. Thomas Hutchinson (Oxford: Oxford University Press, 1970), 344.

9. Hazlitt, *Characters of Shakespear's Plays*, 214. 'Arbitrary' here refers to the arbitrary rule of hereditary power, especially monarchy.

10. Ibid.

11. Jonathan Sachs, 'Republicanism: Ancient Rome and Literary Modernity in British Romanticism', in *Romans and Romantics*, ed. Timothy Saunders, Charles Martindale, Ralph Pite and Mathilde Skole (Oxford: Oxford University Press, 2012), 41.

12. Ibid., 28.

13. Stanley Cavell, *Disowning Knowledge in Seven Plays of Shakespeare* (Cambridge: Cambridge University Press, 2003), 163.

14. Cavell takes this idea from Adelman's psychoanalytic reading of the play (on which see below).

15. Cavell, *Disowning Knowledge*, 162.

16 John Dennis, *Original Letters: Familiar, Moral, and Critical* (London, 1721), 71–2.
17 Joseph Addison, *The Spectator*, num. 40 (16 April 1711).
18 Margaret Cavendish, 'Letter 123' from *CCXI Sociable Letters, written by the Thrice Noble, Illustrious, and Excellent Princess, the Lady Marchioness of Newcastle* [1664], ed. James Fitzmaurice (London: Routledge, 1997), 130.
19 John Dryden, 'Heads of an Answer to Rymer' [*c*. 1677], in *Shakespeare: The Critical Heritage*, Vol. 1: 1623–1692, ed. Brian Vickers (London: Routledge, 1974), 201.
20 Thomas Rymer, 'The Tragedies of the Last Age' [1677], in *Shakespeare: The Critical Heritage*, Vol. 1: 1623–1692, ed. Brian Vickers, 196.
21 Charles Gildon, 'Remarks on the Plays of Shakespeare' [1710], in *Shakespeare: The Critical Heritage*, Vol. 2: 1693–1733, ed. Brian Vickers, 253.
22 Samuel Johnson, 'Preface' to *The Plays of William Shakespeare in Eight Volumes* (1765), in *Shakespeare: The Critical Heritage*, Vol. 5: 1765–1774, ed. Brian Vickers (London: Routledge, 1979), 60.
23 Samuel Johnson (ed.), *The Plays of William Shakespeare*, Vol. 6 (London, 1765), 627.
24 John Dennis, *An Essay on the Genius and Writings of Shakespear: With Some Letters of Criticism to* The Spectator (London, 1712), 4.
25 Ibid., 7.
26 Ibid.
27 Ibid.
28 Lytton Strachey, *Books and Characters* (London: Chatto and Windus, 1922), 51–2. Strachey is writing about the literary scholar Walter Raleigh, not the Elizabethan courtier of the same name.
29 A. C. Bradley, *Shakespearean Tragedy: Lectures on* Hamlet, Othello, King Lear *and* Macbeth [1904] (Harmondsworth: Penguin, 1991), 25.
30 Ibid., 29.

31 A. C. Bradley, '*Coriolanus*: British Academy Lecture' (1912), in Coriolanus: *Critical Essays*, ed. David Wheeler (London: Routledge, 1995), 26. Most of Bradley's published work was originally in the form of lectures.

32 Ibid., 34.

33 Ibid.

34 Ibid., 34–5.

35 Ibid., 36.

36 Ibid., 40.

37 Inchbald, 'Remarks', 3.

38 Gildon, 'Remarks', 252.

39 Janet Adelman, *Suffocating Mothers: Fantasies of Maternal Origin in Shakespeare's Plays* (London: Routledge, 1992), 152.

40 Ibid., 146.

41 Ibid., 147.

42 Bruce Smith, *Homosexual Desire in Shakespeare's England: A Cultural Poetics* (Chicago, IL: The University of Chicago Press, 1991), 76.

43 Ibid., 35 (silently correcting Smith's erroneous phrase 'Coriolanus's speech to Aufidius'). Smith is quoting from Thomas North's 1579 translation of Plutarch's *Lives of the Noble Grecians and Romans*.

44 Paul Hammond, *Figuring Sex Between Men from Shakespeare to Rochester* (Oxford: Oxford University Press, 2002), 111.

45 Jonathan Goldberg, 'The Anus in *Coriolanus*', in *Historicism, Psychoanalysis, and Early Modern Culture*, ed. Carla Mazzio and Douglas Trevor (New York and London: Routledge, 2000), 267.

46 Ibid., 261.

47 Ibid., 268–9.

48 Jason Edwards, '*Coriolanus*: "Tell Me Not Wherein I Seem Unnatural": Queer Meditations on *Coriolanus* in the Time of War', in *Shakesqueer: A Queer Companion to the Complete Works of Shakespeare*, ed. Madhavi Menon (Durham, NC: Duke University Press, 2011), 80–8; James Kuzner, 'Unbuilding

the City: *Coriolanus* and the Birth of republican Rome', *Shakespeare Quarterly* 58 (2007): 174–99.

49 Kuzner, 'Unbuilding the City', 175.

50 Edwards, '*Coriolanus*: "Tell Me Not Wherein I Seem Unnatural"', 87.

Chapter 2

1 See Lee Bliss and Bridget Escolme, 'Introduction', in *Coriolanus* by William Shakespeare, ed. Lee Bliss (Cambridge: Cambridge University Press, 2010), 63–111; Peter Holland, 'Introduction', in *Coriolanus* by William Shakespeare, ed. Peter Holland (London: Bloomsbury, 2013), 1–141; R. B. Parker, 'Introduction', in *Coriolanus* by William Shakespeare, ed. R. B. Parker (Oxford: Oxford University Press, 1994), 86–136; John Ripley, Coriolanus *on Stage in England and America, 1609–1994* (London: Associated University Presses, 1998); and Robert Ormsby, *Coriolanus* (Manchester: Manchester University Press, 2014). The following sections of this essay employ material from my *Coriolanus* volume: '*Coriolanus* on the early modern stage' and '*Coriolanus*, the Jacobite cause and the Kemble tradition' draw on 1–27 of the monograph; 'Politics, star actors and *Coriolanus*'s "relevance" on twentieth-century stages' draws on 28–156 and 172–89 of the monograph; the paragraph on Robert Lepage's 1992–4 productions draws on 190–207 of the monograph. Many thanks to Manchester University Press for permission to reuse material from that book for this essay. I gratefully acknowledge the many archivists and theatre companies who provided material for this essay. I thank Canada's Social Sciences and Humanities Research Council for funding to support research for this essay.

2 For more on these relationships, see Parker, 'Introduction', 43–70.

3 For more on its early modern staging related to arguments in this section, see Ormsby, *Coriolanus*, 1–11.

4 See David George, '*Coriolanus* at the Blackfriars?', *Notes and Queries* 38 (1991): 489–92; Parker, 'Introduction', 86–8; Holland, 'Introduction', 71–7.

5 For a summary of this literature, see Ormsby, *Coriolanus*, 2.

6 Parker, 'Introduction', 11.

7 Ormsby, *Coriolanus*, 5.

8 Ibid., 6.

9 Oliver Arnold, *The Third Citizen: Shakespeare's Theater and the Early Modern House of Commons* (Baltimore, MD: Johns Hopkins University Press, 2007), 187. See also Ormsby, *Coriolanus*, 7.

10 Cynthia Marshall, 'Wound-man: *Coriolanus*, Gender, and the Theatrical Construction of Interiority', in *Feminist Readings of Early Modern Culture: Emerging Subjects*, ed. Valerie Traub, M. Lindsay Kaplan and Dympna Callaghan (Cambridge: Cambridge University Press, 1996), 101. See also Ormsby, *Coriolanus*, 7.

11 Ormsby, *Coriolanus*, 8.

12 Ibid., 9.

13 Ibid.

14 Coppélia Kahn, *Roman Shakespeare: Warriors, Wounds, and Women* (London and New York: Routledge, 1997), 147; Danielle Clarke, 'Renaissance Eloquence and Female Exemplarity: *Coriolanus* and the *matrona docta*', *Renaissance Studies* 28 (2014): 128–46. See also Ormsby, *Coriolanus*, 10.

15 For more on Tate's adaptation, see Ruth McGugan, *Nahum Tate and the* Coriolanus *Tradition in English Drama. With a Critical Edition of Tate's* The Ingratitude of A Common-Wealth (New York and London: Garland, 1987); Ormsby, *Coriolanus*, 11–14; Ripley, Coriolanus, 54–70.

16 Ripley, Coriolanus, 55.

17 Ormsby, *Coriolanus*, 11–12.

18 Ibid., 12–13.

19 Ibid., 13–14.

20 For more, see ibid., 14–17; Ripley, Coriolanus, 70–94.

21 Ormsby, *Coriolanus*, 14, 15–16.
22 Ibid., 15–16.
23 Ibid., 14–17.
24 Ripley, Coriolanus, 95. For more on Kemble's performances, see Ormsby, *Coriolanus*, 17–23.
25 Ormsby, *Coriolanus*, 18.
26 Ripley, Coriolanus, 96.
27 Ormsby, *Coriolanus*, 18–22.
28 Ripley, Coriolanus, 117.
29 Ormsby, *Coriolanus*, 21–3.
30 For more on these productions, see ibid., 23–7; Ripley, Coriolanus, 160–239.
31 Ripley, Coriolanus, 236–9.
32 Ormsby, *Coriolanus*, 24.
33 Ibid.
34 Ibid., 24–5.
35 Ibid., 25–6.
36 Ripley, Coriolanus, 240–69.
37 Ormsby, *Coriolanus*, 27.
38 Holland, 'Introduction', 20.
39 Felicia Hardison Londré, '*Coriolanus* and Stavisky: The Interpenetration of Art and Politics', *Theatre Research International* 11 (1986): 122.
40 Isabelle Schwartz-Gastine, '*Coriolanus* in France from 1933 to 1977: Two Extreme Interpretations', *Shakespeare and European Politics*, ed. Dirk Delabastita, Jozef De Vos and Paul Franssen (Newark: University of Delaware Press, 2008), 128.
41 Ibid.
42 Ibid., 128–9.
43 Ibid., 133.
44 Londré, '*Coriolanus*', 129.
45 Ibid., 119–23.
46 Ibid., 119–20.

47 Schwartz-Gastine, *Coriolanus*, 131.
48 Londré, *Coriolanus*, 127.
49 Ibid., 128–9.
50 Ibid., 129–30; Holland, 'Introduction', 22.
51 For more on the production, see Ormsby, *Coriolanus*, 28–45; Ripley, Coriolanus, 290–98.
52 Ripley, Coriolanus, 270.
53 Ormsby, *Coriolanus*, 30, 30–2.
54 Ibid., 28.
55 Ibid., 36–9.
56 Ibid., 40–1.
57 Ibid., 43–5.
58 For more on Brecht's adaptation, see ibid., 46–53; Ripley, Coriolanus, 307–11.
59 Ormsby, *Coriolanus*, 48.
60 Arrigo Subiotto, *Bertolt Brecht's Adaptations for the Berliner Ensemble* (London: MHRA, 1975), 150. See also Ormsby, *Coriolanus*, 48.
61 Steven Parker, *Bertolt Brecht: A Literary Life* (London: Bloomsbury, 2014), 540. See also Ormsby, *Coriolanus*, 48–51.
62 Ormsby, *Coriolanus*, 49–50.
63 Darko Suvin, *To Brecht and Beyond: Soundings in Modern Dramatology* (Brighton: Harvester, 1984), 200–1. See also Ormsby, *Coriolanus*, 51–52.
64 Ormsby, *Coriolanus*, 52–3.
65 For more on this production, see ibid., 53–65.
66 Lawrence Gunter, 'Brecht and Beyond: Shakespeare on the East German Stage', in *Foreign Shakespeare: Contemporary Performance*, ed. Dennis Kennedy (Cambridge: Cambridge University Press, 1993), 114. See also Ormsby, *Coriolanus*, 54.
67 Darko Suvin, 'Brechtian or Pseudo-Brechtian: Mystical Estrangement in the Berliner Ensemble Adaptation of *Coriolanus*', *ASSAPH Section 3: Studies in Theatre* 3 (1986): 150, 152. See also Ormsby, *Coriolanus*, 54.

68 James Smith, 'Brecht, the Berliner Ensemble, and the British Government', *New Theatre Quarterly* 22 (2006): 321. See also Ormsby, *Coriolanus*, 61.

69 Ormsby, *Coriolanus*, 62.

70 Ibid., 57.

71 Ibid., 55.

72 Ibid., 53–8.

73 Ibid., 57–61.

74 Ibid., 59–60.

75 Ibid., 61–5.

76 For more on this production, see ibid., 66–73; Ripley, Coriolanus, 311–12.

77 Ormsby, *Coriolanus*, 68–9.

78 Ibid., 69–71.

79 For more on this production, see ibid., 73–85.

80 Ibid., 73–6.

81 Ibid., 79.

82 Ibid., 80–3.

83 Ibid., 83–5.

84 See Margaret Eddershaw, *Performing Brecht: Forty Years of British Performance* (London and New York: Routledge, 1996), 1–4; Dan Rebellato, *1956 and All That* (London and New York: Routledge, 1999), 150; Maro Germanou, 'Brecht and the English Theatre', in *Brecht in Perspective*, ed. Graham Bartram and Anthony Waine (London and New York: Longman, 1982), 213. For more on these RSC productions, see Ormsby, *Coriolanus*, 86–115; Ripley, Coriolanus, 316–23.

85 Ormsby, *Coriolanus*, 86.

86 Ibid., 93–5.

87 Ibid., 97–104.

88 John Higgins, 'Hands Full for Terry Hands', *The Times*, 19 October 1977. See also Ormsby, *Coriolanus*, 106.

89 Ormsby, *Coriolanus*, 105–15.

90 For more on this production, see Kristina Bedford, Coriolanus *at the National* (London and Toronto: Associated University

Presses, 1992); Ormsby, *Coriolanus*, 140–56; Ripley, *Coriolanus*, 323–8.

91 Ormsby, *Coriolanus*, 140–4.
92 Ibid., 145–8.
93 Ibid., 148–53.
94 Ibid., 153–6.
95 For more on this production, see ibid., 172–89.
96 Mervyn Rothstein, 'Trims and New Twists for a "Coriolanus"', *New York Times*, 30 November 1988. See also Ormsby, *Coriolanus*, 176.
97 Steven Berkoff, *Free Association: An Autobiography* (London: Faber, 1996), 368.
98 Ormsby, *Coriolanus*, 177–8. See also Ormsby, *Coriolanus*, 176.
99 Ibid., 178–83.
100 Ibid., 183–7.
101 Ibid., 186–8.
102 John Simon, 'The Ignoblest Roman', *New York Magazine*, 5 December 1988, 194; Ormsby, *Coriolanus*, 188.
103 Christian M. Billing, 'The Roman Tragedies', *Shakespeare Quarterly* 61 (2010): 415–16.
104 Jozef De Vos, 'The Sweep of History: Ivo van Hove's Roman Tragedies', *Cahiers Élisabéthains* 75 (2009): 55.
105 Billing, 'The Roman', 419–20.
106 Thomas Cartelli, 'High-tech Shakespeare in a Mediatized Globe: Ivo van Hove's Roman Tragedies and the Problem of Spectatorship', in *The Oxford Handbook of Shakespeare and Performance*, ed. James C. Bulman (Oxford: Oxford University Press, 2017), 275.
107 Billing, 'The Roman', 425.
108 Ibid., 422.
109 Cartelli, 'High-tech', 271.
110 James R. Ball, 'Staging the Twitter War: Toneelgroep Amsterdam's Roman Tragedies', *TDR: The Drama Review* 57 (2013): 167.
111 Cartelli, 'High-tech', 280, 277.

112 Rafaella Marcus and David Ralf, 'Roman Tragedies at the Barbican'. Available online: http://exeuntmagazine.com/reviews/review-roman-tragedies-barbican/ (accessed 2 December 2019).

113 For more on Lepage's production, see Ormsby, *Coriolanus*, 190–207.

114 Ibid., 191.

115 See Annie, Brisset, *A Sociocritique of Translation: Theatre and Alterity in Quebec, 1968–1988*, trans. Rosalind Gill and Roger Gannon (Toronto: University of Toronto Press, 1996), 196; Susan Knutson, '"Tradaptation" dans le sens Québécois: A Word for the Future', in *Translation, Adaption, and Transformation*, ed. Laurence Raw (London and New York: Continuum, 2012), 114. See also Ormsby, *Coriolanus*, 192.

116 Ormsby, *Coriolanus*, 192–4.

117 Ibid., 193–4.

118 Ibid., 195–9.

119 Ibid., 201.

120 Ibid., 202–3.

121 Ibid., 204.

122 Ibid., 204–7.

123 Michael Dobson, 'Shakespeare Performances in England', *Shakespeare Survey* 61 (2008): 345–6.

124 Kawai Shoichiro, 'Ninagawa Yukio', in *The Routledge Companion to Director's Shakespeare*, ed. John Russell Brown (London and New York: Routledge, 2008), 270–80.

125 Ibid., 272.

126 Tomonari Kuwayama, 'Reviewing the Reception of Yukio Ninagawa's Shakespeare Productions (1999–2009) in the British and Japanese Press', *Cahiers Élisabéthains* 82 (2012): 88–91.

127 Motoi Miura, 'Coriolanus Comes Home to Kyoto'. Available online: https://www.japantimes.co.jp/culture/2013/01/23/stage/coriolanus-comes-home-to-kyoto/ (accessed 19 June 2019).

128 Motoi Miura, 'Artist Interview'. Available online: https://performingarts.jp/E/art_interview/1002/1.html (accessed 12 October 2019). See also Deana Rankin, 'Bread and Circuses: Chiten, Japan and *Coriolanus*', in *Shakespeare Beyond English:*

A Global Experiment, ed. Susan Bennett and Christie Carson (Cambridge: Cambridge University Press, 2013), 225.

129 Production details are derived from the video of the performance available from the Globe Player. Chiten Theatre Company, *Coriolanus*. Available online: https://globeplayer.tv/ (accessed 15 November 2019).

130 Susan Bennett and Christie Carson, 'Introduction: Shakespeare Beyond English', in *Shakespeare Beyond English: A Global Experiment*, ed. Susan Bennett and Christie Carson (Cambridge: Cambridge University Press, 2013), 5.

131 Rose Elfman, 'Expert Spectatorship and Intra-Audience Relationships at Globe to Globe 2012', in *Shakespeare on the Global Stage: Performance and Festivity in the Olympic Year*, ed. Paul Prescott and Erin Sullivan (London: Bloomsbury, 2015), 166–7.

132 Production details are derived from the DVD of the live performance: Royal Shakespeare Company, *Coriolanus* (London: BBC/Opus Arte, 2018).

133 Angus Jackson, 'Q&A with Coriolanus Director Angus Jackson'. Available online: https://www.rsc.org.uk/news/archive/qanda-with-angus-jackson (accessed 1 November 2019).

134 Sope Dirisu, '"Being Back at the RSC as a Professional Feels Like a Validation"'. Available online: https://www.thestage.co.uk/features/sope-dirisu-being-back-at-the-rsc-as-a-professional-feels-like-validation (accessed 25 October 2019).

135 Delia Jarrett-Macauley (ed.), *Shakespeare, Race and Performance: The Diverse Bard* (Abingdon and New York: Routledge, 2017); Jami Rogers, 'The Shakespearean Glass Ceiling: The State of Colorblind Casting in Contemporary British Theatre', *Shakespeare Bulletin* 31 (2013): 405–30; Sita Thomas, '"The Dog, the Guard, the Horses and the Maid": Diverse Casting at the Royal Shakespeare Company', *Contemporary Theatre Review* 24 (2014): 475–85.

136 Ayanna Thompson, *Passing Strange: Shakespeare, Race, and Contemporary America* (Oxford: Oxford University Press, 2011), 76–80.

137 Dirisu, '"Being Back"'.

138 Jackson, 'Q&A'.

139 Geoff Mills, 'Coriolanus at the Royal Shakespeare Theatre, Stratford upon Avon'. Available online: http://exeuntmagazine.com/reviews/review-coriolanus-royal-shakespeare-theatre-stratford-upon-avon/ (accessed 2 November 2019); Dominic Cavendish, 'A Grimy, Gory Coriolanus with Thrilling Hand-to-Hand Combat'. Available online: https://www.telegraph.co.uk/theatre/what-to-see/grimy-gory-coriolanus-thrilling-hand-to-hand-combat-review/ (accessed 19 June 2019); Neil Allan, 'Review of *Coriolanus*', *Cahiers Élisabéthains* 95 (2018): 112.

140 Thompson, *Passing*, 94.

141 Rogers, 'The Shakespearean', 418.

142 Details about the Stratford production are derived from live viewings and video of the production in the Festival's archives.

143 'Identity, Representation and Casting in Contemporary Theater'. Available online: https://www.youtube.com/watch?v=XRTrs9hH6a0 (accessed 10 June 2019).

144 Peter Taylor, 'Bringing Boring Theatre to the Masses'. Available online: https://www.therecord.com/opinion-story/8723515-bringing-boring-theatre-to-the-masses/ (accessed 20 October 2019).

Chapter 3

1 Michael Bristol, 'Lenten Butchery: Legitimization Crisis in *Coriolanus*', in *Shakespeare Reproduced: the Text in History and Ideology*, ed. Jean Howard and Marion O'Connor (London: Methuen, 1987), 207.

2 Annabel Patterson, *Shakespeare and the Popular Voice* (London: Blackwell, 1989).

3 Ibid., 127.

4 Ibid.

5 Ibid.

6 Richard Wilson, 'Against the Grain: Representing the Market in *Coriolanus*', *The Seventeenth Century* 6, no. 2 (1991): 111–48.

7   Wilson, 'Against the Grain', 111.
8   Alex Garganigo, '*Coriolanus*, the Union Controversy, and Access to the Royal Person', *SEL Studies in English Literature 1500–1900* 42, no. 2 (2002): 335–59.
9   Steve Hindle, 'Imagining Insurrection in Seventeenth-Century England: Representations of the Midland Rising of 1607', *History Workshop Journal* 66 (2008): 21–61.
10 Ibid., 24.
11 Maurice Hunt, 'The Physiology of Peace and *Coriolanus*', *The Ben Jonson Journal* 26, no. 1 (2019): 78–96. Patrick Gray advances similar arguments in *Shakespeare and the Ethics of War* (Oxford and New York: Berghahn Books, 2019), 12–13.
12 Terence Hawkes, *Meaning By Shakespeare* (London: Routledge, 1992).
13 Peter Campbell and Richard Jordan, 'Forming the Grand Strategist According to Shakespeare', *Texas National Security Review* 3, no. 1 (Winter 2019/2020): 13–33.
14 Patrick Gray and Maurice Samely, 'Shakespeare and Henri Lefebvre's "right to the city": Subjective Alienation and Mob Violence in *Coriolanus, Julius Caesar* and *2 Henry VI*', *Textual Practice* 33, no. 1 (2019): 73–98.
15 Ibid., 73.
16 Ibid., 77.
17 Ibid., 80.
18 Ibid., 86.
19 Nicholas Taylor-Collins, 'The City's Hostile Bodies: *Coriolanus*'s Rome and Carson's Belfast', *Modern Language Review* 115 (2020): 17–45.
20 Ibid., 17.
21 Ibid., 25, 18.
22 Ibid., 45.
23 Thomas Ward, '*Coriolanus* and the Voice of Cynicism', *Renaissance Drama* 47 (2019): 95–121.
24 Ibid., 96.
25 Ibid., 97–8.

26 Ibid., 120.
27 Harry Newman, '"The stamp of Martius": Commoditized Character and the Technology of Theatrical Impression in *Coriolanus*', *Renaissance Drama* 45 (2017): 41.
28 Ibid., 42.
29 Ibid.
30 Ibid., 43.
31 See 'The *Coriolanus* Myth', in my *Tales from Shakespeare: Creative Collisions* (Cambridge: Cambridge University Press, 2014) for a similar engagement with physics. For Shakespeare in new media, see Douglas Lanier, *Shakespeare and Modern Popular Culture* (Oxford: Oxford University Press, 2012).
32 Clifford Werier, 'The Hungry Meme and Political Contagion in *Coriolanus*', in *Contagion and the Shakespearean Stage*, ed. Darryl Chalk and Mary Floyd-Wilson (London: Palgrave, 2019), 191–211.
33 Richard Dawkins, qtd in Werier, 'The Hungry Meme', 193.
34 Ibid., 191.
35 Ibid.
36 Ibid., 196.
37 Ibid.
38 Ibid., 201.
39 Ibid., 194.
40 Janet Adelman, *Suffocating Mothers: Fantasies of Maternal Origin in Shakespeare's Plays*, Hamlet to The Tempest (New York: Routledge, 1992).
41 Janet, Adelman, '"Anger's my Meat": Feeding, Dependency and Aggression in *Coriolanus*', in *Shakespeare: Pattern of Excelling Nature*, ed. David Bevington and Jay Halio (Newark, DE: University of Delaware Press, 1978), 108–24.
42 Adelman, *Suffocating Mothers*, 4.
43 Ibid., 17.
44 Ibid., 146.
45 Ibid., 162.

46 Coppélia Kahn, 'The Milking Babe and the Bloody Man in *Coriolanus* and *Macbeth*', in *Man's Estate: Masculine Identity in Shakespeare* (Berkeley, CA: University of California Press, 1981), 151–92.

47 Ibid., 160.

48 Janet Adelman, 'Shakespeare's Romulus and Remus: Who Does the Wolf Love?', in *Identity, Otherness and Empire in Shakespeare's Rome*, ed. Maria Del Sapio Garbero (Farnham: Ashgate, 2009), 19–34.

49 Ibid., 20.

50 Ibid., 29.

51 For further interesting recent work on masculinity in *Coriolanus*, see Eve Rachele Sanders, 'The Body of the Actor in *Coriolanus*', *Shakespeare Quarterly* 57 (2006): 387–412; R. B. Parker's edition of *Coriolanus* (Oxford: Oxford University Press, 1994); and Joo Young Dittman, '"Tear him to pieces": De-Suturing Masculinity in *Coriolanus*', *English Studies* 90 (2009): 653–72.

52 Lisa S. Starks-Estes, '"One whole wound": *Virtus*, Vulnerability, and the Emblazoned Male Body in *Coriolanus*', in L. S. Starks-Estes, *Violence, Trauma, and* Virtus *in Shakespeare's Roman Poems and Plays: Transforming Ovid* (London: Palgrave, 2014).

53 Ibid., 159.

54 Michela Compagnoni, 'Blending Motherhoods: Volumnia and the Representation of Maternity in William Shakespeare's *Coriolanus*', in *Roman Women in Shakespeare and His Contemporaries*, ed. Domenico Lovascio (Berlin: de Gruyter, 2020), 39–57.

55 Ibid., 39.

56 Ibid., 40.

57 Ibid., 42.

58 Kent R. Lehnhof, 'Acting, Integrity and Gender in *Coriolanus*', *Shakespeare Bulletin* 31, no. 3 (2013): 353–73.

59 Ibid., 354.

60 Willy Maley, '"She done *Coriolanus* at the Convent": Empowerment and Entrapment in Teresa Deevy's *In Search of Valour*', *Irish University Review* 49 (2019): 356–69.

61 Ibid., 358.

62 Ibid., 359.

63 Ibid., 363. Michael D. Friedman has studied stage productions of *Coriolanus* in order to demonstrate the overwhelmingly 'queer' sexuality generated by the ambiguous relationships dramatized in the play. See his '"Let me twine my arms about that body": The Queerness of *Coriolanus* and Recent British Stage Productions', *Shakespeare Bulletin* 33, no. 3 (Fall 2015): 359–419. In a separate article Friedman argues that 'cinemacasting', the live transmission of a stage performance into cinemas, has produced a 'new genre' of Shakespeare production. See 'The Shakespeare Cinemacast: *Coriolanus*', *Shakespeare Quarterly* 67, no. 4 (Winter 2016): 457–80.

64 A further example of adaptation theory applied to *Coriolanus* would be Anna Blackwell's 'Adapting *Coriolanus*: Tom Hiddleston's Body and Action Cinema', *Adaptation* 7 (2014): 344–52.

65 Graham Holderness, 'Introduction: Creating Shakespeare', *Critical Survey* 25 (2013), 1.

66 Graham Holderness, 'Editorial', *Critical Survey* 28, no. 2 (2016), 1.

67 Scott Maisano and Rob Conkie, 'Introduction: Creative Critical Shakespeares', in *Shakespeare and Creative Criticism*, ed. Maisano and Conkie (Oxford: Berghahn Books, 2019), 3.

68 Peter Holland, 'Introduction' to William Shakespeare, *Coriolanus* (London: Bloomsbury, 2013), 6–22.

69 T. S. Eliot, *Collected Poems 1909–1962* (London: Faber, 1963), 137–44.

70 Holland, 'Introduction', 15.

71 Bertolt Brecht, *Collected Plays*, vol. 9: *Adaptations*, ed. Ralph Mannheim and John Willett (New York: Random House, 2000), 377.

72 Günter Grass, *The Plebeians Rehearse the Uprising*, trans. Ralph Mannheim (London: Secker and Warburg, 1967).

73 Valerie C. Rudolph, 'Going to Grass; or, *Coriolanus* Revisited', *Educational Theatre Journal* 27 (2003), 503.

74 Penelope Cole, 'Becoming the Mob: Mike Brookes and Mike Pearson's *Coriolan/us*', *Theatre History Studies* 38 (2019): 104–16.

75 Ibid., 105.

76 John Osborne, *A Place Calling Itself Rome* (London: Faber, 1973).

77 Ibid., 31.

78 Holland, 'Introduction', 133.

79 Holderness, *Tales from Shakespeare*, 126–76.

80 L. Monique Pittman, 'Heroes, Villains and Balkans: Intertextual Masculinities in Ralph Fiennes's *Coriolanus*', *Shakespeare Bulletin* 33, no. 2 (2015): 215–44. Such intertextual reference presupposes of course the spectators' knowledge of these contingent textual relations. While well aware of *300* as a relevant context, having never seen a *Harry Potter* film I saw nothing in the film of *Coriolanus* of Voldemort.

81 Catherine Baker, '"Ancient Volscian Border Dispute Flares": Representations of Militarism, Masculinity and the Balkans in Ralph Fiennes's *Coriolanus*', *International Feminist Journal of Politics* 18, no. 3 (2016): 429–48.

Chapter 4

1 Nathalie Vienne-Guerrin, '*Coriolanus*, or The arraignment of an unruly tongue', in Coriolan *de William Shakespeare: Langages, interprétations, politique(s)* (Tours: Presses Universitaires François-Rabelais, 2007), 133–53.

2 Stanley Fish, *Is there a Text in this Class? The Authority of Interpretive Communities* (Cambridge, MA: Harvard University Press, 1980), 203.

3 Cynthia Marshall, 'Shakespeare, Crossing the Rubicon', *Shakespeare Survey* 53 (2000): 73.

4 John Plotz, '*Coriolanus* and the Failure of Performatives', *ELH* 63, no. 4 (1996): 811.

5   Eve Rachele Sanders, 'The Body of the Actor in *Coriolanus*', *Shakespeare Quarterly* 57, no. 4 (2006): 387–412.
6   Ibid., 387.
7   Peter Kishore Saval, *Shakespeare in Hate: Emotion, Passion, Selfhood* (New York: Routledge, 2015), 32.
8   Fish, *Is there a Text in this Class?*, 200.
9   Alun Thomas, '*Coriolanus*', in *A Year of Shakespeare: Re-living the World Shakespeare Festival*, ed. Paul Edmondson, Paul Prescott and Erin Sullivan (London: Bloomsbury, 2013), 54.
10 Sanders, 'The Body of the Actor in *Coriolanus*', 399.
11 Ibid., 411.
12 Eve Kosofsky Sedgwick, *Between Men: English Literature and Male Homosocial Desire* (New York: Columbia University Press, 1985).
13 Christina Luckyj, 'Volumnia's Silence', *Studies in English Literature* 31, no. 2 (1991): 327–42.
14 Plotz, '*Coriolanus* and the Failure of Performatives', 823.
15 Janet Adelman, *Suffocating Mothers: Fantasies of Maternal Origin in Shakespeare's Plays, Hamlet to The Tempest* (New York: Routledge, 1992).
16 Saval, *Shakespeare in Hate*, 24–5.
17 Miranda Fay Thomas, *Shakespeare's Body Language: Shaming Gestures and Gender Politics on the Renaissance Stage* (London: Bloomsbury, 2019), 164.
18 Coppélia Kahn, *Roman Shakespeare: Warriors, Wounds and Women* (London: Routledge, 1997), 157.

Chapter 5

I am grateful to Liam Semler for his generous feedback on this chapter; I am appreciative of infelicities from which the series editors and Liam saved me. This chapter has its origins in a paper I delivered at the Round Table 'Whither Ecofeminism?' together with Jennifer Munroe, Rebecca Laroche, Steve Mentz and Tiffany Werth at the annual meeting of the Shakespeare

Association of America in Washington, DC, in April 2019; I feel fortunate that Jennifer invited me to participate. I am indebted to Gary Lindeburg's invaluable research assistance. I should note that I submitted this chapter for publication shortly after Trump's impeachment by the US House of Representatives and before the global coronavirus pandemic became widely publicized.

1   William Shakespeare, *Coriolanus*, 5.6.117. All quotations of Shakespeare's *Coriolanus* and *King Lear* are drawn from the Arden Shakespeare, Third Series. Quotations of Shakespeare's other texts are drawn from *The Arden Shakespeare Complete Works*, revised edition (2001).

2   Donald Trump, 'Acceptance Speech', Republican National Convention, Cleveland, Ohio, 21 July 2016. The complete sentence is as follows: 'Nobody knows the system better than me – which is why I alone can fix it.'

3   Hugh Grady, *Shakespeare, Machiavelli, and Montaigne: Power and Subjectivity from* Richard II *to* Hamlet (Oxford: Oxford University Press, 2002), 2.

4   Terence Hawkes, *Shakespeare in the Present* (London: Routledge, 2002), 22. For further definitions and explanations of presentism as a critical theory and a critical practice, see Terence Hawkes, 'Introduction' and 'The Heimlich Manoeuvre', in *Shakespeare in the Present*, 1–5 and 6–22; Ewan Fernie, 'The Prospect of Presentism', *Shakespeare Survey* 58 (2005): 169–84; Hugh Grady and Terence Hawkes, 'Introduction: Presenting Presentism', in *Presentist Shakespeares*, ed. Hugh Grady and Terence Hawkes (London: Routledge, 2007), 1–5; Evelyn Gajowski, 'The Presence of the Past', in *Presentism, Gender, and Sexuality in Shakespeare*, ed. Evelyn Gajowski (Basingstoke: Palgrave Macmillan, 2009), 1–22; Evelyn Gajowski, 'Beyond Historicism: Presentism, Subjectivity, Politics', *Literature Compass* 7/8 (2010): 674–91; Cary DiPietro and Hugh Grady, 'Introduction', in *Shakespeare and the Urgency of Now: Criticism and Theory in the 21st Century*, ed. Cary DiPietro and Hugh Grady (Basingstoke: Palgrave Macmillan, 2013), 1–8; and Miguel Ramalhete Gomes, 'Presentist Studies', in *The Arden Research Handbook of Contemporary Shakespeare Criticism*, ed. Evelyn Gajowski (London: Bloomsbury, 2020), 233–46.

5   Gajowski, 'The Presence of the Past'; Gajowski, 'Beyond Historicism'; Sharon O'Dair, 'Is It Shakespearean Ecocriticism

If It Isn't Presentist?', in *Ecocritical Shakespeare*, ed. Lynne Bruckner and Dan Brayton (Farnham: Ashgate, 2011), 71–85.

6 Laroche and Munroe, *Ecofeminist Theory*, 78.

7 Stacy Alaimo, *Bodily Natures: Science, Environment, and the Material Self* (Bloomington and Indianapolis: Indiana University Press, 2010), 2, 4.

8 Laroche and Munroe, *Ecofeminist Theory*, 80.

9 Ibid., 88. See also Craig Dionne, *Posthuman Lear: Reading Shakespeare in the Anthropocene* (Santa Barbara, CA: Punctum Books, 2016).

10 Val Plumwood, *Feminism and the Mastery of Nature* (London and New York: Routledge, 1993), 49. While she doesn't hyphenate the term here, she does hyphenate it hereafter.

11 Val Plumwood, *Environmental Culture: The Ecological Crisis of Reason* (London: Routledge, 2002), 9.

12 Ibid., 19.

13 See William Cummings, 'Podiatrist's Daughters Say Bone Spur Diagnosis that Helped Trump Avoid Vietnam Draft was "Favor"', *USA Today*, 27 December 2018.

14 See Maggie Haberman and Richard A. Oppel, Jr, 'Donald Trump Criticizes Muslim Family of Slain U.S. Soldier, Drawing Ire', *New York Times*, 30 July 2016.

15 See Katherine Gallagher Robbins, Rejane Frederick, Angela Hanks, Rachel West and Michela Zonta, '5 Ways President Trump and Congressional Republicans Are Betraying Veterans', Center for American Progress, 26 September 2017.

16 See Idrees Ali and Phil Stewart, 'More than 100 US Troops Diagnosed with Brain Injuries from Iran Attack', Reuters, 10 February 2020; and Lolita C. Baldor, 'Number of U.S. Troops Who Suffered Traumatic Brain Injury From Iran Missile Strike Rises to 109', *Time*, 10 February 2020.

17 Donald Trump, 'The State of the Union Address to the US Congress', Washington, DC, 4 February 2020.

18 See Simon Mollan and Beverly Geesin, 'Donald Trump and Trumpism: Leadership, Ideology and Narrative of the Business Executive turned Politician', *Organization* 26 (2019): 1–14; and Ethlyn A. Williams, Rajnandini Pillai, Kate McCombs, Kevin B. Lowe and Bryan J. Deptula, 'Adaptive

and Maladaptive Narcissism, Charisma, and Leadership Performance: A Study of Perceptions of the Presidency of Donald Trump', *Leadership* 16 (2020): 1–22.

19 Theodore F. Kaouk, 'Homo Faber, Action Hero Manque: Crafting the State in *Coriolanus*', *Shakespeare Quarterly* 66 (2015): 439; and Cathy Shrank, 'Civility and the City in *Coriolanus*', *Shakespeare Quarterly* 54 (2003): 423.

20 My reading of Martius here is influenced by that of Katharine Eisaman Maus, '*Coriolanus*' [Introduction], *The Norton Shakespeare based on the Oxford Edition*, ed. Stephen Greenblatt, Walter Cohen, Jean E. Howard and Katharine Eisaman Maus (New York and London: Norton, 1997), 2785–92.

21 Trump, 'State of the Union'.

22 Janet Adelman, *Suffocating Mothers: Fantasies of Maternal Origin in Shakespeare's Plays*, Hamlet *to* The Tempest (London: Routledge, 1992), 154, 164.

23 Shrank, 'Civility and the City', 420–1.

24 Robin Headlam Wells, '"Manhood and Chevalrie": *Coriolanus*, Prince Henry, and the Chivalric Revival', *Review of English Studies* 51 (2000): 421.

25 See, for example, Bill Maher, *Real Time with Bill Maher*, HBO-TV, 15 September 2017; Masha Gessen, 'The Trump-Russia Investigation and the Mafia State', *New Yorker*, 31 January 2019; Max Boot, 'The Republicans Have Become the Party of Russia. This Makes Me Sick', *Washington Post,* 4 December 2019; Ronald Brownstein, 'The Russification of the Republican Party', *Atlantic*, 5 December 2019; and David Frum, 'A Gangster in the White House', *Atlantic*, 28 December 2019.

26 More than 160 high-ranking members of the Executive Office of the President alone (excluding the Office of the Vice President, the Cabinet and the various departments of the executive branch) have left their positions since Trump's inauguration. See 'List of Trump Administration Dismissals and Resignations' at Wikipedia.org.

27 Shashank Bengali and Ramin Mostaghim, 'Iran Reacts to Pompeo as Trump's Secretary of State Pick: "Cowboyish" and "eager to start a war"', *Los Angeles Times*, 14 March 2018.

28 John Brennan, Interview, *Hardball with Chris Matthews*, MSNBC TV, 12 February 2020.

29 Adelman, *Suffocating Mothers*, 158.
30 Ibid., 147.
31 Ibid.
32 Plumwood, *Feminism*, 51.
33 Tony Schwartz, Interview, *Hardball with Chris Matthews*, MSNBC TV, 5 February 2019.
34 Trump, Tweet, Twitter, 6 January 2018. The complete sentence is: 'I think that would qualify as not smart, but genius… and a very stable genius at that! I'm a very stable genius.'
35 Stephen Greenblatt, *Tyrant: Shakespeare on Politics* (New York and London: Norton, 2018), 173.
36 Shrank, *Civility and the City*, 422.
37 Wells, 'Manhood and Chevalrie', 398–9.
38 See Tim O'Brien's *Time* magazine cover illustration, 'King Me', depicting Trump looking in a mirror that reflects a crowned monarch, 18 June 2018.
39 See, for example, Rebecca Solnit, 'President Trump is at War with the Rule of Law. This won't End Well', *Guardian*, 9 October 2019; and Steve Denning, 'How Trump's Cabinet Now Undermines The Rule Of Law', *Forbes*, 19 May 2019.
40 Wells, 'Manhood and Chevalrie', 398.
41 Greenblatt, *Tyrant*, 164.
42 The publicity for Ralph Fiennes's film prominently features Martius's blood-covered face. *Coriolanus,* film production, dir. Ralph Fiennes, Hermetof Pictures, Piccadilly Pictures and Icon Entertainment International (2011).
43 For an analysis of the significance of the repeated phrase, 'It shall be so', in Martius's banishment and in influencing the plebeians, see Margaret Sinclair, '"It Shall Be So": Grammatical usage as political intent in *Coriolanus*', *Journal of Aesthetic Education* 36 (2002): 32–6.
44 Greenblatt, *Tyrant,* 178.
45 Philip Rucker, Robert Costa and Josh Dawsey, 'Trump Seeks to Bend the Executive Branch as Part of Impeachment Vendetta', *Washington Post*, 12 February 2020.
46 Schwartz, Interview.

47   Bill Maher, *Real Time*.
48   Jason V. Morgan, 'We Have a President who Denigrates People and Hugs Flags', Letters to the Editor, *Washington Post*, 8 March 2019.
49   Trump, Tweet, Twitter, 23 July 2019.
50   Interview, *Andrea Mitchell Reports*, MSBNC TV, 7 February 2020.
51   *Church and State Magazine*, 'God and Trump: The Offensive Notion of Divine Anointment', Editorial, June 2019.
52   Randall Martin, 'Ecocritical Studies', in *The Arden Research Handbook of Contemporary Shakespeare Criticism*, 193. For an extended meditation on the commons, the relationship of humans and the land, and the questions, 'Who shall have the right to vote? The landed gentry? Or all Englishmen?' that characterized the Putney Debates during the English Civil War, see Caryl Churchill's dramatic text, *Light Shining in Buckinghamshire* (London: Nick Hern Books, 2015).
53   David Hawkes, *Shakespeare and Economic Theory* (London: Bloomsbury, 2015), 92. See also Peter Holland's discussion, 'Hunger and Unrest in the Midlands' (56–68), in his Introduction to the Arden Third edition of *Coriolanus*. For a discussion of the commodification of water, as well as land, see Martin, 'Ecocritical Studies', 189–204.
54   Gregory Doran's stage production of *2 Henry 4* for the Royal Shakespeare Company, Stratford-upon-Avon (2014) offered a stark representation of the pitiful state of the poverty-stricken troops.
55   Hawkes, *Economic Theory*, 95–6.
56   Kirk Semple, 'Central American Farmers Head to the US, Fleeing Climate Change', *New York Times*, 13 April 2019.
57   Katrina Vanden Heuvel, *The Thom Hartmann Program*, Satellite XM Radio, 9 January 2020. See also Ian Bremmer, 'The "Strongman Era" Is Here: Here's What It Means For You', *Time*, 3 May 2018.
58   Trump, 'State of the Union'.
59   E. M. Forster, *Howards End*, ed. Alistair M. Duckworth (Boston, MA: Bedford/St. Martins, 1997), 188, 21.

60 Liam Semler, email correspondence with the author, 2 February 2020.
61 James Kuzner, 'Unbuilding the City: *Coriolanus* and the Birth of republican Rome', *Shakespeare Quarterly* 58 (2007): 186.
62 Plumwood, *Environmental Culture*, 8–9.
63 Alaimo, *Bodily Natures*, 5, 158.

Chapter 6

1 Hegel, *Philosophy of History*, trans. J. Sibree (New York: Dover, 1956), 275–340; Hegel, *Phenomenology of Spirit*, trans. A. V. Miller (Oxford: Oxford University Press, 1977), 290–4.
2 For Hegel, endlessness is bad (a 'spurious infinite') when it is incomprehensible to a finite self/city/State; endlessness is good when a finite self/city/State's self-mediation is comprehensible, when '[t]he outward shape, the form of finitude, in no way deprives the content ... of its substantiality and the infinity inherent within it' (Hegel, *Philosophy of Right*, trans. T. M. Knox [Oxford: Oxford University Press, 1967], 101). Importantly, this issue of endlessness arises when we try to comprehend the play *Coriolanus* as a whole. For example, this is my second reading of this play using Hegel: for the other, see Bates, *Hegel and Shakespeare on Moral Imagination* (Albany, NY: State University of New York Press, 2010), 37–53. These different readings underscore 'the inevitable provisionality of any comment on or approach to the play' (Peter Holland, 'Introduction', *Coriolanus* [London, New York: Bloomsbury, 2013], 6). Unlike the Roman spurious infinites of self and city depicted *in* the play, this provisionality of the play as a whole, when properly understood, is a good endlessness. Arriving at an experience of this good endlessness is possible if one is careful to assess the way that spurious infinites of self- and social-mediation work. The play educates us about social mediation. A final note: I apply Hegel's ideas about Rome *to* Shakespeare's *Coriolanus*; this is not Hegel's account of the play. Hegel only briefly mentions the *historical* figure: see Bates, *Hegel and Shakespeare*, note 7, 305–6.

3   Hegel, *Philosophy of History*, 276.
4   Ibid., 280.
5   Ibid., 284.
6   For a discussion of 'pathological excesses of Roman honour' in *Coriolanus*, see Robert S. Miola, *Shakespeare's Rome* (Cambridge: Cambridge University Press, 1983), 171. Cantor explains that austerity and virtue were more significant for the Republic, largely a thing of the past for the Empire; Shakespeare was well aware of this in his Roman plays, depicting Coriolanus in terms of Roman heroic virtues, and Antony (in *Antony and Cleopatra*) as *recalling* these virtues. Paul A. Cantor, *Shakespeare's Rome: Republic and Empire* (Chicago, IL and London: University of Chicago Press, 1976), 10–15, 59.
7   Hegel, *Philosophy of History*, 288.
8   Ibid., 288.
9   Sophocles' *Antigone* as cited in Hegel, *Phenomenology*, 261.
10 Hegel, *Philosophy of History*, 289.
11 Ibid.
12 Ibid., 290.
13 The Greek Pantheon was 'the embodiment of a rich intellectual material, and adorned ... with bright fancies ... ', but 'the Romans' adoption of the Greek gods is reductive .... Their talk of Jupiter, Juno, Minerva, sounds like a mere theatrical mention of them' (Ibid., 291, 293). '[I]n Shakespeare's Rome even the gods are in some sense included within the precincts of the city' (Cantor, *Shakespeare's Rome*, 56–7).
14 Hegel, *Phenomenology*, 56.
15 Ibid., 492.
16 Coherence is necessary but relative, and so always entails 'more', even in Hegel's expression 'The True is the Whole' (*Phenomenology*, 11).
17 Ibid., 294; bracketed text my addition.
18 Ibid., 294–363.
19 Ibid., 49.

20 For example, 'He's a disease that must be cut away' (3.1.296).

21 Hegel, *Phenomenology*, 292–3.

22 For differences between Republic and Empire in *Coriolanus*, *Julius Caesar* and *Antony and Cleopatra*, see Cantor, *Shakespeare's Rome*. According to Cantor, the Roman Republic cannot be characterized by one form of government (monarchy, aristocracy or democracy); Shakespeare, whose 'knowledge of Rome is evidently better than that of many of his critics', designed the Rome of *Coriolanus* as a 'mixed regime' (9–10).

23 See G. W. F. Hegel, *The Phenomenology of Mind*, trans. J. B. Baillie (New York, Evanston, San Francisco, London: Harper & Row, Publishers, 1967), 241.

24 Hegel, *Phenomenology*, 205.

25 Ibid., 291.

26 For a different reading of Coriolanus in relation to stoicism, see Patrick Gray, *Shakespeare and the Fall of the Roman Republic: Selfhood, Stoicism and Civil War* (Edinburgh: Edinburgh University Press, 2019), 181.

27 Hegel, *Phenomenology*, 456.

28 Ibid., 7–8, 14.

29 Ibid., 453–78. See H. S. Harris, *Hegel's Ladder* (Indianapolis, Cambridge: Hackett Publishing Company, 1997), vol. 2, 771.

30 '[I]t seems necessary to reinforce the coherence of a way of thinking that takes into account the event of Christian mystery as an absolute singularity, a religion par excellence and an irreducible condition for a joint history of the subject, responsibility, and Europe', Jacques Derrida, *The Gift of Death*, trans. David Wills (Chicago, IL and London: University of Chicago Press, 1995), 2. The resolution of the first and second unhappy consciousnesses each seems final, but is not: there is always a remainder. Thus, according to Hegel, the resolution of the second unhappy consciousness is the birth of Christian Europe, a solution originating the alienations of the Holy Roman Empire, and thus requiring solution(s) to come.

31 For the role of places (outside, and as mental maps), see Richard Raspa's 'Place in Shakespeare's *Coriolanus*: The Intersection of Geography, Culture, and Identity', in

Mediterranean Studies 26 (2018): 213–28. According to Raspa, the tragedy is in part due to Coriolanus's failure to understand Rome. In my reading, the ground of tragedy is the *social* failure of individuals in Rome to comprehend their incarnation in and as the city (Menenius: 'You know neither me, yourselves, nor anything' [2.1.65]).

32 See also, Shakespeare, *Julius Caesar*, ed. David Daniell (London and New York: Bloomsbury, 1998), 3.1.259–61 and 3.2.221–3.

33 In 'Legal Status' there is no *explicit* discussion of a Roman secret. Phenomenologically, the secret is the unrevealed truth about what 'the mediator' is, the drive to make sense of the mediator. In Roman 'Legal Status', an advance has been made over the first unhappy consciousness: individuals are no longer relying on a mediator per se, but on social *media*; the phenomenon is no longer unconsciously orchestrated custom/identity, but rather *alienated social self-determination*. This problem of the secret to self-determination in media also functions to produce multiple and contradictory political *appropriations* of Shakespeare's play: '[t]here is nothing before quite like *Coriolanus*'s unremitting study of the political landscape of Rome, nothing too that has allowed a Shakespeare tragedy to be appropriated by political right and left with equal success' (Holland, 'Introduction', 3).

34 Hegel, *Phenomenology*, 485.

35 Stratford Festival Production of Shakespeare's *Coriolanus*, 2018, dir. and set design Robert Lepage. While Holland discusses the dizzying mix of costumes in Poel's 1931 staging of the play (Holland, 'Introduction', 9–10), Poel was not focusing on the problem of media, he was using costumes to show that '[t]his was no longer a play about Rome but about all ages and the ways in which different societies viewed militarism' (10). By contrast, Lepage brought *media* center stage.

36 Contradiction is true of the play as a whole: '*Coriolanus* becomes a contested space, a text that allows for and encourages contradictory meanings, meanings that can be ascribed to the dominant thinkers of our world but which always remain partial, incomplete ...' (Holland, 'Introduction', 19).

37 Hegel, *Phenomenology*, 292.

38 Ibid., 290. In *Coriolanus*, persons, and Rome, are portrayed as failing to reflect themselves: Menenius to the tribunes, 'O that you could turn your eyes toward the napes of your necks and make but an interior survey of your good selves! O that you could!' (2.1.36–9). Coriolanus fails reflection by declaring himself best at it: 'For the mutable, rank-scented meinie, let them / Regard me, as I do not flatter, and / Therein behold themselves' (3.1.68–70).

39 Creon followed the gods as much as Antigone did. See L. A. MacKay, 'Antigone, Coriolanus, and Hegel', *Transactions and Proceedings of the American Philological Association* 93 (1962): 166.

40 The 'more' of rhetoric is everywhere in the play. Menenius is constantly trying to get in 'one word more' (3.1.312), and Coriolanus's peeks of anger are often at words, for example at the tribune's word 'Shall' (3.1.89–113) or Aufidius's 'Boy' (5.6.104). Hamamra has good reason to frame the play a 'tragedy of language', among other kinds of tragedy. See Bilal Tawfiq Hamamra, '"Never shame to hear / What you have nobly done": The Representation of Existential Shame in Shakespeare's *Coriolanus*', *Rupkatha Journal on Interdisciplinary Studies in Humanities* IX, no. 2 (2017): 104. However, I think that the 'more' is in more than rhetoric.

41 Virgilia presents an interesting figure in this respect. Coriolanus refers to her as 'My gracious silence' (2.1.170); Holland notes that Plutarch connects the muse revered by Romans above all to one '"who was called *Tacita*, as ye would saye, Ladye silence"' (Holland, editorial notes in *Coriolanus*, 227). The secret of the play could be argued to be silent Virgilia. For a similar conclusion, see Bernard Freydberg, '"No" as Affirmation: A Continental-Philosophical Reading of *Coriolanus*', in *Shakespeare and Continental Philosophy*, ed. Jennifer Ann Bates and Richard Wilson (Edinburgh: Edinburgh University Press, 2016), 236–46. Freydberg concludes that the ground of tragedy is Virgilia's tacit affirmation of marital love (246). I think the ground is rather the Roman unhappy consciousness about the remainder of the person, their unknowable secret. For comparison of Cordelia's silence with Virgilia's, see Hamamra, '"Never shame to hear"', 104.

For a feminist (Kristeva) critique of the predominance, in critical responses to the play, of finding a phallocentrically-conceived lack in Coriolanus, see Cynthia Marshall, 'Woundman: *Coriolanus*, Gender, and the Theatrical Construction of Interiority', in *Feminist Readings of Early Modern Culture: Emerging Subjects*, ed. Valerie Traub, M. Lindsay Kaplan and Dympna Callaghan (Cambridge: Cambridge University Press, 1996), 93–118.

42 Hegel, *Phenomenology*, 493. I address the tragi-comic nature of the *Phenomenology* in *Hegel and Shakespeare*, and 'Hegel's "Instinct of Reason" and Shakespeare's *The Merchant of Venice*: What is a Relevant *Aufhebung* of Nature? Of Justice?', in *The Philosophy of Theatre, Drama and Acting*, ed. Tom Stern (London: Roman and Littlefield, 2017), 15–41.

43 Hegel, *Philosophy of History*, 290. *Religare* means to restrain, tie back (https://www.merriam-webster.com/dictionary/religion).

44 For a discussion of T. S. Eliot's 'objective correlative' (through Shakespeare, Hegel, Žižek and Brandom), see Andrew Cutrofello's *All for Nothing: Hamlet's Negativity* (Cambridge, MA and London: MIT Press, 2014), 148–54.

45 Hegel, *Philosophy of History*, 294.

46 Spurious measures appear throughout *Coriolanus*: e.g. war is said to be good because it enacts overcoming, whereas 'peace is a great maker of cuckolds' (4.5.230–1); war makes men need one another, peace makes them hate one another (4.5.232–4).

47 Hegel, *Phenomenology*, 493.

48 Ibid., 493.

49 Ibid.

Chapter 7

1 Gary Taylor, John Jowett, Terri Bourus and Gabriel Egan, eds, *The New Oxford Shakespeare* (Oxford: Oxford University Press, 2016–17).

2   Hugh Craig and Brett Greatley-Hirsch, *Style, Computers, and Early Modern Drama: Beyond Authorship* (Cambridge: Cambridge University Press, 2017), 101–8.

3   See the introduction to this method in Craig and Greatley-Hirsch, *Style*, 30–9.

4   Table 7.1 and Figures 7.1 and 7.2 in this chapter are not included in the Craig and Greatley-Hirsch book, but are prepared from the original data set underlying the discussion there, by permission of the authors.

5   Craig and Greatley-Hirsch, *Style*, 102.

6   Ibid.

7   Ibid., 103.

8   The corpus has eleven plays from 1606, twelve from 1607, six from 1608, one from 1609, nine from 1610 and eleven from 1611. The details of the plays included are in the Supplementary Materials to this chapter, available at http://hdl.handle.net/1959.13/1410040.

9   This is the first step in the authorial attribution method known as 'Craig's Zeta'. See Hugh Craig and Arthur Kinney, 'Methods', in *Shakespeare, Computers, and the Mystery of Authorship*, ed. Hugh Craig and Arthur F. Kinney (Cambridge: Cambridge University Press, 2009), 15–25, for an introduction. This procedure is a variant of 'Burrows's Zeta' (John Burrows, 'All the Way Through: Testing for Authorship in Different Frequency Strata', *Literary and Linguistic Computing* 22 [2007]: 27–47).

10 For a possible model, see Yla R. Tausczik and James W. Pennebaker, 'The Psychological Meaning of Words: LIWC and Computerized Text Analysis Methods', *Journal of Language and Social Psychology* 29 (2010): 24–54.

11 *Has* is heavily weighted in the positive direction on the First Principal Component of the PCA described above, and *hath* is heavily weighted in the negative direction, and three of the four *Coriolanus* characters have low scores on PC1, aligning them with high counts of *hath* and low counts of *has*, which seems to contradict the Zeta finding. This reminds us that character scores are combinations of all 100 word-variables, with

corresponding local variations, and that these character parts form only part of the entire dialogue of the play, whereas in the Zeta calculations we look at one word at a time, and take segments of the play as a whole.

12. For a survey of these changes, see Terttu Nevalainen, *An Introduction to Early Modern English* (Edinburgh: Edinburgh University Press, 2006).

13. The list of 180 comprises all the verbs apart from *doth* and *hath* which appear in whatever form in more than one play in the 275-play corpus and five or more times overall. The full list is in the Supplementary Materials file at http://hdl.handle.net/1959.13/1410040.

14. Hugh Craig, 'Shakespeare's Style, Shakespeare's England', in *Fashioning England and the English*, ed. Rahel Orgis and Matthias Heim (London: Palgrave Macmillan, 2018), 71–96.

15. Marina Tarlinskaja, *Shakespeare's Verse: Iambic Pentameter and the Poet's Idiosyncrasies* (New York: Peter Lang, 1987), 137–8; and George T. Wright, *Shakespeare's Metrical Art* (Oakland, CA: University of California Press, 1988), 294–5.

16. Dates are taken from Martin Wiggins and Catherine Richardson, *British Drama 1533–1642: A Catalogue* (Oxford: Oxford University Press, 2012–present). Collaborative plays are excluded, as is *Merry Wives of Windsor*, which is mostly prose. Tarlinskaja has made an error in the figure she gives for *Othello*: her percentage score for this play does not correspond to the raw number of shared lines she quotes. The error is repeated when she reprints the same table as Table B5 in Appendix B of *Shakespeare and the Versification of English Drama 1561–1642* (London: Ashgate, 2014).

17. Wright, *Shakespeare's Metrical Art*, 140, 120.

18. Hartmut Ilsemann, 'More Statistical Observations on Speech-Lengths in Shakespeare's Plays', *Literary and Linguistic Computing* 23 (2008): 397–407; Hartmut Ilsemann, 'Some Statistical Observations on Speech Lengths in Shakespeare's Plays', *Shakespeare Jahrbuch* 141 (2005): 158–68; MacDonald P. Jackson, 'A New Chronological Indicator for Shakespeare's Plays and for Hand D of *Sir Thomas More*', *Notes and Queries* 54 (252), no. 3 (2007): 304–7; Pervez Rizvi, 'Speech Lengths

in Early Modern Plays', *ANQ: A Quarterly Journal of Short Articles, Notes and Reviews* 33 (2020): 143–7.

19 Mikhail Gasparov, 'Boris Yarkho's Works on Literary Theory', trans. Michael Lavery and Marina Tarlinskaja, *Studia Metrica et Poetica* 3 (2016): 141.

20 Howard Giles, 'Accent Mobility: A Model and Some Data', *Anthropological Linguistics* 15 (1973): 87–109; Nikolas Coupland and Adam Jaworski, 'Relevance, Accommodation, and Conversation: Modeling the Social Dimension of Communication', *Multilingua* 16 (1997): 235–58.

Chapter 8

1 Brian Vickers, 'Teaching *Coriolanus*: The Importance of Perspective', in *Teaching Shakespeare*, ed. Walter Edens (Princeton, NJ: Princeton University Press, 2015), 228–9.

2 Ralph Alan Cohen, *ShakesFear and How to Cure It: The Complete Handbook for Teaching Shakespeare* (London: Arden Shakespeare, 2018), 12. See 129–36 for *Coriolanus* teaching activities.

3 Vickers, 'Teaching *Coriolanus*', 266.

4 Graham Holderness, 'The Coriolanus Myth', in *Tales from Shakespeare: Creative Collisions* (Cambridge: Cambridge University Press, 2014), 89.

5 Peter Holland, 'Introduction', in William Shakespeare, *Coriolanus*, ed. Holland (London: Bloomsbury, 2013), 1.

6 Cohen, *ShakesFear*, 129.

7 Sarah Roberts, '"Alone", "constant", and "(in)visible": Staging Leadership in *Coriolanus*', *Shakespeare in Southern Africa* 29 (2017): 28.

8 Tanya Van Der Walt, 'Making Shakespeare Useful: A Pared-down, Portable *Coriolanus*', *Shakespeare in Southern Africa* 28 (2016): 99. For more on Shakespeare in South Africa, see Chris Thurman, 'Shakespeare.za: digital Shakespeares and education in South Africa', *Research in Drama Education: The Journal of Applied Theatre and Performance* 25, no. 1 (2020): 49–67.

9   Michael Brooke, 'The Spread of the Eagle (1963)', BFI Screen Online. Available online: http://www.screenonline.org.uk/tv/id/466545/index.html (accessed 9 March 2020).

10 Emily Griffiths Jones, '"Beloved of all the trades in Rome": Oeconomics, Occupation, and the Gendered Body in *Coriolanus*', *Shakespeare Studies* 43 (2015): 154.

11 Holland, 'Introduction', 107–8.

12 Zvi Jagendorf, '*Coriolanus*: Body Politic and Private Parts', *Shakespeare Quarterly* 41, no. 4 (1990): 457.

13 Simon Palfrey, *Doing Shakespeare*, 2nd edn (London: Bloomsbury, 2011), 36.

14 See Holland, 'Introduction', 35, and Cathy Shrank, 'Civility and the City in *Coriolanus*', *Shakespeare Quarterly* 54, no. 4 (2003): 413–14.

15 Andrew Gurr, '*Coriolanus* and the Body Politic', *Shakespeare Survey* 28 (1975): 65.

16 Gert Biesta and Deborah Osberg, 'Complexity, Education and Politics from the Inside-Out and the Outside-In: An Introduction', in *Complexity Theory and the Politics of Education*, ed. Gert Biesta and Deborah Osberg (Rotterdam: Sense Publishers, 2010), 2.

17 Keith Morrison, *School Leadership and Complexity Theory* (London and New York: Routledge, 2002), 2.

18 Claire Hansen, *Shakespeare and Complexity Theory* (London and New York: Routledge, 2017), 9–10.

19 Morrison, *School Leadership and Complexity Theory*, 18.

20 Darcy Wudel, 'Shakespeare's *Coriolanus* in the Political Science Classroom', *PS: Political Science and Politics* 35, no. 2 (2002): 217.

21 Biesta and Osberg, 'Complexity, Education and Politics', 2.

22 Liam E. Semler, *Teaching Shakespeare and Marlowe: Learning versus the System* (London: Bloomsbury, 2013), 53.

23 Morrison, *School Leadership and Complexity Theory*, 18.

24 Ibid.

25 Roberts, 'Staging Leadership', 38.

26 Catherine Lisak, '"O, me alone!": *Coriolanus* in the Face of Collective Otherness', *Actes des congrès de la Société française Shakespeare* 28 (2011): 226.

27 Robert N. Watson, '*Coriolanus* and the "Common Part"', *Shakespeare Survey* 69 (2016): 182; Shrank, 'Civility and the City in *Coriolanus*', 420.

28 Holland, 'Introduction', 119.

29 Hansen, *Shakespeare and Complexity Theory*, 9.

30 Cohen, *ShakesFear*, 129.

31 Alex Garganigo, '*Coriolanus*, the Union Controversy, and Access to the Royal Person', *Studies in English Literature, 1500–1900* 42, no. 2 (2002): 336.

32 Cohen, *ShakesFear*, 89.

33 Andrew Hadfield, 'Shakespeare and Politics in the Time of the Gunpowder Plot', *The Review of Politics* 78 (2016): 572.

34 Holland, 'Introduction', 99, 101.

35 Ian Munro, *The Figure of the Crowd in Early Modern London: The City and its Double* (London: Palgrave Macmillan, 2005), 194.

36 Munro, *The Figure of the Crowd*, 186.

37 Ibid., 192.

38 Robert Maslen, 'Introduction', in Thomas Dekker and Thomas Middleton, 'News from Gravesend: Sent to Nobody', in *Thomas Middleton: The Collected Works*, ed. Gary Taylor and Robert Maslen (Oxford: Oxford University Press, 2007), 128.

39 Ralph Alan Cohen, 'The Most Convenient Place: The Second Blackfriars Theatre and its Appeal', *The Oxford Handbook of Early Modern Theatre*, ed. Richard Dutton (Oxford: Oxford University Press, 2009), 209.

40 Andrew Gurr, *The Shakespearean Stage 1574–1642* (Cambridge: Cambridge University Press, 2009), 190.

41 Ibid., 190–1, 193.

42 Ibid., 195.

43 Cohen, 'The Most Convenient Place', 223–4.

44 Cohen, *ShakesFear*, 39.

45 Holderness, 'The Coriolanus Myth', 89.
46 Kate Wilkinson, 'Shakespeare's Citizens and the 99%: Accommodating the Occupy Movement in Productions of *Coriolanus*', *Early Modern Literary Studies* 19 (2016): 1.
47 Hugh Grady and Terence Hawkes, eds, *Presentist Shakespeares* (London and New York: Routledge, 2007), 5.
48 Wilkinson, 'Shakespeare's Citizens and the 99%', 2.
49 'Our demands', Extinction Rebellion, https://rebellion.earth/the-truth/demands/ (accessed 18 February 2020).
50 Ibid.
51 Thurman, 'Shakespeare.za', 55.
52 Ibid., 57.
53 Ibid., 56.
54 Ibid., 55–6.
55 Robin Headlam Wells, '"Manhood and chevalrie": *Coriolanus*, Prince Henry, and the Chivalric Revival', *The Review of English Studies* 51, no. 203 (2000): 397.
56 Shrank, 'Civility and the City in *Coriolanus*', 406.
57 Stephen Greenblatt, *Tyrant: Shakespeare on Politics* (New York: W. W. Norton and Co, 2019), 171.
58 Jagendorf, '*Coriolanus:* Body Politic and Private Parts', 457.
59 John J. Joughin, 'Shakespeare and Politics: An Introduction', in *Shakespeare and Politics*, ed. Catherine M. S. Alexander (Cambridge: Cambridge University Press, 2004), 13.
60 Holderness, 'The Coriolanus Myth', 104.
61 Roberts, 'Staging Leadership', 31.
62 John. O Whitney and Tina Packer, *Power Plays: Shakespeare's Lessons in Leadership and Management* (London: Macmillan, 2000), 26–9.
63 Roberts, 'Staging Leadership', 34.
64 Munro, *The Figure of the Crowd*, 192; Watson, '*Coriolanus* and the "Common Part"', 189–90.
65 Jan Kott, *Shakespeare our Contemporary* (London: Methuen, 1983), 142.

66 Roberts, 'Staging Leadership', 28.
67 Marjorie Garber, *Shakespeare and Modern Culture* (New York: Anchor Books, 2008), 72.
68 Kent R. Lehnhof, 'Acting, Integrity, and Gender in *Coriolanus*', *Shakespeare Bulletin* 31, no. 3 (2013): 367.
69 Vickers, 'Teaching *Coriolanus*', 247.
70 Joo Young Dittmann, '"Tear him to pieces": De-Suturing Masculinity in *Coriolanus*', *English Studies* 90 (2009): 661.
71 Shrank, 'Civility and the City in *Coriolanus*', 409.
72 Jeremy Lopez, *The Arden Introduction to Reading Shakespeare: Close Reading and Analysis* (London: Arden Shakespeare, 2019), 12, 64.
73 Jean MacIntyre, 'Words, Acts, and Things: Visual Language in *Coriolanus*', *English Studies in Canada* 10, no. 1 (1984): 1.
74 John Garrison, 'Queer Desire and Self-Erasure in *Coriolanus* (2011)', *Literature/Film Quarterly* 42, no. 2 (2014): 427.
75 Michael D. Friedman, '"Let me twine/Mine arms about that body": The Queerness of *Coriolanus* and Recent British Stage Productions', *Shakespeare Bulletin* 33, no. 3 (2015): 396.
76 Coppélia Kahn, 'Mother of Battles: Volumnia and Her Son in *Coriolanus*', in *Roman Shakespeare: Warriors, Wounds and Women* (London and New York: Routledge, 1997), 144–59.
77 Young Dittmann, '"Tear him to pieces"', 655.
78 Lehnhof, 'Acting, Integrity, and Gender in *Coriolanus*', 354.
79 Griffiths Jones, '"Beloved of all the trades in Rome"', 156.
80 Alan Galey and Ray Siemens, 'Introduction: Reinventing Shakespeare in the Digital Humanities', *Shakespeare* 4, no. 3 (2008): 272–3.
81 Thurman, 'Shakespeare.za', 53.
82 Christie Carson and Peter Kirwan, eds, *Shakespeare and the Digital World: Redefining Scholarship and Practice* (Cambridge: Cambridge University Press, 2014), 2.
83 Jeremy Ehrlich, 'Back to Basics: Electronic Pedagogy from the (Virtual) Ground Up', *Shakespeare* 4, no. 3 (2008): 273.
84 Ayanna Thompson and Laura Turchi, *Teaching Shakespeare with Purpose: A Student-Centred Approach* (London: Bloomsbury, 2016), 15.

85 Thompson and Turchi, *Teaching Shakespeare with Purpose*, 15.
86 Ibid.
87 See https://web.hypothes.is/ (accessed 18 February 2020).
88 Palfrey, *Doing Shakespeare*, 22–3.
89 See https://storymap.knightlab.com/ and https://vue.tufts.edu/ (both accessed 2 July 2020).
90 Mikko Kanninen, Tiina Syrjä and Tom Gorman, 'The Coriolanus Online Project' (paper presented at the *Academic Mindtrek 2016*, Tampere, Finland, 2016).
91 Tim Gorman, Tiina Syrjä and Mikko Kanninen. 'There is a World Elsewhere: Rehearsing and Training through Immersive Telepresence', *Theatre, Dance and Performance Training* 10, no. 2 (2019): 208, 212.
92 Kanninen, Syrjä and Gorman, 'The Coriolanus Online Project', 1.
93 Gorman, Syrjä and Kanninen, 'There is a World Elsewhere', 216.
94 Ibid., 225.
95 Kanninen, Syrjä and Gorman, 'The Coriolanus Online Project', 1.
96 Sheila Cavanagh, '"Come, and learn of us": Shakespeare in an Age of Global Communication', *CEA Critic* 78, no. 2 (2016): 243–4.
97 Peter Kirwan, '"From the Table of my Memory": Blogging Shakespeare In/Out of the Classroom', in Carson and Kirwan, 106.
98 Ibid., 108.
99 Ibid., 110.
100 Ibid.; Ehrlich, 'Back to Basics', 277.
101 See Maurizio Calbi and Stephen O'Neill, 'Introduction', *Borrowers and Lenders* 10, no. 1 (2016), which includes a discussion of social media as teaching platforms, and Kyle DiRoberto, '"Oh, teach me how I should forget to think": The Pedagogical Problems of Pleasure and Rigor in Social Media and Shakespeare', *Borrowers and Lenders* 10, no. 1 (2016).
102 Holderness, 'The Coriolanus Myth', 89.
103 Ibid., 105.

104 Holland, 'Introduction', 139.
105 Jon Dawson qtd in Michael D. Friedman, 'The Hurt Roman: Homoeroticism, Intimacy, and Fratriarchy in Ralph Fiennes's Coriolanus', *Literature/Film Quarterly* 43, no. 2 (2015): 89.
106 Friedman, 'The Hurt Roman', 98.
107 Holderness, 'The Coriolanus Myth', 116, 90–1.
108 Sarah Soncini, '"In Hunger for Bread, Not in Thirst for Revenge": Belly, Bellum and Rebellion in *Coriolanus* and the *Hunger Games* Trilogy', *Altre Modernità* 13, no. 5 (2015): 100–20.

BIBLIOGRAPHY

Adamson, Sylvia, Lynette Hunter, Lynne Magnusson, Ann Thompson and Katie Wales. *Reading Shakespeare's Dramatic Language*. London: Methuen Drama, 2001.
Addison, Joseph. *The Spectator* 40 (16 April 1711).
Adelman, Janet. '"Anger's my Meat": Feeding, Dependency and Aggression in *Coriolanus*'. In *Shakespeare, Pattern of Excelling Nature: Shakespeare Criticism in Honor of America's Bicentennial from the International Shakespeare Association Congress, Washington, D.C., April 1976*, edited by David Bevington and Jay Halio, 108–24. Newark, DE: University of Delaware Press, 1978.
Adelman, Janet. *Suffocating Mothers: Fantasies of Maternal Origin in Shakespeare's Plays*, Hamlet to The Tempest. New York: Routledge, 1992.
Adelman, Janet. 'Shakespeare's Romulus and Remus: Who Does the Wolf Love?' In *Identity, Otherness and Empire in Shakespeare's Rome*, edited by Maria del Sapio Garbero, 19–34. Farnham: Ashgate, 2009.
Alaimo, Stacy. *Bodily Natures: Science, Environment, and the Material Self*. Bloomington and Indianapolis: Indiana University Press, 2010.
Ali, Idrees and Phil Stewart. 'More than 100 U.S. Troops Diagnosed with Brain Injuries from Iran Attack'. Reuters, 10 February 2020. Available online: https://www.reuters.com/article/us-usa-pentagon-tbi-exclusive/exclusive-more-than-100-u-s-troops-diagnosed-with-brain-injuries-from-iran-attack-officials-idUSKBN2041ZK (accessed 1 March 2020).
Allan, Neil. 'Review of *Coriolanus*'. *Cahiers Élisabéthains* 95 (2018): 111–13.
Arnold, Oliver. *The Third Citizen: Shakespeare's Theater and the Early Modern House of Commons*. Baltimore, MD: Johns Hopkins University Press, 2007.

Baker, Catherine. '"Ancient Volscian Border Dispute Flares": Representations of Militarism, Masculinity and the Balkans in Ralph Fiennes's *Coriolanus*'. *International Feminist Journal of Politics* 18, no. 3 (2016): 429–48.

Baldor, Lolita C. 'Number of U.S. Troops Who Suffered Traumatic Brain Injury From Iran Missile Strike Rises to 109'. *Time*, 10 February 2020.

Ball, James R. 'Staging the Twitter War: Toneelgroep Amsterdam's *Roman Tragedies*'. *TDR: The Drama Review* 57, no. 4 (2013): 163–70.

Barlow, William. *A Sermon preached at Paules Crosse*. London: Mathew Law. 1601. Early English Books Online Text Creation Partnership. Available online: https://quod.lib.umich.edu/e/eebo/A04416.0001.001?view=toc (accessed 18 February 2020).

Barton, Anne. 'Livy, Machiavelli and Shakespeare's *Coriolanus*'. *Shakespeare Survey* 38 (1985): 115–29.

Bates, Jennifer Ann. *Hegel and Shakespeare on Moral Imagination*. Albany, NY: State University of New York Press, 2010.

Bates, Jennifer Ann. 'Hegel's "Instinct of Reason" and Shakespeare's *The Merchant of Venice*: What is a Relevant *Aufhebung* of Nature? Of Justice?' In *The Philosophy of Theatre, Drama and Acting*, edited by Tom Stern, 15–41. London: Roman and Littlefield, 2017.

Bedford, Kristina. Coriolanus *at the National*. London and Toronto: Associated University Presses, 1992.

Bengali, Shashank and Ramin Mostaghim. 'Iran Reacts to Pompeo as Trump's Secretary of State Pick: "Cowboyish" and "eager to start a war"'. *Los Angeles Times*, 14 March 2018.

Bennett, Susan and Christie Carson. 'Introduction: Shakespeare beyond English'. In *Shakespeare beyond English: A Global Experiment*, edited by Susan Bennett and Christie Carson, 1–11. Cambridge: Cambridge University Press, 2013.

Berkoff, Steven. *Free Association: An Autobiography*. London: Faber, 1996.

Biesta, Gert and Deborah Osberg, eds. *Complexity Theory and the Politics of Education*. Rotterdam: Sense Publishers, 2010.

Billing, Christian M. 'The Romans Tragedies'. *Shakespeare Quarterly* 61, no. 3 (2010): 415–39.

Blackwell, Anna. 'Adapting *Coriolanus*: Tom Hiddleston's Body and Action Cinema'. *Adaptation* 7 (2014): 344–52.

Bliss, Lee and Bridget Escolme. 'Introduction'. In William Shakespeare, *Coriolanus*, edited by Lee Bliss, 1–111. 2nd edn. Cambridge: Cambridge University Press, 2010.

Boot, Max. 'The Republicans Have Become the Party of Russia. This Makes Me Sick'. *Washington Post*, 4 December 2019. Available online: https://www.washingtonpost.com/opinions/2019/12/04/republicans-have-become-party-russia-this-makes-me-sick/?fbclid=IwAR0AoqE3Nnxg0i3z2mlY57_NXKatlK-BLys60YfaQbJJndmv6abKfv-YUcL (accessed 5 December 2019).

Braden, Gordon. 'Shakespeare's Roman Tragedies'. In *A Companion to Shakespeare's Works, Volume 1: The Tragedies*, edited by Richard Dutton and Jean E. Howard, 199–218. Oxford: Blackwell Publishing, 2003.

Bradley, A. C. *Shakespearean Tragedy: Lectures on* Hamlet, Othello, King Lear *and* Macbeth. 1904. Reprinted. Harmondsworth: Penguin, 1991.

Bradley, A. C. '*Coriolanus*: British Academy Lecture'. 1912. Reprinted in Coriolanus: *Critical Essays*, edited by David Wheeler, 25–45. London: Routledge, 1995.

Brecht, Bertolt. *Collected Plays. Vol. 9: Adaptations*. Edited by Ralph Mannheim and John Willett. New York: Random House, 1972.

Bremmer, Ian. 'The "Strongman Era" Is Here: Here's What It Means For You'. *Time*, 3 May 2018. Available online: https://time.com/5264170/the-strongmen-era-is-here-heres-what-it-means-for-you/ (accessed 19 July 2020).

Brennan, John. Interview. *Andrea Mitchell Reports*. MSBNC TV, 7 February 2020.

Brennan, John. Interview. *Hardball with Chris Matthews*. MSNBC TV, 12 February 2020.

Brisset, Annie. *A Sociocritique of Translation: Theatre and Alterity in Quebec, 1968–1988*. Translated by Rosalind Gill and Roger Gannon. Toronto: University of Toronto Press, 1996.

Bristol, Michael. 'Lenten Butchery: Legitimization Crisis in *Coriolanus*'. In *Shakespeare Reproduced: The Text in History and Ideology*, edited by Jean Howard and Marion O'Connor, 207–24. London: Methuen, 1987.

British Library. Discovering Literature. *Coriolanus*-related materials. Available online: https://www.bl.uk/works/coriolanus (accessed 18 February 2020).

Brooke, Michael. 'The Spread of the Eagle (1963)'. BFI Screen Online. Available online: http://www.screenonline.org.uk/tv/id/466545/index.html (accessed 9 March 2020).

Brownstein, Ronald. 'The Russification of the Republican Party'. *Atlantic*, 5 December 2019. Available at: https://www.theatlantic.com/politics/archive/2019/12/impeachment-republican-party-russia/603088/?fbclid=IwAR1NUlEfAz8N8mIpd73P8bo31FFRGPnMmnYsP4_tP012LAjhbXKmpLZXnWE (accessed 6 December 2019).

Bullough, Geoffrey, ed. *Narrative and Dramatic Sources of Shakespeare, Vol. 5: The Roman Plays*. London: Routledge and Kegan Paul, 1964, 1966.

Burke, Kenneth. '*Coriolanus* – and the Delights of Faction'. *The Hudson Review* 19, no. 2 (1966): 185–202.

Burrows, John. 'All the Way Through: Testing for Authorship in Different Frequency Strata'. *Literary and Linguistic Computing* 22 (2007): 27–47.

Campbell, Peter and Richard Jordan. 'Forming the Grand Strategist According to Shakespeare'. *Texas National Security Review* 3, no. 1 (Winter 2019/2020): 13–33.

Cantor, Paul A. *Shakespeare's Rome: Republic and Empire*. Chicago, IL and London: University of Chicago Press, 1976.

Carson, Christie and Peter Kirwan, eds. *Shakespeare and the Digital World: Redefining Scholarship and Practice*. Cambridge: Cambridge University Press, 2014.

Cartelli, Thomas. 'High-tech Shakespeare in a Mediatized Globe: Ivo van Hove's *Roman Tragedies* and the Problem of Spectatorship'. In *The Oxford Handbook of Shakespeare and Performance*, edited by James C. Bulman, 267–83. Oxford: Oxford University Press, 2017.

Cavanagh, Sheila. '"Come, and Learn of Us": Shakespeare in an Age of Global Communication'. *CEA Critic* 78, no. 2 (2016): 242–55.

Cavell, Stanley. '"Who does the Wolf Love?" Reading *Coriolanus*'. *Representations* 3 (1983): 1–20.

Cavell, Stanley. *Disowning Knowledge in Seven Plays of Shakespeare*. Cambridge: Cambridge University Press, 2003.

Cavendish, Dominic. 'A Grimy, Gory Coriolanus with Thrilling Hand-to-Hand Combat'. Available online: https://www.telegraph.co.uk/theatre/what-to-see/grimy-gory-coriolanus-thrilling-hand-to-hand-combat-review/ (accessed 19 June 2019).

Cavendish, Margaret. 'Letter 123'. In *CCXI Sociable Letters, written by the Thrice Noble, Illustrious, and Excellent Princess, the Lady Marchioness of Newcastle*. 1664. Reprinted in *Sociable Letters*, edited by James Fitzmaurice. London: Routledge, 1997.

Chiten Theatre Company. *Coriolanus*. Available online: https://globeplayer.tv/ (accessed 15 November 2019).

Churchill, Caryl. *Light Shining in Buckinghamshire*. London: Nick Hern Books, 2015.

Clarke, Danielle. 'Renaissance Eloquence and Female Exemplarity: *Coriolanus* and the *matrona docta*'. *Renaissance Studies* 28, no. 1 (2014): 128–46.

Cohen, Ralph Alan. 'The Most Convenient Place: The Second Blackfriars Theatre and its Appeal'. In *The Oxford Handbook of Early Modern Theatre*, edited by Richard Dutton, 209–23. Oxford: Oxford University Press, 2009.

Cohen, Ralph Alan. *ShakesFear and How to Cure It: The Complete Handbook for Teaching Shakespeare*. London: Bloomsbury, 2018.

Cohn, Ruby. *Modern Shakespeare Offshoots*. Princeton, NJ: Princeton University Press, 1976.

Cole, Penelope. 'Becoming the Mob: Mike Brookes and Mike Pearson's *Coriolan/us*'. *Theatre History Studies* 38 (2019): 104–16.

Compagnoni, Michela. 'Blending Motherhoods: Volumnia and the Representation of Maternity in William Shakespeare's *Coriolanus*'. In *Roman Women in Shakespeare and His Contemporaries*, edited by Domenico Lovascio, 39–57. Berlin: de Gruyter, 2020.

Conkie, Rob and Scott Maisano, eds. *Shakespeare and Creative Criticism*. London: Berghahn Books, 2019.

Cornell, Tim. 'Coriolanus: Myth, History and Performance'. In *Myth, History and Culture in Republican Rome: Studies in Honour of T. P. Wiseman*, edited by David Braund and Christopher Gill, 73–97. Exeter: University of Exeter Press, 2003.

Coupland, Nikolas and Adam Jaworski. 'Relevance, Accommodation, and Conversation: Modeling the Social Dimension of Communication'. *Multilingua* 16 (1997): 235–58.

Craig, Hugh. 'Shakespeare's Style, Shakespeare's England'. In *Fashioning England and the English*, edited by Rahel Orgis and Matthias Heim, 71–96. London: Palgrave Macmillan, 2018.

Craig, Hugh and Brett Greatley-Hirsch. *Style, Computers, and Early Modern Drama: Beyond Authorship*. Cambridge: Cambridge University Press, 2017.

Craig, Hugh and Arthur F. Kinney. 'Methods'. In *Shakespeare, Computers, and the Mystery of Authorship*, edited by Hugh Craig and Arthur F. Kinney, 15–39. Cambridge: Cambridge University Press, 2009.

Cummings, William. 'Podiatrist's Daughters Say Bone Spur Diagnosis that Helped Trump Avoid Vietnam Draft was "Favor"'. *USA Today*, 27 December 2018. Available online: https://www.usatoday.com/story/news/politics/onpolitics/2018/12/27/trump-vietnam-war-bone-spur-diagnosis/2420475002/ (accessed 1 March 2020).

Cutrofello. Andrew. *All for Nothing: Hamlet's Negativity*. Cambridge, MA and London: MIT Press, 2014.

Davis, Brent and Dennis Sumara. *Complexity and Education: Inquiries into Learning, Teaching, and Research*. New York and London: Routledge, 2006.

Dawkins, Richard. *The Selfish Gene*. Oxford: Oxford University Press, 1976, 1989.

Dekker, Thomas and Thomas Middleton. 'News from Gravesend: Sent to Nobody'. In *Thomas Middleton: The Collected Works*, edited by Gary Taylor and Robert Maslen, 128–48. Oxford: Oxford University Press, 2007.

Denning, Steve. 'How Trump's Cabinet Now Undermines The Rule Of Law'. *Forbes*, 19 May 2019. Available online: https://www.forbes.com/sites/stevedenning/2019/05/19/how-trumps-cabinet-now-undermines-the-rule-of-law/#27c6874b1dea (accessed 1 March 2020).

Dennis, John. *An Essay on the Genius and Writings of Shakespear: With Some Letters of Criticism to* The Spectator. London: Bernard Lintott, 1712.

Dennis, John. *The Invader of His Country, or The Fatal Resentment*. London: J. Pemberton, 1720.

Dennis, John. *Original Letters: Familiar, Moral, and Critical*. London: W. Mears, 1721.

Derrida, Jacques, translated by David Wills. *The Gift of Death*. Chicago, IL and London: University of Chicago Press, 1995.

De Vos, Jozef. 'The Sweep of History: Ivo van Hove's *Roman Tragedies*'. *Cahiers Élisabéthains* 75, no. 1 (2009): 55–8.

Dionne, Craig. *Posthuman Lear: Reading Shakespeare in the Anthropocene*. Santa Barbara, CA: Punctum Books, 2016.

DiPietro, Cary and Hugh Grady, eds. *Shakespeare and the Urgency of Now: Criticism and Theory in the 21st Century*. Basingstoke: Palgrave Macmillan, 2013.

Dirisu, Sope. '"Being Back at the RSC as a Professional Feels Like a Validation."' Available online: https://www.thestage.co.uk/features/sope-dirisu-being-back-at-the-rsc-as-a-professional-feels-like-validation (accessed 25 October 2019).

Dittman, Joo Young. '"Tear him to pieces": De-Suturing Masculinity in *Coriolanus*'. *English Studies* 90 (2009): 653–72.

Dobson, Michael. 'Shakespeare Performances in England'. *Shakespeare Survey* 61 (2008): 318–50.

Drogula, Fred K. *Commanders and Command in the Roman Republic and Early Roman Empire*. Chapel Hill, NC: University of North Carolina Press, 2015.

Dryden, John. 'Heads of an Answer to Rymer'. *c.* 1677. In *Shakespeare: The Critical Heritage* Vol. 1: 1623–1692, edited by Brian Vickers. London: Routledge, 1974.

DuBois, Page. 'A Disturbance of Syntax at the Gates of Rome'. *Stanford Literature Review* 2 (1985): 185–208.

Eastman, Nate. 'The Rumbling Belly Politic: Metaphorical Location and Metaphorical Government in *Coriolanus*'. *Early Modern Literary Studies* 13, no. 1 (May 2007): 2.1–39.

Eddershaw, Margaret. *Performing Brecht: Forty Years of British Performance*. London and New York: Routledge, 1996.

Edwards, Jason. '"Tell Me Not Wherein I Seem Unnatural": Queer Meditations on *Coriolanus* in the Time of War'. In *Shakesqueer: A Queer Companion to the Complete Works of Shakespeare*, edited by Madhavi Menon, 80–8. Durham, NC: Duke University Press, 2011.

Ehrlich, Jeremy. 'Back to Basics: Electronic Pedagogy from the (Virtual) Ground Up'. *Shakespeare* 4, no. 3 (2008): 271–83.

Elfman, Rose. 'Expert Spectatorship and Intra-Audience Relationships at Globe to Globe 2012'. In *Shakespeare on the Global Stage: Performance and Festivity in the Olympic Year*, edited by Paul Prescott and Erin Sullivan, 163–90. London: Bloomsbury, 2015.

Eliot, T. S. 'Hamlet'. In *Selected Essays*, 141–6. 3rd edn. London: Faber and Faber, 1951, 1961.

Eliot, T. S. *Collected Poems 1909–1962*. London: Faber, 1963.
Escolme, Bridget. *Emotional Excess on the Shakespearean Stage: Passion's Slaves*. London: Bloomsbury, 2013.
Fernie, Ewan. 'Shakespeare and the Prospect of Presentism'. *Shakespeare Survey* 58 (2005): 169–84.
Fiennes, Ralph, dir. [film] *Coriolanus*. Icon Entertainment International/BBC Films, 2011.
Film Education. *Coriolanus* Teachers' Notes. Available online: http://www.filmeducation.org/coriolanus/index.html (accessed 18 February 2020).
Fish, Stanley. *Is There a Text in this Class? The Authority of Interpretive Communities*. Cambridge, MA: Harvard University Press, 1980.
Flaherty, Jennifer. 'Filming Shakespeare's Rome: The "Preposterous Contemporary" Eternal City'. *Interdisciplinary Literary Studies* 17, no. 2 (2015): 228–40.
Folger Shakespeare Library. *Coriolanus* Resources and Texts. Available online: https://www.folger.edu/coriolanus (accessed 18 February 2020).
Forster, E. M. *Howards End*. Edited by Alistair M. Duckworth. Case Studies in Contemporary Criticism. Boston, MA: Bedford/St. Martins, 1997.
French, Philip. 'Review of Coriolanus'. *Observer*, 22 January 2012.
Freydberg. Bernard. '"No" as Affirmation: A Continental-Philosophical Reading of *Coriolanus*'. In *Shakespeare and Continental Philosophy*, edited by Jennifer A. Bates and Richard Wilson, 236–46. Edinburgh: Edinburgh University Press, 2016.
Friedman, Michael D. '"Let Me Twine/Mine Arms About That Body": The Queerness of *Coriolanus* and Recent British Stage Productions'. *Shakespeare Bulletin* 33, no. 3 (2015): 395–419.
Friedman, Michael D. 'The Hurt Roman: Homoeroticism, Intimacy, and Fratriarchy in Ralph Fiennes's *Coriolanus*'. *Literature/Film Quarterly* 43, no. 2 (2015): 86–103.
Friedman, Michael D. 'The Shakespeare Cinemacast: *Coriolanus*'. *Shakespeare Quarterly* 67, no. 4 (2016): 457–80.
Frum, David. 'A Gangster in the White House'. *Atlantic*, 28 December 2019. Available online: https://www.theatlantic.com/ideas/archive/2019/12/donald-trumps-gangster-whitehouse/604216/?fbclid=IwAR0uY3GE4fCR4oIxzJUv4uGjF0w53XsjTXQm25RVUgV-dqUUnt48qvEXNpw (accessed 29 December 2019).

Frye, Northrop. *The Double Vision: Language and Meaning in Religion*. Toronto: University of Toronto Press, 1991.
Gajowski, Evelyn, ed. *Presentism, Gender, and Sexuality in Shakespeare*. Basingstoke: Palgrave Macmillan, 2009.
Gajowski, Evelyn. 'Beyond Historicism: Presentism, Subjectivity, Politics'. *Literature Compass* 7/8 (2010): 674–91.
Gajowski, Evelyn, ed. *The Arden Research Handbook of Contemporary Shakespeare Criticism*. London: Bloomsbury, 2020.
Galey, Alan and Ray Siemens. 'Introduction: Reinventing Shakespeare in the Digital Humanities'. *Shakespeare* 4, no. 3 (2008): 201–7.
Garber, Marjorie. *Shakespeare and Modern Culture*. New York: Anchor Books, 2008.
Garganigo, Alex. '*Coriolanus*, the Union Controversy, and Access to the Royal Person'. *Studies in English Literature 1500–1900* 42, no. 2 (2002): 335–59.
Garrison, John. 'Queer Desire and Self-Erasure in *Coriolanus* (2011)'. *Literature/Film Quarterly* 42, no. 2 (2014): 427–37.
Gasparov, Mikhail, translated by Michael Lavery and Marina Tarlinskaja. 'Boris Yarkho's Works on Literary Theory'. *Studia Metrica et Poetica* 3, no. 2 (2016): 130–50.
George, David. '*Coriolanus* at the Blackfriars?' *Notes and Queries* 38 (1991): 489–92.
George, David. 'Plutarch, Insurrection and Dearth in *Coriolanus*'. *Shakespeare Survey* 53 (2000): 60–72.
George, David, Thomas Clayton, Niels Herold, Megan-Marie Johnson and Ashley Spriggs, eds. *A New Variorum Edition of Shakespeare*: Coriolanus. 2 vols. Accurance, 2019.
Germanou, Maro. 'Brecht and the English Theatre'. In *Brecht in Perspective*, edited by Graham Bartram and Anthony Waine, 208–24. London and New York: Longman, 1982.
Gessen, Masha. 'The Trump-Russia Investigation and the Mafia State'. *New Yorker*, 31 January 2019. Available online: https://www.newyorker.com/news/our-columnists/the-trump-russia-investigation-and-the-mafia-state (accessed 1 February 2019).
Gildon, Charles. 'Remarks on the Plays of Shakespeare'. 1710. In *Shakespeare: The Critical Heritage* Vol. 2: 1693–1733, edited by Brian Vickers. London: Routledge, 1974.

Giles, Howard. 'Accent Mobility: A Model and Some Data'. *Anthropological Linguistics* 15 (1973): 87–109.

'God and Trump: The Offensive Notion of Divine Anointment'. Editorial. *Church and State Magazine*, June 2019. Available online: https://www.au.org/church-state/june-2019-church-state-magazine/editorial/god-and-trump-the-offensive-notion-of-divine (accessed 2 April 2020).

Goldberg, Jonathan. 'The Anus in *Coriolanus*'. In *Historicism, Psychoanalysis, and Early Modern Culture*, edited by Carla Mazzio and Douglas Trevor, 260–71. New York and London: Routledge, 2000.

Gomes, Miguel Ramalhete. 'Presentist Studies'. In *The Arden Research Handbook of Contemporary Shakespeare Criticism*, edited by Evelyn Gajowski, 233-46. London: Bloomsbury, 2020.

Gorman, Tim, Tiina Syrjä and Mikko Kanninen. 'There is a World Elsewhere: Rehearsing and Training through Immersive Telepresence'. *Theatre, Dance and Performance Training* 10, no. 2 (2019): 208–26.

Grady, Hugh. *Shakespeare, Machiavelli, and Montaigne: Power and Subjectivity from* Richard II *to* Hamlet. Oxford: Oxford University Press, 2002.

Grady, Hugh and Terence Hawkes, eds. *Presentist Shakespeares*. London and New York: Routledge, 2007.

Granville-Barker, Harley. 'Verse and Speech in *Coriolanus*', *Review of English Studies* 23, no. 89 (1947): 1–15.

Grass, Günter. *The Plebeians Rehearse the Uprising*. Translated by Ralph Mannheim. London: Secker and Warburg, 1967.

Gray, Patrick. *Shakespeare and the Ethics of War*. Oxford and New York: Berghahn Books, 2019.

Gray, Patrick. *Shakespeare and the Fall of the Roman Republic: Selfhood, Stoicism and Civil War*. Edinburgh Critical Studies in Shakespeare and Philosophy. Edinburgh: Edinburgh University Press, 2019.

Gray, Patrick, and Maurice Samely. 'Shakespeare and Henri Lefebvre's "right to the city": Subjective Alienation and Mob Violence in *Coriolanus, Julius Caesar* and *2 Henry VI*'. *Textual Practice* 33, no. 1 (2019): 73–98.

Greenblatt, Stephen. 'A Man of Principle'. *New York Review of Books*, 8 March 2012.

Greenblatt, Stephen. *Tyrant: Shakespeare on Politics*. New York and London: Norton, 2018, 2019.
Gunter, Lawrence. 'Brecht and Beyond: Shakespeare on the East German Stage'. In *Foreign Shakespeare: Contemporary Performance*, edited by Dennis Kennedy, 109–39. Cambridge: Cambridge University Press, 1993.
Gurr, Andrew. '*Coriolanus* and the Body Politic'. *Shakespeare Survey* 28 (1975): 63–9.
Gurr, Andrew. *The Shakespearean Stage 1574–1642*. Cambridge: Cambridge University Press, 2009.
Haberman, Maggie, and Richard A. Oppel, Jr. 'Donald Trump Criticizes Muslim Family of Slain U.S. Soldier, Drawing Ire'. *New York Times*, 30 July 2016. Available online: https://www.nytimes.com/2016/07/31/us/politics/donald-trump-khizr-khan-wife-ghazala.html (accessed 15 December 2019).
Hackel, Heidi Brayman and Ian Frederick Moulton, eds. *Teaching Early Modern English Literature from the Archives*. New York: Modern Language Association of America, 2015.
Hadfield, Andrew. 'Shakespeare and Politics in the Time of The Gunpowder Plot'. *The Review of Politics* 78 (2016): 571–88.
Hamamra, Bilal Tawfiq. '"Never shame to hear / What you have nobly done": The Representation of Existential Shame in Shakespeare's *Coriolanus*'. *Rupkatha Journal on Interdisciplinary Studies in Humanities* IX, no. 2 (2017): 101–9.
Hammer, Paul E. J. 'Devereux, Robert, second earl of Essex (1565–1601), soldier and politician'. *Oxford Dictionary of National Biography*. Oxford: Oxford University Press, 2008.
Hammond, Paul. *Figuring Sex between Men from Shakespeare to Rochester*. Oxford: Oxford University Press, 2002.
Hansen, Claire. *Shakespeare and Complexity Theory*. New York and London: Routledge, 2017.
Haraway, Donna. *Simians, Cyborgs, and Women: The Reinvention of Nature*. New York: Routledge, 1991.
Harris, H. S. *Hegel's Ladder*. Volumes 1 and 2. Indianapolis, Cambridge: Hackett Publishing Company, 1997.
Hawkes, David. *Shakespeare and Economic Theory*. London: Bloomsbury, 2015.
Hawkes, Terence. *Meaning By Shakespeare*. London: Routledge, 1992.
Hawkes, Terence. *Shakespeare in the Present*. London: Routledge, 2002.

Hazlitt, William. *Characters of Shakespear's Plays*. 1817. In *The Complete Works of William Hazlitt in Twenty-One Volumes*, Vol. 4, edited by P. P. Howe. London and Toronto: J. M. Dent and Sons, 1930.

Hegel, G. W. F., translated by J. Sibree. *Philosophy of History*. New York: Dover Publications, 1956.

Hegel, G. W. F., translated by T. M. Knox. *Philosophy of Right*. Oxford: Oxford University Press, 1967.

Hegel, G. W. F., translated by J. B. Baillie. *The Phenomenology of Mind*. New York, Evanston, San Francisco, London: Harper & Row, Publishers, 1967.

Hegel, G. W. F., translated by A. V. Miller. *Phenomenology of Spirit*. Oxford: Oxford University Press, 1977.

Higgins, John. 'Hands Full for Terry Hands'. *The Times*, 19 October 1977.

Hindle, Steve. 'Imagining Insurrection in the Seventeenth-Century England: Representations of the Midland Rising of 1607'. *History Workshop Journal* 66 (2008): 21–61.

Holderness, Graham. 'Introduction: Creating Shakespeare'. *Critical Survey* 25 (2013): 1–3.

Holderness, Graham. *Tales from Shakespeare: Creative Collisions*. Cambridge: Cambridge University Press, 2014.

Holderness, Graham. 'The Coriolanus Myth'. In *Tales from Shakespeare: Creative Collisions*, 89–125. Cambridge: Cambridge University Press, 2014.

Holderness, Graham. 'Editorial'. *Critical Survey* 28, no. 2 (2016): 1–2.

Holland, Peter. 'Introduction'. In William Shakespeare, *Coriolanus*, edited by Peter Holland, 1–141. London: Bloomsbury, 2013.

Holloway, Carson. 'Shakespeare's *Coriolanus* and Aristotle's Great-Souled Man'. *Review of Politics* 69, no. 3 (2007): 353–74.

Holstun, James. 'Tragic Superfluity in *Coriolanus*'. *ELH* 50, no. 3 (1983): 485–507.

Hopkins, Lisa. 'Gender Studies and Queer Theory'. In *Beginning Shakespeare*, 134–61. Manchester: Manchester University Press, 2005.

Houston, John Porter. 'Syndeton and Asyndeton in *Coriolanus*'. In *Shakespearean Sentences: A Study in Style and Syntax*, 159–78. Baton Rouge, LA and London: Louisiana State University Press, 1988.

Hunt, Maurice. 'The Physiology of Peace and *Coriolanus*'. *The Ben Jonson Journal* 26, no. 1 (2019): 78–96.

'Identity, Representation and Casting in Contemporary Theater'. Available online: https://www.youtube.com/watch?v=XRTrs9hH6a0 (accessed 10 June 2019).

Ilsemann, Hartmut. 'Some Statistical Observations on Speech Lengths in Shakespeare's Plays'. *Shakespeare Jahrbuch* 141 (2005): 158–68.

Ilsemann, Hartmut. 'More Statistical Observations on Speech-Lengths in Shakespeare's Plays'. *Literary and Linguistic Computing* 23, no. 4 (2008): 397–407.

Inchbald, Elizabeth Ann. 'Remarks' [on *Coriolanus*]. In *The British Theatre, or A Collection of Plays Which Are Acted at the Theatres Royal, Drury Lane, Covent Garden, and Haymarket*, Volume 5. London, 1808.

Jackson, MacD. P. 'A New Chronological Indicator for Shakespeare's Plays and for Hand D of *Sir Thomas More*'. *Notes and Queries* 54 (252), no. 3 (2007): 304–7.

Jagendorf, Zvi. '*Coriolanus*: Body Politic and Private Parts'. *Shakespeare Quarterly* 41, no. 4 (1990): 455–69.

James I and VI, King. *Plague Orders*. London: Robert Barker, 1603. Early English Books Online Text Creation Partnership. Available online: https://quod.lib.umich.edu/e/eebo/A22700.0001.001?view=toc (accessed 18 February 2020).

Jarrett-Macauley, Delia, ed. *Shakespeare, Race and Performance: The Diverse Bard*. Abingdon and New York: Routledge, 2017.

Johnson, Samuel. 'Preface' to *The Plays of William Shakespeare in Eight Volumes*. 1765. In *Shakespeare: The Critical Heritage* Vol. 5: 1765–1774, edited by Brian Vickers. London: Routledge, 1979.

Jones, Emily Griffiths. '"Beloved of All the Trades in Rome": Oeconomics, Occupation, and the Gendered Body in *Coriolanus*'. *Shakespeare Studies* 43 (2015): 154–78.

Joughin, John J. 'Shakespeare and Politics: An Introduction'. In *Shakespeare and Politics*, edited by Catherine M. S. Alexander, 1–21. Cambridge: Cambridge University Press, 2004.

Kahn, Coppélia. *Man's Estate: Masculine Identity in Shakespeare*. Berkeley, CA: University of California Press, 1981.

Kahn, Coppélia. 'Mother of Battles: Volumnia and Her Son in *Coriolanus*'. In *Roman Shakespeare: Warriors, Wounds and Women*, 144–59. London and New York: Routledge, 1997.

Kahn, Coppélia. *Roman Shakespeare: Warriors, Wounds, and Women*. London and New York: Routledge, 1997.

Kanninen, Mikko, Tiina Syrjä and Tom Gorman. 'The *Coriolanus* Online Project'. Paper presented at the *Academic Mindtrek 2016*, Tampere, Finland, 2016.

Kaouk, Theodore F. 'Homo Faber, Action Hero Manque: Crafting the State in *Coriolanus*'. *Shakespeare Quarterly* 66 (2015): 409–39.

Kastan, David Scott. '"A rarity most beloved": Shakespeare and the Idea of Tragedy'. In *A Companion to Shakespeare's Works, Volume 1: The Tragedies*, edited by Richard Dutton and Jean E. Howard, 4–22. Oxford: Blackwell Publishing, 2003.

Kelsey, Holly. 'Sovereign and the sick city in 1603'. Shakespeare Birthplace Trust, 23 August 2016. Available online: https://www.shakespeare.org.uk/explore-shakespeare/blogs/sovereign-and-sick-city-1603/ (accessed 18 February 2020).

Kemble, John Philip. *Coriolanus; or The Roman Matron. A Tragedy. Altered from Shakespeare*. London: J. Christie, 1789.

Kirwan, Peter. '*Coriolanus* Performed by the Donmar Warehouse (Review)'. *Shakespeare Bulletin* 32, no. 2 (2014): 275–8.

Kirwan, Peter. '"From the Table of My Memory": Blogging Shakespeare in/out of the Classroom'. In *Shakespeare and the Digital World: Redefining Scholarship and Practice*, edited by Christie Carson and Peter Kirwan, 100–12. Cambridge: Cambridge University Press, 2014.

Knight, Wilson. G. 'The Royal Occupation: An Essay on *Coriolanus*'. In *The Imperial Theme: Further Interpretations of Shakespeare's Tragedies Including the Roman Plays*, 156–98. Oxford: Oxford University Press, 1963.

Knutson, Susan. '"Tradaptation" dans le sens Québécois: A Word for the Future'. In *Translation, Adaption, and Transformation*, edited by Laurence Raw, 112–22. London and New York: Continuum, 2012.

Kott, Jan. *Shakespeare Our Contemporary*. 1964. Reprinted. London: Methuen, 1983.

Kuwayama, Tomonari. 'Reviewing the Reception of Yukio Ninagawa's Shakespeare Productions (1999-2009) in the British and Japanese Press'. *Cahiers Élisabéthains* 82 (2012): 87–92.

Kuzner, James. 'Unbuilding the City: *Coriolanus* and the Birth of Republican Rome'. *Shakespeare Quarterly* 58, no. 2 (2007): 174–99.

Lampert, Jay. 'Why is there no Category of the City in Hegel's Aesthetics?' *British Journal of Aesthetics* 41, no. 3 (2001): 312–24.

Langis, Unhae. '*Coriolanus*: Inordinate Passions and Powers in Personal and Political Governance'. *Comparative Drama* 44, no. 1 (2010): 1–27.

Lanier, Douglas. *Shakespeare and Modern Popular Culture*. Oxford: Oxford University Press, 2012.

Laroche, Rebecca and Jennifer Munroe. *Shakespeare and Ecofeminist Theory*. London: Bloomsbury, 2017.

Lehnhof, Kent R. 'Acting, Integrity and Gender in *Coriolanus*'. *Shakespeare Bulletin* 31, no. 3 (2013): 353–73.

Lepage, Robert, [performance] dir. *Coriolanus*. Stratford Festival Production, 2018.

Lisak, Catherine. '"O, Me Alone!": *Coriolanus* in the Face of Collective Otherness'. *Actes des congrès de la Société française Shakespeare* 28 (2011): 225–55.

'List of Trump Administration Dismissals and Resignations'. Wikipedia.org. Available online: https://en.wikipedia.org/wiki/List_of_Trump_administration_dismissals_and_resignations#cite_ref-12 (accessed 31 January 2020).

Londré, Felicia Hardison. '*Coriolanus* and Stavisky: The Interpenetration of Art and Politics'. *Theatre Research International* 11 (1986): 119–32.

Lopez, Jeremy. *The Arden Introduction to Reading Shakespeare: Close Reading and Analysis*. London: Bloomsbury, 2019.

Lowe, Lisa. '"Say I Play the Man I Am": Gender and Politics in *Coriolanus*'. *The Kenyon Review* 8, no. 4 (1986): 86–95.

Luckyj, Christina. 'Volumnia's Silence'. *Studies in English Literature 1500–1900* 31, no. 2 (1991): 327–42.

MacIntyre, Jean. 'Words, Acts, and Things: Visual Language in *Coriolanus*'. *English Studies in Canada* 10, no. 1 (1984): 1–10.

MacKay, L. A. 'Antigone, Coriolanus, and Hegel'. *Transactions and Proceedings of the American Philological Association* 93 (1962): 166–74.

Mackenzie, Stanley D. '"Unshout the noise that banish'd Martius": Structural Paradox and Dissembling in *Coriolanus*'. *Shakespeare Studies* 18 (1986): 189–204.

Maher, Bill. *Real Time with Bill Maher*. HBO-TV, 15 September 2017.

Maley, Willy. '"She done *Coriolanus* at the Convent": Empowerment and Entrapment in Teresa Deevy's *In Search of Valour*'. *Irish University Review* 49 (2019): 356–69.

Marcus, Rafaella and David Ralf. 'Review: *Roman Tragedies* at the Barbican'. Available online: http://exeuntmagazine.com/reviews/review-roman-tragedies-barbican/ (accessed 2 December 2019).

Marlowe, Christopher. *Tamburlaine the Great, Part Two*. In *The Complete Plays*, edited by Frank Romany and Robert Lindsey. Harmondsworth: Penguin, 2003.

Marshall, Cynthia. 'Wound-man: *Coriolanus*, Gender, and the Theatrical Construction of Interiority'. In *Feminist Readings of Early Modern Culture: Emerging Subjects*, edited by Valerie Traub, M. Lindsay Kaplan and Dympna Callaghan, 98–118. Cambridge: Cambridge University Press, 1996.

Marshall, Cynthia. 'Shakespeare, Crossing the Rubicon'. *Shakespeare Survey* 53 (2000): 73–88.

Marshall, Cynthia. 'Coriolanus and the Politics of Theatrical Pleasure'. In *A Companion to Shakespeare's Works: The Tragedies*, edited by Richard Dutton and Jean E. Howard, 452–72. Oxford: Blackwell Publishing, 2003.

Martin, Randall. 'Ecological Studies'. In *The Arden Research Handbook of Contemporary Shakespeare Criticism*, edited by Evelyn Gajowski. London: Bloomsbury, 2020.

Mason, Mark, ed. *Complexity Theory and the Philosophy of Education*. Malden, MA and Oxford: Wiley-Blackwell, 2008.

Maus, Katharine Eisaman. '*Coriolanus*' [Introduction]. In *The Norton Shakespeare based on the Oxford Edition*, edited by Stephen Greenblatt, Walter Cohen, Jean E. Howard and Katharine Eisaman Maus, 2785–92. New York and London: Norton, 1997.

McDonald, Russ. 'The Idioms of the Late Tragedies'. In *Shakespeare's Late Style*, 52–66. Cambridge: Cambridge University Press, 2006, 2009.

McGugan, Ruth. *Nahum Tate and the* Coriolanus *Tradition in English Drama. With a Critical Edition of Tate's* The Ingratitude of A Common-Wealth. New York and London: Garland, 1987.

McGuire, Philip C. *Shakespeare: The Jacobean Plays*. London: Macmillan, 1994.

Menon, Madhavi. 'Coriolanus and I'. *Shakespeare* 7, no. 2 (2011): 156–69.

Menon, Madhavi. 'Queer Shakes'. In *Shakesqueer*, edited by Madhavi Menon, 1–27. Durham, NC: Duke University Press, 2011.

Miles, Geoffrey. *Shakespeare and the Constant Romans*. Oxford: Clarendon, 1996.

Mills, Geoff. '*Coriolanus* at the Royal Shakespeare Theatre, Stratford upon Avon'. Available online: http://exeuntmagazine.com/reviews/review-coriolanus-royal-shakespeare-theatre-stratford-upon-avon/ (accessed 2 November 2019).

Miola, Robert S. *Shakespeare's Rome*. Cambridge: Cambridge University Press, 1983.

Miura, Motoi. 'Artist Interview'. Available online: https://performingarts.jp/E/art_interview/1002/1.html (accessed 12 October 2019).

Miura, Motoi. 'Coriolanus Comes Home to Kyoto'. *Japan Times*, 23 January 2013. Available online: https://www.japantimes.co.jp/culture/2013/01/23/stage/coriolanus-comes-home-to-kyoto/ (accessed 19 June 2019).

Mollan, Simon and Beverly Geesin. 'Donald Trump and Trumpism: Leadership, Ideology and Narrative of the Business Executive turned Politician'. *Organization* 26 (2019): 1–14.

Morgan, Jason V. 'We Have a President Who Denigrates People and Hugs Flags'. Letters to the Editor, *Washington Post*, 8 March 2019. Available online: https://www.washingtonpost.com/opinions/we-have-a-president-who-denigrates-people-and-hugs-flags/2019/03/08/d03f2e4c-407c-11e9-85ad-779ef05fd9d8_story.html (accessed 1 March 2020).

Morrison, Keith. *School Leadership and Complexity Theory*. London and New York: Routledge, 2002.

Muir, Kenneth. 'Menenius's Fable'. *Notes & Queries* 198 (1953): 240–2.

Muir, Kenneth. *The Sources of Shakespeare's Plays*. New Haven, NJ: Yale University Press, 1977, 1978.

Munro, Ian. *The Figure of the Crowd in Early Modern London: The City and Its Double*. London: Palgrave Macmillan, 2005.

Munro, Lucy. '*Coriolanus* and the Little Eyases: The Boyhood of Shakespeare's Hero.' In *Shakespeare and Childhood*, edited by Kate Chedgzoy, Susanne Greenhalgh and Robert Shaughnessy, 80-95. Cambridge: Cambridge University Press, 2007.

Nevalainen, Terttu. *An Introduction to Early Modern English*. Edinburgh: Edinburgh University Press, 2006.

Newman, Harry. '"The stamp of Martius": Commoditised Character and the Technology of Theatrical Impression in *Coriolanus*'. *Renaissance Drama* 45, no. 1 (2017): 41–68.

O'Dair, Sharon. 'Is It Shakespearean Ecocriticism If It Isn't Presentist?' In *Ecocritical Shakespeare*, edited by Lynne Bruckner and Dan Brayton, 71–85. Farnham: Ashgate, 2011.

Ormsby, Robert. *Coriolanus*. Manchester: Manchester University Press, 2014.

Osborne, John. *A Place Calling Itself Rome*. London: Faber, 1972.

Palfrey, Simon. *Doing Shakespeare*. 2nd edn. London: Bloomsbury, 2011.

Parker, R. B. 'Introduction'. In William Shakespeare, *Coriolanus*, edited by R. B. Parker, 1–148. Oxford: Oxford University Press, 1994.

Parker, Steven. *Bertolt Brecht: A Literary Life*. London: Bloomsbury, 2014.

Patterson, Annabel. *Shakespeare and the Popular Voice*. London: Blackwell, 1989.

Pittman, L. Monique. 'Heroes, Villains and Balkans: Intertextual Masculinities in Ralph Fiennes's *Coriolanus*'. *Shakespeare Bulletin* 33, no. 2 (2015): 215–44.

Plotz, John. '*Coriolanus* and the Failure of Performatives'. *ELH* 63, no. 4 (1996): 809–32.

Plumwood, Val. *Feminism and the Mastery of Nature*. London and New York: Routledge, 1993.

Plumwood, Val. *Environmental Culture: The Ecological Crisis of Reason*. London and New York: Routledge, 2002.

Plutarch. *Plutarch's Lives*. Translated by Thomas North. 1579. Reprinted. London: J.M. Dent, 1910. Available online: https://oll.libertyfund.org/titles/plutarch-plutarchs-lives-englished-by-sir-thomas-north-in-ten-volumes (accessed 18 February 2020).

Rankin, Deana. 'Bread and Circuses: Chiten, Japan and *Coriolanus*'. In *Shakespeare beyond English: A Global Experiment*, edited by Susan Bennett and Christie Carson, 223–6. Cambridge: Cambridge University Press, 2013.

Raspa, Richard. 'Place in Shakespeare's *Coriolanus*: The Intersection of Geography, Culture, and Identity'. *Mediterranean Studies* 26, no. 2 (2018): 213–28.

Rebellato, Dan. *1956 and All That*. London and New York: Routledge, 1999.

'Religion'. *Merriam-Webster.com Dictionary*. Available online: https://www.merriam-webster.com/dictionary/religion (accessed 1 April 2020).

Ripley, John. Coriolanus *on Stage in England and America, 1609–1994*. London and Cranbury, NJ: Associated University Press, 1998.

Riss, Arthur. 'The Belly Politic: *Coriolanus* and the Revolt of Language'. *ELH* 59, no. 1 (1992): 53–75.

Rizvi, Pervez. 'Speech Lengths in Early Modern Plays'. *ANQ: A Quarterly Journal of Short Articles, Notes and Reviews* 33 (2020): 143–7.

Robbins, Katherine Gallagher, Rejane Frederick, Angela Hanks, Rachel West and Michela Zonta. '5 Ways President Trump and Congressional Republicans Are Betraying Veterans'. Center for American Progress, 26 September 2017. Available online: https://www.americanprogress.org/issues/poverty/reports/2017/09/26/439661/5-ways-president-trump-congressional-republicans-betraying-veterans/%20%3c/ (accessed 23 November 2019).

Roberts, Sarah. '"Alone", "constant", and "(in)visible": Staging Leadership in *Coriolanus*'. *Shakespeare in Southern Africa* 29 (2017): 27–49.

Rogers, Jami. 'The Shakespearean Glass Ceiling: The State of Colorblind Casting in Contemporary British Theatre'. *Shakespeare Bulletin* 31, no. 3 (2013): 405–30.

Rothstein, Mervyn. 'Trims and New Twists for a "Coriolanus"'. *New York Times*, 30 November 1988.

Royal Shakespeare Company. *Coriolanus*. London: BBC/Opus Arte, 2018.

Royal Shakespeare Company. *Coriolanus* Resources and Production Information. Available online: https://www.rsc.org.uk/coriolanus/ (accessed 18 February 2020).

Royal Shakespeare Company. *Coriolanus* Teacher Pack. 2017. Available online: https://cdn2.rsc.org.uk/sitefinity/education-pdfs/teacher-packs/edu-coriolanus-teacherpack-2017.pdf?sfvrsn=7c110321_2 (accessed 18 February 2020).

Rucker, Philip, Robert Costa and Josh Dawsey. 'Trump Seeks to Bend the Executive Branch as Part of Impeachment Vendetta'. *Washington Post*, 12 February 2020.

Rudolph, Valerie C. 'Going to Grass; or, *Coriolanus* Revisited'. *Educational Theatre Journal* 27 (2003): 498–503.

Rymer, Thomas. 'The Tragedies of the Last Age'. 1677. In *Shakespeare: The Critical Heritage* Vol. 1: 1623-1692, edited by Brian Vickers. London: Routledge, 1974.

Sachs, Jonathan. 'Republicanism: Ancient Rome and Literary Modernity in British Romanticism'. In *Romans and Romantics*, edited by Timothy Saunders, Charles Martindale, Ralph Pite and Mathilde Skoie, 23–42. Oxford: Oxford University Press, 2012.

Salkeld, Duncan. 'Shakespeare Studies, Presentism, and Micro-History'. *Cahiers Élisabéthains* 76, no. 1 (2009): 35–43.

Sanders, Eve Rachele. 'The Body of the Actor in *Coriolanus*'. *Shakespeare Quarterly* 57, no. 4 (2006): 387–412.

Sanders, Wilbur. 'An Impossible Person: Caius Martius Coriolanus'. In Wilbur Sanders and Howard Jacobson, *Shakespeare's Magnanimity: Four Tragic Heroes, Their Friends and Families*, 136–87. London: Chatto and Windus, 1978.

Saval, Peter Kishore. *Shakespeare in Hate: Emotion, Passion, Selfhood*. New York: Routledge, 2015.

Schwartz, Tony. Interview. *Hardball with Chris Matthews*. MSNBC TV, 5 February 2019.

Schwartz-Gastine, Isabelle. '*Coriolanus* in France from 1933 to 1977: Two Extreme Interpretations'. In *Shakespeare and European Politics*, edited by Dirk Delabastita, Jozef De Vos and Paul Franssen, 124–42. Newark, DE: University of Delaware Press, 2008.

Sears, P. *Deserts on the March*. Norman, OK: University of Oklahoma Press, 1935.

Sedgwick, Eve Kosofsky. *Between Men: English Literature and Male Homosocial Desire*. New York: Columbia University Press, 1985.

Semler, Liam E. *Teaching Shakespeare and Marlowe: Learning versus the System*. London: Bloomsbury, 2013.

Semple, Kirk. 'Central American Farmers Head to the US, Fleeing Climate Change'. *New York Times*, 13 April 2019.

Shakespeare, William. *Mr William Shakespeares Comedies, Histories and Tragedies*. London: Isaac Jaggard and Edward Blount for William Jaggard et al., 1623. [The First Folio.]

Shakespeare, William. *The Plays of William Shakespeare*. Edited by Samuel Johnson. Volume 6. London, 1765.

Shakespeare, William. *Coriolanus*. Penguin Classics. Edited by G. R. Hibbard. London: Penguin, 1967, 2005.

Shakespeare, William. *Coriolanus*. Edited by R. B. Parker. Oxford: Oxford University Press, 1994.

Shakespeare, William. *King Lear*. Edited by R. A. Foakes. The Arden Shakespeare, Third Series. London: Bloomsbury, 1997.
Shakespeare, William. *Julius Caesar*. Edited by David Daniell. The Arden Shakespeare, Third Series. London, New York: Bloomsbury, 1998.
Shakespeare, William. *Coriolanus*. Cambridge School Shakespeare. 2nd edition. Cambridge: Cambridge University Press, 1999.
Shakespeare, William. *The Arden Shakespeare Complete Works*. Revised edition. Edited by Richard Proudfoot, Ann Thompson and David Scott Kastan. London: The Arden Shakespeare, 2001.
Shakespeare, William. *Hamlet*. Edited by Anne Thompson and Neil Taylor. The Arden Shakespeare, Third Series. London: Bloomsbury, 2006.
Shakespeare, William. *Complete Works*. Edited by Jonathan Bate and Eric Rasmussen. RSC Editions. Basingstoke: Macmillan, 2007.
Shakespeare, William. *Coriolanus*. Edited by Lee Bliss. 2nd edn. Cambridge: Cambridge University Press, 2010.
Shakespeare, William. *Coriolanus*. Oxford School Shakespeare. Oxford: Oxford University Press, 2012.
Shakespeare, William. *Coriolanus*. Edited by Peter Holland. The Arden Shakespeare, Third Series. London: Bloomsbury, 2013.
Shakespeare, William. *King Henry IV, Part 2*. Edited by James C. Bulman. The Arden Shakespeare, Third Series. London: Bloomsbury, 2016.
Shakespeare, William. *The New Oxford Shakespeare*. Edited by Gary Taylor, John Jowett, Terri Bourus and Gabriel Egan. Oxford: Oxford University Press, 2016–present.
Shakespeare on Film. *Coriolanus* Study Guide. Available online: http://www.thefilmspace.org/shakespeare-on-film/resources/coriolanus/docs/coriolanus_studyguide.pdf (accessed 18 February 2020).
Shakespeare Theatre. *Coriolanus* Teacher and Student Resource Guide. Available online: http://www.shakespearetheatre.org/_pdf/first_folio/Folio-coriolanus.pdf (accessed 18 February 2020).
Shannon, C. E. 'A Mathematical Theory of Communication'. *Bell System Technical Journal* 27 (1948): 379–423, 623–56.
Shelley, Percy Bysshe. *Poetical Works*. Edited by Thomas Hutchinson. Oxford: Oxford University Press, 1970.
Sheridan, Thomas. *Coriolanus: or, the Roman Matron. A Tragedy. Altered from Shakespeare*. London: A. Millar, 1755.

Shoichiro, Kawai. 'Ninagawa Yukio'. In *The Routledge Companion to Director's Shakespeare*, edited by John Russell Brown, 269–83. London and New York: Routledge, 2008.

Shrank, Cathy. 'Civility and the City in *Coriolanus*'. *Shakespeare Quarterly* 54, no. 4 (2003): 406–23.

Simmons, J. L. *Shakespeare's Pagan World: The Roman Tragedies*. Charlottesville, VA: University of Virginia Press, 1973.

Simon, John. 'The Ignoblest Roman'. *New York Magazine* (5 December 1988): 194–5.

Sinclair, Margaret. '"It Shall Be So": Grammatical Usage as Political Intent in *Coriolanus*'. *Journal of Aesthetic Education* 36, no. 4 (2002): 32–6.

Smith, Bruce. *Homosexual Desire in Shakespeare's England: A Cultural Poetics*. Chicago, IL: The University of Chicago Press, 1991.

Smith, Bruce R. *Shakespeare and Masculinity*. Oxford: Oxford University Press, 2000.

Smith, Emma. *This is Shakespeare*. Harmondsworth: Penguin, 2019.

Smith, James. 'Brecht, the Berliner Ensemble, and the British Government'. *New Theatre Quarterly* 22, no. 4 (2006): 307–23.

Solnit, Rebecca. 'President Trump is at War with the Rule of Law. This won't End Well'. *The Guardian*, 9 October 2019. Available online: https://www.theguardian.com/commentisfree/2019/oct/09/trump-government-executive-branch-rebecca-solnit (accessed 1 March 2020).

Starks-Estes, Lisa S. *Violence, Trauma, and Virtus in Shakespeare's Roman Poems and Plays: Transforming Ovid*. London: Palgrave Macmillan, 2014.

Strachey, Lytton. *Books and Characters*. London: Chatto and Windus, 1922.

Stratford Festival. *Coriolanus* Digital Study Guide. Available online: https://www.stratfordfestival.ca/learn/studyguides/2018/coriolanus-study-guide (accessed 18 February 2020).

Subiotto, Arigo. *Bertolt Brecht's Adaptations for the Berliner Ensemble*. London: MHRA, 1975.

Suvin, Darko. *To Brecht and Beyond: Soundings in Modern Dramatology*. Brighton: Harvester, 1984.

Suvin, Darko. 'Brechtian or Pseudo-Brechtian: Mystical Estrangement in the Berliner Ensemble Adaptation of *Coriolanus*'. *ASSAPH Section 3: Studies in Theatre* 3 (1986): 135–58.

Tarlinskaja, Marina. *Shakespeare's Verse: Iambic Pentameter and the Poet's Idiosyncrasies*. New York: Peter Lang, 1987.

Tarlinskaja, Marina. *Shakespeare and the Versification of English Drama, 1561–1642*. London: Ashgate, 2014.

Tate, Nahum. *The Ingratitude of a Common-Wealth: or the Fall of Caius Martius Coriolanus*. London: T. M. for Joseph Hindmarsh, 1682.

Tausczik, Yla R. and James W. Pennebaker. 'The Psychological Meaning of Words: LIWC and Computerized Text Analysis Methods'. *Journal of Language and Social Psychology* 29, no. 1 (2010): 24–54.

Taylor, Peter. 'Bringing Boring Theatre to the Masses'. Available online: https://www.therecord.com/opinion-story/8723515-bringing-boring-theatre-to-the-masses/ (accessed 20 October 2019).

Taylor-Collins, Nicholas. 'The Cities' Hostile Bodies: *Coriolanus*'s Rome and Carson's Belfast'. *Modern Language Review* 115 (2020): 17–45.

Teach Shakespeare. Shakespeare's Globe. Available online: https://teach.shakespearesglobe.com/ (accessed 18 February 2020).

TES. *Coriolanus* Lesson Plan, Key Stage 4 Module. Available online: https://www.tes.com/teaching-resource/coriolanus-william-shakespeare-scheme-of-work-6030978 (accessed 18 February 2020).

Thomas, Alun. '*Coriolanus*'. In *A Year of Shakespeare: Re-living the World Shakespeare Festival*, edited by Paul Edmondson, Paul Prescott and Erin Sullivan. London: Bloomsbury, 2013.

Thomas, Miranda Fay. *Shakespeare's Body Language: Shaming Gestures and Gender Politics on the Renaissance Stage*. London: Bloomsbury, 2019.

Thomas, Sita. '"The Dog, the Guard, the Horses and the Maid": Diverse Casting at the Royal Shakespeare Company'. *Contemporary Theatre Review* 24, no. 4 (2014): 475–85.

Thompson, Ayanna. *Passing Strange: Shakespeare, Race, and Contemporary America*. Oxford: Oxford University Press, 2011.

Thompson, Ayanna and Laura Turchi. *Teaching Shakespeare with Purpose: A Student-Centred Approach*. London: Bloomsbury, 2016.

Thomson, James. *Coriolanus. A Tragedy*. London: A. Millar, 1749.

Thurman, Chris. 'Shakespeare.za: digital Shakespeares and education in South Africa'. *Research in Drama Education: The*

Journal of Applied Theatre and Performance 25, no. 1 (2020): 49–67.

Trump, Donald. 'Acceptance Speech'. Republican National Convention. Cleveland, Ohio, 21 July 2016.

Trump, Donald. 'The State of the Union Address to the US Congress'. Washington, DC, 4 February 2020.

Vanden Heuvel, Katrina. *The Thom Hartmann Program*. Satellite XM Radio, 9 January 2020.

Van Der Walt, Tanya. 'Making Shakespeare Useful: A Pared-Down, Portable *Coriolanus*'. *Shakespeare in Southern Africa* 28 (2016): 99–101.

Vickers, Brian. 'Teaching *Coriolanus*: The Importance of Perspective'. In *Teaching Shakespeare*, edited by Walter Edens, Christopher Durer, Walter Eggers, Duncan Harris and Keith Hull, 228–70. Princeton, NJ: Princeton University Press, 1977, 2015.

Vienne-Guerrin, Nathalie. '*Coriolanus*, or "The arraignment of an unruly tongue"'. In *Coriolan de William Shakespeare: Langages, interprétations, politique(s)*, edited by Richard Hillman, 133–53. Tours: Presses Universitaires François-Rabelais, 2007.

Ward, Thomas. '*Coriolanus* and the Voice of Cynicism'. *Renaissance Drama* 47, no. 1 (2019): 95–121.

Watson, Robert N. '*Coriolanus* and the "Common Part"'. *Shakespeare Survey* 69 (2016): 181–97.

Wells, Robin Headlam, '"Manhood and Chevalrie": *Coriolanus*, Prince Henry, and the Chivalric Revival'. *Review of English Studies* 51 (2000): 395–422.

Wells, Robin Headlam. *Shakespeare's Politics: A Contextual Introduction*. London: Continuum, 2009.

Werier, Clifford. 'The Hungry Meme and Political Contagion in *Coriolanus*'. In *Contagion and the Shakespearean Stage*, edited by Darryl Chalk and Mary Floyd-Wilson, 191–211. London: Palgrave, 2019.

West, Michael and Myron Silberstein. 'The Controversial Eloquence of Shakespeare's Coriolanus – An Anti-Ciceronian Orator?' *Modern Philology* 102, no. 3 (2005): 307–31.

Wheeler, David, ed. Coriolanus: *Critical Essays*. 1995. Milton Park and New York: Routledge, 2015.

White, R. S. and Ciara Rawnsley. 'Discrepant Emotional Awareness in Shakespeare'. In *The Renaissance of Emotion: Understanding Affect in Shakespeare and his Contemporaries*, edited by Richard Meek and Erin Sullivan, 241–63. Manchester: Manchester University Press, 2015.

Whitney, John O. and Tina Packer. *Power Plays: Shakespeare's Lessons in Leadership and Management*. London: Macmillan, 2000.

Wiggins, Martin and Catherine Richardson. *British Drama 1533–1642: A Catalogue*. 9 volumes. Oxford: Oxford University Press, 2012.

Wilkinson, Kate. 'Shakespeare's citizens and the 99%: Accommodating the Occupy Movement in Productions of *Coriolanus*'. *Early Modern Literary Studies* 19, special issue (2016).

Williams, Ethlyn A., Rajnandini Pillai, Kate McCombs, Kevin B. Lowe and Bryan J. Deptula. 'Adaptive and Maladaptive Narcissism, Charisma, and Leadership Performance: A Study of Perceptions of the Presidency of Donald Trump'. *Leadership* 16 (2020): 1–22.

Wilson, Richard. 'Against the Grain: Representing the Market in *Coriolanus*'. *Seventeenth Century* 6, no. 2 (1991): 111–48.

Wright, George T. *Shakespeare's Metrical Art*. Oakland, CA: University of California Press, 1988.

Wu, Duncan. *William Hazlitt: The First Modern* Man. Oxford: Oxford University Press, 2008.

Wudel, Darcy. 'Shakespeare's *Coriolanus* in the Political Science Classroom'. *PS: Political Science and Politics* 35, no. 2 (2002): 217–22.

INDEX

Abbey, Graham 69
acting 11, 12, 51, 59–61, 86, 95–116
Adamson, Sylvia 210
adaptation studies 87–8, 91–2
Addison, Joseph 25–6
Adelman, Janet 20, 35–6, 40, 82–4, 111, 122, 125
Agamben, Giorgio 41, 78
Alaimo, Stacy 119, 137
Alcibiades 5
Alexandre 53
Allan, Neil 68
Amyot, Jacques 5
Antium 8, 48, 51, 130, 186, 200, 212
Aquinas, Thomas 76
'ardenspaces' 199, 202
Aristotle 13, 27
Arnold, Oliver 47
Ashcroft, Peggy 58
Astor Place riots 51
Atkins, Robert 52
Aufidius (character) 3–6, 8, 13, 15–6, 28–30, 55, 109, 113–16, 141, 149, 154–5, 162
Augustine 76, 77, 85
Averell, William 5

Baker, Catherine 92
Bakhtin, Mikhail 76–8
Barlow, William 203

Barr, William 124
Bates, Jennifer 11, 14
Baudrillard, Jean 75
Belfast 78–9
Benson, Frank 51
Berkoff, Steven 60–1, 194
Berliner Ensemble 55–8
Biesta, Gert 198
Blackfriars' Theatre 7, 86, 204–5
Bolsonaro, Jair 132, 135
Bombardier, Louise 69
Booth, Barton 49
Braden, Gordon 7
Bradley, A. C. 20, 32–4, 36
Brandon, Samuel 179
Brecht, Bertolt 55–8, 88–91
Brennan, John 124
Bridges-Adams, William 52
Bristol, Michael 74–6
Brooks, Mike 104
Burbage, Richard 48, 100
Burke, Edmund 21
Burke, Kenneth 3
Butler, Gerard 91

Cadieux, Anne-Marie 63
Camden, William 197
Campbell, Peter 76
Cantor, Paul A. 7
Carson, Christie 211
Carson, Ciaran 78
Cartelli, Thomas 62
Cavanagh, Sheila 213

Cavell, Stanley 23, 36, 40
Cavendish, Dominic 68
Cavendish, Margaret 26
Chapman, George 178
'character criticism' 20
Charles II, King 49
Chiten Company 65
Cohen, Ralph Alan 192, 203, 205
Cole, Penelope 90
Coleridge, Samuel Taylor 21
Comédie-Française 11, 52–5
Cominius (character) 8, 50, 99–101, 108–9, 111, 120, 129, 131, 188–9, 213
Compagnoni, Michela 85
complexity theory 197–202
Conkie, Rob 88
Conway, William 51
Cooper, Thomas Abthorpe 51
Coriolanus (character)
    death 2, 4, 12–13, 15–16, 47, 52, 55–9, 62, 65, 67, 69, 105, 116, 157, 215
    failure 11, 34, 83, 87, 125, 127, 141, 151, 162, 201
    and Hitler 53, 207
    humour 4, 8–9
    nobility 4, 7, 16, 33, 50, 53, 109, 115–16, 174
    relationship with Aufidius 4, 6, 37–40, 48, 63, 67, 84, 90, 105–6, 108–9, 114–16, 187, 200, 212
    relationship with Volumnia 6, 9, 10, 12, 19, 35–7, 48, 83–4, 108–13, 124–5
    singularity 3–4, 46–7, 122–3, 199–200
    soliloquies 8, 113–14, 152, 212
    and Trump 11, 117–37
    wounds and scars 4, 47, 97, 101–2, 129, 153, 159, 196
Coriolanus (play)
    the body 95–116
    climaxes 4, 46, 55, 112–13
    composition date 6
    deviations from Plutarch 5–6, 39, 101, 122, 127
    editions 192
    food and hunger motif 6, 23, 36–7, 40, 81, 125, 148, 203
    'Fable of the Belly' 3, 5, 22–4, 40, 96, 194–9
    film versions 91–2, 193–4, 215–16
    language 5, 7–8, 13, 23, 39, 46, 79, 98, 106, 140–1, 162, 165–90, 196, 209–10
    on stage 10–11, 45–70
    opening scene 1, 3, 6, 47, 126, 194–7
    paradoxes 10, 15–16, 18–19, 31, 33–4, 36–7, 41–3, 78–9, 83, 196, 201
    silence 8, 12, 55, 109–10, 112–13
    story from Plutarch 5, 12, 72
    teaching and learning 191–216
Corioles 2, 8, 57, 104, 105, 155, 174–5, 187–9, 205
Corrigan, James 66
Costa, Robert 130
Craig, Hugh 11, 14
creative criticism 88–91
Cultural Materialism 73
Cummings, Constance 57
Cynicism 79

Davis, Brent 198
Dawkins, Richard 81
Dawsey, Josh 130
Deevy, Teresa 86
Dekker, Thomas 204
democracy 9–10, 20–1, 41, 43, 50–1, 60, 62, 72, 74, 79, 118, 121, 137, 207
Dennis, John 10, 16, 25–9, 32, 36, 38, 49
Derrida, Jacques 78
Dickson, Andrew 214
digital technologies 211–14
Dirisu, Sope 66
Dittman, Joo Young 211
Dobson, Michael 214
Doctor Who 14
Dollimore, Jonathan 73
Dryden, John 26
Duterte, Rodrigo 132

Eagleton, Terry 73
Eastman, Nate 197
ecocriticism 118
ecofeminism 117–20
Edwards, Jason 41–3
Ehrlich, Jeremy 211–12, 214
Eisenhower, Dwight D. 76
Eliot, T. S. 2, 88
El-Sisi, Abdel Fattah 132
Erdoğan, Recep 132
Essex, earl of 202, 203
Evans, Dame Edith 54–5
The Examiner 21
Extinction Rebellion movement 206

Fabre, Émile 53–4
Fiennes, Ralph 91, 193, 215
Fish, Stanley 97, 103–4
Fletcher, John 27, 171, 176, 178

Flörchinger, Martin 57
Forrest, Edwin 11, 51–2
Forster, E. M. 135
Foucault, Michel 75
French Revolution 16, 18, 22, 50
Friedman, Michael D. 194, 210, 215

Gagnon, Gérald 63
Gajowski, Evelyn 11, 14
Garber, Marjorie 208
Garganigo, Alex 75, 197
Garneau, Michel 63
Garrison, John 210
gender 11, 67, 82–7, 210–1
George, David 6
Gildon, Charles 27, 35
Globe Theatre 6, 65, 204
Globe to Globe Festival 65, 194
Goldberg, Jonathan 40–2
Gordon, Alexis 69–70
Grady, Hugh 118, 206
Graham, Franklin 133
grain shortages 6, 127
Granville-Barker, Harley 2
Grass, Günter 58, 89, 91
Gray, Patrick 77
Greatley-Hirsch, Brett 167, 171
Greece, ancient 141–5, 147, 151, 156, 158, 160–1
Greenblatt, Stephen 73, 127, 129, 207
Griffiths, Huw 10
Guerinik, Reda 69
Gurr, Andrew 196, 197, 204
Gwynne, Hadyn 66

Hadfield, Andrew 203
Hall, Peter 54, 59, 61
Hamblin, Thomas 51
Hammond, Paul 39

Hands, Terry 59
Hansen, Claire 13, 14
Haraway, Donna 131
Harry Potter (film) 92
Hawkes, David 133–4
Hawkes, Terence 73, 76, 118, 206
Hazlitt, William 18–22, 33, 36
Hegel, G. W. F. 11, 77, 78, 139–64
Heywood, Thomas 178
Hicks, Greg 59
Hiddleston, Tom 194
Hindle, Steve 75
Hobbes, Thomas 75
Hogg, Ian 58–9
Holderness, Graham 11, 192, 205, 207, 215–16
Holland, Peter 5, 79, 88, 90, 192, 195, 200
Holstun, James 13
homoeroticism 37–9, 63, 69, 108–9, 114
Hopkins, Anthony 57
Hopkins, Lisa 210
Howard, Alan 59
The Hunger Games (film) 216
Hunt, Maurice 76
The Hurt Locker (film) 216
Hutcheon, Linda 87
hyper-separation 119–20, 135–7

Ibsen, Henrik 88
Inchbald, Elizabeth 17–19, 22, 33, 35
Irving, Henry 51, 214

Jackson, Angus 66, 194, 214
Jacobitism 30
Jagendorf, Zvi 195, 207
James I, King 75, 196, 204
James II, King 49
James, Emrys 58
Johnson, Samuel 27–8
Jones, David 58
Jones, Emily Griffiths 211
Jordan, Richard 76

Kabuki 66
Kaczyński, Jarosław 132
Kahn, Coppélia 83, 112–13, 210
Kamaralli, Anna 11, 14
Kant, Immanuel 78
Kaouk, Theodore 121
Kastan, David Scott 13
Kean, Edmund 51
Kemble, John Philip 11, 17, 21, 35, 50–2
Kenzari, Chico 62
Khan, Humayun 121
Khorram, Ali 124
Kim, Jong-un 132
Kirwan, Peter 194, 211, 213–14
Kuwayama, Tomonari 64
Kuzner, James 41–2, 137

Laird, Martina 66
Laroche, Rebecca 118
Laughton, Charles 54
Lefebvre, Henri 77, 78
Lehnhof, Kent R. 85, 211
Leitch, Thomas 87
Lepage, Robert 62–3, 68–70
Lisak, Catherine 199
Livy 5, 72, 91
Lopez, Jeremy 209–10
Luckyj, Christina 109

Macready, Charles 51
Magna Carta 124, 128

Maher, Bill 131
Maisano, Scott 88
Maley, Willy 86–7
Mars 51
Marshall, Cynthia 5, 10, 47, 98
Martin, Randall 133
Marx, Karl 78
masculinity 1, 4, 5, 10, 36–9, 83–6, 100, 115–16, 125–6, 128, 132, 211
Mason, John 178
Mason, Mark 198
Matthews, Chris 126
MacIntyre, Jean 210
Mbeki, Thabo 206
McCain, John 121
McGann, Jerome 73
McKellen, Ian 59
mediation and self-mediation 11, 12, 98, 104, 140, 150–2, 154–7, 161–4
meme theory 81–2
Menenius (character) 3, 4, 6, 7, 8, 10, 22–3, 27–9, 40, 99–100, 103, 111, 132, 141, 171, 194–6, 198–9, 215
Menon, Madhavi 210
Middleton, Thomas 178, 204
Midlands Rising 6–7, 74–6, 78, 203
Miles, Geoffrey
Mills, Geoff 68
Monk, Nugent 52
Montrose, Louis 73
Morrison, Jackie 66–7
Moshinsky, Elijah 194
Miura, Motoi 65, 194
Muir, Kenneth 5, 12
Munro, Ian 204, 208

Munro, Lucy 86
Munroe, Jennifer 118

Naumann, Günter 57
Nazism 53, 55, 57
neoclassicism 10, 27–8, 32, 50
neo-Stoicism 84–5
New Historicism 73, 118
Newman, Harry 80
Nicholls, Anthony 55
Ninagawa, Yukio 64, 66
Normil, Widemir 69
North, Sir Thomas 5, 12, 203
Nunn, Trevor 58–9

Occupy movement 206
O'Dair, Sharon 118
Olivier, Laurence 54–5
'one (or few) and the many' 3, 10, 20–3, 37, 41, 208–9
Orbán, Viktor 132
Ormsby, Robert 10
Osberg, Deborah 198
Osborne, John 90–1

Packer, Tina 208
Paine, Thomas 21
Palfrey, Simon 196, 210, 212
Papp, Joseph 60
Parker, R. B. 46, 203
Parscale, Brad 133
Patterson, Annabel 41, 74–6
Peacock, Lucy 69
Pearson, Mike 104
Peele, George 171, 178
Pelosi, Nancy 126
Peterloo Massacre 21
Phelps, Samuel 51
Philip, Jules 63
Piachaud, René-Louis 52, 88

Pitoors, Frieda 62
Pittman, L. Monique 91–2
plague 6–7, 204
Plotz, John 9, 98, 110
Plumwood, Val 119–20, 125–6, 137
Plutarch 5, 39, 91, 203
Poel, William 88
politics 3, 4, 9, 10, 13, 18, 20–4, 41–3, 50, 52–60, 62, 66, 71–82, 89–91, 117–18, 121, 143, 193, 197–8, 202, 205–9, 215
  Shakespeare as political theorist 7
  teaching approach 207–9
Pompeo, Mike 124
Pope, Alexander 25
presentism 76, 78, 86, 92–3, 117–18, 134–7, 205–7
psychoanalytic criticism 20, 35–7, 40, 82–3
Putin, Vladimir 132

queer readings 37–43, 210–11
Quilley, Dennis 58
Quin, James 49

Rabelais, François 77
race 66–70, 120
Ralegh, Sir Walter 202
Raleigh, Walter (critic) 32
Rancière, Jacques 79
reason 120, 150–1
recognition and misrecognition 12–3, 114, 125
  'politics of recognition' 77
the Restoration 24
rhetoric 6–9, 48, 59, 85, 95–116, 154, 195, 197–8, 204, 209

Ripley, John 45, 50, 54
Riss, Arthur 197
Roberts, Sarah 192, 208
Robeson, Paul 54
Rogers, Jami 68
Rome 2, 9–11, 71–2, 78, 118, 120–5, 130, 137, 139–64, 197–8
  'Conflict of the Orders' 4
Romantic movement 17, 20, 29, 32
Romulus and Remus 84
Rourke, Josie 194, 215
Rucker, Philip 130
Rudolf, Valerie C. 89
Russia 130–1
Rymer, Thomas 27

Sachs, Jonathan 21–2
Salvini, Tomasso 51
Samely, Maurice 77
Sanders, Eve Rachele 100–1, 105
Sanders, Julie 87
Sanders, Wilbur 8
satire 13
Saval, Peter Kishore 100, 102, 104, 111–12
Schall, Ekkehard 57
Schwartz, Delmore 88
Schwartz, Tony 126, 131
Schwartz-Gastine, Isabelle 52
Sedgwick, Eve Kosofsky 108
selfhood and self-knowledge 7, 11–12, 33–4, 41–2, 100–3, 105–6, 111, 121–6, 146–7, 153–4
Semler, Liam 136, 199
Shakespeare, William
  Antony and Cleopatra 2, 7, 33, 61, 71, 194

As You Like It 97
Coriolanus, see separate entry
'four great tragedies' 33
Hamlet 2, 8, 12, 27, 36, 80, 97, 175
1 Henry IV 179
2 Henry IV 134
2 Henry VI 134
Julius Caesar 3, 7, 61, 71, 106, 194
King Lear 3, 12, 26, 65, 119, 134, 136
Macbeth 36–7, 51, 62, 83, 106
Othello 102, 176
'Plutarchan plays' 7
Richard III 97, 102, 195
The Taming of the Shrew 102
The Tempest 62, 134
Timon of Athens 13
Troilus and Cressida 106, 108
The Two Noble Kinsmen 176
The Winter's Tale 134, 176
Shannon, Claude 181
Shelley, Percy Bysshe 21
Sheridan, Richard Brinsley 17, 38
Shiriashi, Kayoto 64
Shrank, Cathy 121–2, 127, 200, 207, 209
Shrewsbury, earl of 203
Siddons, Sarah 50
Sills, André 69–70
Simmons, J. L. 7
Sinclair, Margaret 210
Skyfall (film) 216
Smith, Bruce 38–9

Smith, Emma 18
Snipes, Wesley 68
Sondland, Gordon 131
Sophocles 144, 151, 155
Spivak, Larry 60
Stalin, Joseph 56
Starks-Estes, Lisa S. 84
Stavisky, Alexandre 53
Strachey, Lytton 31–2, 36
'strongman' leaders 11, 132–7
Stow, John 203
Sturgeon, Nicola 67
stylometry 11–12, 165–90
Sumara, Dennis 198
Suvin, Darko 56
Suzuki, Tadashi 65

Tarlinskaja, Marina 179–80
Tate, Nahum 10, 26, 30, 38, 39, 48–9
Taylor, Peter 69
Taylor-Collins, Nicholas 78
Tenschert, Joachim 56–7
Terry, Ellen 51
Thatcher, Margaret 59
Thate, Hilmar 57
Thomas, Alun 104–5
Thomas, Miranda Fay 112
Thomé, Georges 54
Thompson, Ayanna 67, 212
Thompson, James 49
300 (film) 92
Thurman, Chris 206, 211
Titus Lartius (character) 132
Toneelgroep 61–2
tragedy 3, 10, 12, 13, 16, 26, 32, 43, 52, 83, 137, 139–64
trans-corporeality 119–20, 136–7

INDEX

tribunes 4, 6, 9, 30, 47, 52, 57, 76, 103, 127–9, 148, 153, 201
Turchi, Laura 212

Udall, Nicholas 179
Ulbricht, Walter 56

Van der Walt, Tanya 192
Van Hove, Ivo 61–2
Van Huet, Fredja 62
Vanden Heuvel, Katrina 135
Vickers, Brian 3, 192, 208–9
Vienne-Guerrin, Nathalie 97, 111
Vietnam War 120–1
Vindman, Alexander 131
Virgilia (character) 49, 109–11, 124, 202
'voices' 8, 47, 77, 79, 153, 185–6, 201
Voldemort 92
Voltaire 27
Volumnia (character) 3, 6, 8, 35–7, 48, 50, 55, 56, 84–5, 99, 109–10, 112–13, 175, 181, 210–1, 215

Walken, Christopher 60
Ward, Thomas 79
Warwickshire 6
Watson, Robert N. 200, 208
Weigel, Helene 55–6, 58
Wekwerth, Manfred 56–7
Wells, Robin Headlam 123, 207
Werier, Clifford 81
White, Paula 133
Whitney, John O. 208
Wilkinson, Kate 205–6
Williamson, Nichol 59
Wilson, Richard 6, 75
Worth, Irene 59, 61
Wright, George T. 179–80
Wu, Duncan 20
Wudel, Darcy 198

X, Malcolm 68
Xi, Jinping 132

Yarkho, Boris 181
Young Martius (character) 6, 49, 124

www.ingramcontent.com/pod-product-compliance
Lightning Source LLC
Chambersburg PA
CBHW052151300426
44115CB00011B/1623